FIGHT FAT & WIN!

HOW TO EAT A LOW-FAT DIET *WITHOUT* CHANGING YOUR LIFESTYLE

By Elaine Moquette-Magee, M.P.H.,R.D.

Fight Fat & Win! © 1990
by Elaine Moquette-Magee, M.P.H., R.D.

Library of Congress Cataloging-in-Publication Data

Moquette-Magee, Elaine.
   Fight fat & win.

   Includes index.
   1. Low-fat diet. 2. Low-fat diet—Recipes. I. Title.
   II. Title: Fight fat & win.
   RM237.7.M67 1990   613.2'8   90-3532

Edited by: Donna Hoel
Photography: Jeff Natrop, Thoen Photography
Cover Design & Production: Wenda Johnson, Nancy Bolmgren
Text Design & Production: MacLean & Tuminelly
Printing: Print Craft, Inc.

Printed in the United States of America

10 9 8 7 6 5 4 3 2 1

Published by:

DCI Publishing, Inc.
P. O. Box 47945
Minneapolis, MN 55447-9727

DEDICATION

Dedicated with love and respect to Jim Magee and Robert D. Frowein (Uncle Bob) whose lives were shortened by heart disease and cancer. Both deaths occurred during the years I was writing this book.

ACKNOWLEDGMENTS

I want to thank my parents, Don and Nesly Moquette, who as far back as I can remember always told me "you can do anything you set your mind to." Silly me . . . I actually believed them. I thank God every day for giving me such a wonderful family (including my two sisters, Lynn Moquette O'Leary and Collette Moquette Ricks). It has made all the difference in my life. They've always been there for me with love and encouragement. And now, I can't believe how lucky I am . . . I have married into another exceptional family, the Magees. I love you all very much. Which brings me to my husband, Dennis.

The old saying goes, "Behind every successful man is a woman." Well, all I know is beside this particular nutrition writer is a very special and understanding man. And no matter how tense or frustrated I get before a big deadline, all I have to do is think of Dennis and I can't help but smile.

Now, for all the other wonderful people in my life. When a project like this one spans over three years of one's life, there ends up being countless people who contribute through either emotional or professional support. So this is my attempt to thank some of the people who contributed to the completion of this book.

I would like to thank Lori Kinser, who has not only been the best friend a woman could ever hope for, but who contributed to the book's conception and provided invaluable input throughout.

Several friends reviewed certain portions of the book for accuracy or practicality. Thank you all. Your time and suggestions meant a lot to me: Dr. Lorelei DiSogra, Patty Magee, Matthew Ricks, and Lynn Moquette O'Leary. Thanks also to Paul Rauber, Michael Fullerton, Russ Spencer, and my agent, Micheal Snell, for their editing contributions.

TABLE OF CONTENTS

INTRODUCTION

This is one of those rare occasions where the title actually accurately represents the content of the book. If someone were to ask me "What's your book about in ten words or less?" I would have to answer: "How to eat a low-fat diet without changing your lifestyle." Because that's exactly what you will be prepared to do by the book's end.

Why then the title "Fight Fat & Win"? In today's society with a fast food chain on every corner, 15 minutes to make dinner because both parents are working, and where we eat OUT more than we eat IN, it is a "fight" against "fat." For the most part, "fast" food is "fat" food. And what makes the fight against dietary fat even more tricky is that fat tastes good. It also adds pleasure to our meals by making food feel soft and smooth in our mouths. (All fats help out in this department—it's called improving the "mouth feel.") Let's face it, we can't much argue with slogans like "everything tastes better with butter."

Most people have failed in their attempts to lower the fat in their diet because they are not willing (or able) to change their busy lifestyle. Most of the low-fat diet plans given to people are doomed to fail because they involve making all food from scratch and avoiding all restaurants and fast food chains. Then , too, the "new" low-fat recipes and suggestions given to them probably didn't taste like something they particularly wanted to stick around for. Americans today just aren't willing to give all this up, at least most of the time. Give up time AND taste? Never!

I'll admit it's darn difficult for my cooking to compete head-on with Chez Michel (or some other Italian chef) who uses tons of butter and cream in his Fettucine Alfredo when I'm using low-fat milk with only a touch of butter. Or for my low-fat mint chocolate chip cookies to win the taste test against Mrs. Field's or Grandma's recipe. But my versions definitely taste great and as long as they're not side to side with their fattier competitors, you and your family probably won't even notice.

That's where the "& WIN" part fits into the picture. I admit it's going to be a fight to lower the fat in our diets, but this is one fight you can WIN. Because this book shows you how to do it without giving up good tasting food and your free and easy way of life.

But before we move on to the first chapter and winning the war against fat, I need to warn you about two things that will continually try to distract you from fighting fat. They will tease you at every turn. I'm talking about the media and advertising.

You see, it's too easy for health conscious Americans to become distracted by each individual diet-related claim that comes along. Last year it was oat bran, the year before fish oil capsules. Next year it will probably be rice bran. Don't you get tired of jumping on every nutrient bandwagon that comes along? If you continue to do so you will be "buying into" (literally) the vicious cycle of believing, reading up on, and trying to follow each nutrient claim and trend that hits the media spotlight. They never last too long before something else comes along.

So why focus on fighting fat? For starters, according to the Surgeon General and the National Academy of Sciences recent report (Diet and Health), when it comes to dietary change, cutting our TOTAL fat intake should be America's number one priority. Secondly, when you lower fat, all of the other diet recommendations tend to fall into place.

For example, once you cut the total amount of fat in your diet, you automatically lower the amount of saturated fat and cholesterol too, since both are fatty substances found only in foods containing fat. Take whole milk as one all-American example. Watch the cholesterol (and calories) go down as the amount of fat (percent of calories from fat) goes down:

1 Cup	Calories	Percent Calories from Fat	Cholesterol (mg)
Whole milk	150	49	34
Milk, 2% milkfat	121	35	22
Milk, 1% milkfat	102	22	14
Skim (nonfat)	86	5	5

And, if you eat less of certain foods to lower your fat intake, you need to eat more of other foods (namely complex carbohydrates) in order to fill your plate—and stomach. This is where you automatically start following the other dietary guidelines because eating more carbohydrates (whole grains, starches, fruits, and vegetables) will increase your fiber total, along with supplying necessary vitamins and minerals.

Most books or diet plans have been too detailed in their explanations and don't give practical day-to-day information on HOW to eat a diet low in fat. And the ones that do ask you to completely change your lifestyle and demand unrealistic amounts of time and motivation. The answer? Keep reading "Fight Fat & Win." It's easy to understand and filled with guides and examples. And best of all, it doesn't ask you to give up your busy lifestyle. I'm not willing to give up mine—so why should you!

1

Life in the Fat Lane

The stories you are about to hear could be true. (Then again they could be slightly exaggerated.)

The Working Parent

The buzzer goes off (sigh) . . . you turn over, resting your head comfortably on your pillow, only to realize it's a work day and you have to get up. Between the time you take that first peaceful stretch and the time you race out the door, five minutes late, there seem to be a hundred things to do. You need to shower, get your children ready, iron a shirt, not to mention eating breakfast and packing lunches.

The Single Adult

You finally get off work. Your whole day has been a run-on sentence of appointments and phone calls. Now you have to rush to the automatic teller machine to get some cash so you can get to the dry cleaners before it closes at 5:30 to get your suit for tomorrow's meeting. (Somehow you lost the claim ticket so it takes them extra long to find that suit.) Then you barely make it to your 6 o'clock aerobics class and by the time you're showered, dressed, and on the road again, it's almost 8 P.M. Phew! Then . . .

- You could be meeting someone for a movie or coffee.
- You attend a night class or committee meeting.
- You're anxious to get home to watch your favorite sit-com—or you're just anxious to get home. (To play back the messages on the answering machine, maybe?)

On its own, being a "parent" or "having a career" keeps you busy enough, and some of us even manage to do both. Of course, there are other urgencies to squeeze into your schedule. Like exercise, family and friends, prayer or meditation, studying, and hobbies. Who doesn't consider themselves busy these days?

We might be busy, but aren't Americans today becoming more concerned about their health? Aren't we doing any better at the dinner table? Does the popular word "nutrition" simply represent vitamin supplements or alfalfa sprouts to most people, or has the concept of "improving our health through our diet (the foods we eat)" caught on—even a little?

According to a 1988 article in the *New York Times*, apparently not. The article discussed the results of a national telephone survey ("What Americans Eat: Nutrition Can Wait, Survey Finds") polling more than 1800 people. May I offer a few observations that might help us understand why we aren't eating as well as we think we are?

Observation #1.

One thing for sure, when it comes to nutrition as it relates to preventing disease and enhancing our total health, the interest is definitely there. More than half of the people surveyed said they had changed their eating habits in a major way in the past five years. Most of the women surveyed (60%) said they "Pay attention to salt at every meal." Slightly less than half said they were concerned about fats (46%) or sugar and sweets (42%). More than one-fourth (31%) said they were interested in lowering cholesterol.

I don't know about you, but I think "paying attention to something" (or someone) at "every meal" is quite a commitment. And the fact that a large portion of the American population is willing to do this is . . . well, it's exciting!

The survey noted that what people said they paid attention to at every meal and what they actually did were quite different. But I don't totally blame the confused consumer for this little indiscretion. Certainly all the nutrition and diet misinformation generated by food advertisers (trying to fit their products into the health food market) and pseudo-nutrition professionals (trying to sell their books) hasn't helped. Different health agencies and institutes handing out different diet guidelines (often on the same nutrient) telling us WHAT to do but not HOW to do it doesn't even come close to rescuing the consumer amidst all this confusion.

So, I propose that the problem doesn't lie in the area of consumer awareness or interest in nutrition or health but in the acquisition or availability of "nutritionally correct" and practical information. (Perhaps the average American comes out a little short in the motivation department, too.)

Observation #2.

People must also eat differently when eating out (and most of those people surveyed must have eaten out the day before). Supermarket sales have been showing that beef and egg consumption has persistently decreased since 1976, while fish and poultry sales are on the rise.

Observation #3.

I think there are some Americans eating "lighter meals" that frequently find themselves trapped in a "gourmet reward system." If they're "good" at a couple of meals, they later go for the rich desserts or fatty favorites—guilt free! Not that I'm into inflicting guilt, but I think people deserve to know how rich ice cream, flaky pastries, creamy entrees, deep fried doodads, etc., day after day, influence daily totals of fat, saturated fat, cholesterol, and calories.

Observation #4.

America snacks in a big way. The younger generations seem to "graze" more than the older. But grazing (snacking) as an act isn't bad, it's what we graze on that usually makes it bad. For all generations, the number one snack, according to the *New York Times* survey, is sweets and ice cream. Chips, nuts, and popcorn come in second. When does America snack? Well, 14% said they snacked all day, and 33% said they snacked after dinner or before bed.

Observation #5.

Americans are indeed starting to get the message that excess fat, saturated fat, cholesterol, and sodium may be harmful to their health. A recent Food Marketing Institute survey showed the same consumer trend the *New York Times* survey showed: People are becoming more concerned about specific nutrients rather than the concept of "nutrition" in general. They just don't know how to (and perhaps some just don't want to) translate these concerns into breakfast, lunch, or dinner decisions. Let's take a closer look at the way America is eating at breakfast, lunch, and dinner and why we still have far to go.

Eating in the Fast Lane

When you think "typical American diet" what do you picture? Meat and potatoes? TV dinners? Guess again. In recent years, the average American has doled out $400 to buy fast food. And fast food sales have doubled, at least, over the past seven years.

Even TV dinners take too long to heat up in the oven, compared with the shelves of microwavable gourmet and not-so-gourmet entrees available at supermarkets. And you can take your pick of fast food on your way to just about anywhere.

The 100% pure home-cooked meal (you know, the one demanding hours of preparation time) seems to have become extinct sometime between World War II and the sexual revolution of the 60s. It used to be accepted that mothers or housewives were the ones responsible for buying and making food for the family. But now that the big home-cooked meal is OUT and food in minutes is IN, food buying decisions are up for grabs. It's every person for him or herself, and everyone becomes a "consumer." Kind of makes you feel liberated, doesn't it?

Every time we place a fast food or restaurant order, every time we pull a frozen entree from the freezer case or a can off the shelf, we are making a decision that affects our health. Problem is the typical American let loose to make his or her own food choices isn't doing too well.

Let's find out the fatty truth about America's most loved meals, beginning with how some of us start our days.

MORNINGS

Fast food

1 Sausage Biscuit (McDonalds)
Calories 582
Sodium 1380 mg
61% calories from FAT

Restaurants

Ham and cheese (3 egg) omelette, 3 slices bacon, hash browns, 8 oz. of whole milk
Calories 990
Sodium 2061 mg
62% calories from FAT
Fiber 0.3 gm

TYPICAL LUNCHES

Fast Food

Big Mac, small fries, chocolate shake
Calories 1166
Sodium 1419 mg
41% calories from FAT

Restaurants

Chef salad

(1/4 cup creamy dressing, 2 cups lettuce with egg, ham, cheese, avocado, and tomato)
Calories 785
Sodium 1422 mg
72% calories from FAT
Fiber 6 gm

* Do you carefully order the chef salad, thinking you're not eating the calories and fat that usually comes with restaurant lunches? Try again.

French Dip Sandwich

(6 oz roast beef on a submarine roll, dipped in gravy)
1 cup potato salad
12 oz whole milk
Calories 1628
Sodium 1664 mg
53% calories from FAT
Fiber 4 gm

Bag Lunch

Salami and cheese sandwich
(2 slices white bread, 5 slices dry salami, 2 oz cheese, 2 teaspoons mayonnaise)
2 1/2 oz bag of chips
12 oz fruit soda
Calories 1059
Sodium 1572 mg
55% calories from FAT

Dinners
Fast Food

1 Extra Crispy Dinner (Kentucky Fried Chicken)
Calories 950
Sodium 1915
51% calories from FAT

Restaurants

6 oz T-bone steak (with visible fat)
1 baked potato with butter and sour cream, 1/2 cup mixed
    vegetables, 1 slice apple pie, 12 oz wine
Calories 1886
Sodium 741 mg (with no salt added)
64% calories from FAT
Fiber 14 gm

So what does all this mean in nutrient terms?

Basically, this means the typical American diet is:

>—too high in fat, protein, calories (sometimes), sodium, and cholesterol and too low in complex carbohydrates, fiber, and some vitamins and minerals.

You're thinking, "What a mess!" "I'm never going to remember all these things." Or "There're just too many things to change—so why don't I just forget about it."

Well, relax. It's not as complicated as it seems. All these nutrient problems are related and can be easily understood and solved. Allow me to explain.

For many of us, problems start with our choosing too many high fat foods and meals high in protein. (Meals high in animal protein usually tend to be high in fat too.) And where there's fat, there's a whole bunch of calories. As an example of the problem, in 1979, Americans ate only one pound of fish for every 10 pounds of beef and pork. (Excess meat consumption also is helping to keep our saturated fat intake at an all-time high.)

If someone said to you, "Quick, think of some 'high protein' foods," you might imagine a thick, juicy, medium rare, 6
oz. steak—untrimmed of fat, of course, because as others will
remind you, it's the best part. Did you also imagine it having
805 calories, 83% of which are from fat? Or maybe I'm catch-
ing you on a sunny Saturday morning and you're thinking of a
2-egg omelette filled with 2 ounces of cheese bubbling out of
the side nearest you. Well, the omelette has 370 calories, 71%
of which are from fat—not even mentioning the fried potatoes
or sausage you could be picturing next to it!

And of course, when eating typically American, we add
extra fat to our food one way or another—like oil in our frying
pan, shortening in the mixing bowl, and butter or sour cream
on our table.

So you see, an excess in animal protein (dairy foods,
meats, eggs, etc.) can also lead to a high intake of cholesterol— and excess fat, in general. And in turn this usually
leads to excess calories.

So if we're making our portions of animal protein food
smaller, eating less fatty foods, etc., what should we eat
instead? The answer is complex carbohydrates. By eating
foods such as fruits, vegetables, grains (rice, oats), whole
wheat bread, and pasta, we can't help but increase fiber in our
diet and improve the amount and combinations of vitamins
and minerals.

If you haven't got it all down yet, don't panic. That's what
the rest of the book is for.

I'm not suggesting you never drive through the golden
arches again. I'm not even suggesting the frozen food section
be roped off as a "restricted area—beware." And I'm not saying
fast and frozen food is BAD and home cooked meals are GOOD.
Because there are better, healthier choices out there . . . yes,
even in convenience land. We just need to know what they are.

Once we start pitching our dollars on the healthier choices, we're sending a vote to food companies and restaurants in
favor of selling healthier products. So as time goes on, we may
even have more healthful foods to choose from.

And while we're filling out our ballots, companies need
to realize that any food package without a nutrient informa-

tion label isn't even in the running for us. (These labels are still optional by law, unless a nutritional claim is made in the advertising.) How can we know whether the food meets nutritional guidelines without the label listing this information?

Nutrition is becoming a top priority for more and more people. But so is time and—as long as we all have tastebuds and a desire to enjoy eating—taste.

The top three factors involved in choosing food should be

- Nutrition
- Time
- Taste

If you're wondering why taste is rated third, hear me out. In order to really taste your food, you have to have the time to enjoy eating it, which for some of us means taking less time to make it. And we won't have time or taste buds unless we are alive and well, which is where low-fat eating comes in—and thus the need for this book.

Why Use Percent Calories from Fat and What Does It Mean?

Before we go any further, there's something you should know. You may have already wondered why is she using percent calories from fat and what does it mean anyway? You should know there are two ways of judging whether something is low in fat. You can use grams of fat or the percent of calories from fat. The latter is a percentage based on the proportion of fat calories to total calories and therefore gives you a percentage. The first is an absolute amount based on the weight of fat in a particular product.

Currently, it's an on-going debate between the two. Some dietitians pledge allegiance to the grams of fat camp and others swear percent calories from fat is the best way to go. It really is a choice between the two because paying attention to both is terribly confusing and time consuming. The truth is they both have weaknesses, but using grams of fat as a way of judging fat content has many more weaknesses, in my opinion. So basically this entire book is geared to using the percent of calories from fat criteria because it has fewer problems.

First of all, if the whole point is that you're trying to adhere to the "eat less than 30% calories from fat" daily health guidelines, wouldn't you want to judge your meals by the same criteria? It makes sense that if most of your meals are less than 30% calories from fat your intake overall is less than 30% calories from fat. That's the beauty of using percentages; they cross over boundaries. For example, if every item you put in your mouth during a meal is less than 30% calories from fat, then the whole meal will be less than 30% fat. And if every meal during the day is less than 30% calories from fat, your day's intake will be less than 30% calories from fat!

So because each meal is a separate entity, each one having less than 30% calories from fat, you can move on to the next meal without regard to the last. When using grams of fat, your daily allotment of fat grams has to be added up as the day goes on. For example, if you're supposed to eat 1800 calories a day with less than 30 percent of those calories from fat, you need to have less than 60 grams of fat each day.

Here's how to calculate your fat calorie allowance: Say you eat 1800 calories a day. Multiply 1800 calories by 30%. This tells you you can have 540 fat calories. Each gram of fat has 9 calories, so 540 fat calories divided by 9 gives 60 grams of fat.

Which brings me to another problem with using grams of fat. No one eats exactly the same amount of calories day in and day out. And no one has the time and energy to faithfully keep track of their grams of fat and total calories over a day's time. For example, if you eat 60 grams of fat, but for some reason your meals added up to only 1400 calories that particular day, you will have eating 39% of your calories from fat—hardly close to the less than 30 percent guidelines.

But, if for some reason you've already settled into the grams of fat groove, or if you're just plain curious, you can calculate grams of fat from the percent calories from fat information in this book by:

Step 1. Divide the percent calories from fat by 100

Step 2. Multiply the calories per serving by this fraction.

Step 3. Take this new number and divide by 9—the number of calories in 1 gram of fat.

Your answer tells you the grams of fat per serving.

2

Focus on Fat: Your Life Depends on It

People come up with all sorts of reasons for not caring that the way they eat may be hazardous to their health. "My father lived to be 90." "I've never been overweight." "You have to die of something." I've heard them all!

True, we do have to die of something, but the way we eat may strongly direct whether we die of this "something" at age 50 or 90. True, our genes partly determine our risk for these chronic diseases or possibly our response to the nutritional factors that relate to chronic disease. But for most of these diseases, we have no way of identifying who these susceptible people are.

Besides, who are we kidding? We're not just talking about one or two percent of Americans who happen to be born in a family dying primarily of chronic disease! Seventy percent of all deaths in the U.S. are related to cardiovascular diseases and cancer (number one and two in a distinguished list of chronic diseases).

In 1988, "low-fat eating" made the front page of most major newspapers, thanks to the much appreciated report from the Surgeon General C. Everett Koop on Nutrition and Health. Dr. Koop positioned diet on the front line of defense against chronic disease by saying, "If you are among the two out of three Americans who do not smoke or drink excessively, your choice of diet can influence your long-term health prospects more than any other action you might take."

Koop even confirmed that dietary fat is the number one bad guy, saying: "Of greatest concern is our excessive intake of dietary fat and its relationship to risk of chronic diseases such as coronary heart disease, some types of cancers, diabetes, high blood pressure, stroke and obesity."

So, according to this government report, issued from America's ultimate physician (so to speak) reducing our fat intake is the number one dietary priority of the nation. It's music to my ears. More specifically, the report said a high intake of total dietary fat is associated with increases in risk for obesity, some types of cancer and possibly gallbladder disease. Furthermore, a high intake of saturated fats and, to a lesser degree, of dietary cholesterol is linked to increased risk of coronary heart disease.

Then, in 1989 the National Academy of Sciences released the 1200-some odd page report entitled "Diet and Health— Implications for Reducing Chronic Disease Risk." And what do you know! The committee gave highest priority to the recommendation to reduce the total amount of fat in our diets. The report explained that it gave top billing to fat because "the scientific evidence concerning dietary fats and other lipids and human health is strongest and the likely impact on public health is greatest."

The report recommended Americans "reduce total fat to 30 percent or less of calories, reduce saturated fatty acid intake to less than 10 percent of calories and reduce cholesterol to less than 300 milligrams daily." Well, that sure sounds like a lot of "reducing" needs to go on.

But fear not. There are certain foods we should eat more of. The report points out that most people should compensate for the loss of fat calories by eating greater amounts of complex carbohydrates (by choosing more vegetables, fruits, grains, cereals, and legumes).

The justification for the recommendations these two reports make rests on the role diet (particularly dietary fat) plays in five of the ten leading causes of death: Heart disease (#1), cancer (#2), stroke (#3), diabetes(#7), and atherosclerosis (#10). One statistic from the Surgeon General's report that really impressed me was that of the 2.1 million Americans who died in 1987, nearly 1.5 million (71 percent) were killed by diseases associated with poor diet. What are these alleged associations? Take a look at the chart that follows.

Changes in Diet that Can Reduce the Risks of Certain Diseases

Disease	Eat Less Fat	Control Calories	Increase Starch and Fiber	Reduce Sodium	Control Alcohol
Heart Disease	✔	✔		✔	
Cancer	✔	✔	✔		✔
Stroke	✔	✔		✔	✔
Diabetes	✔	✔	✔		
Gastro-intestinal disease	✔	✔	✔		✔

A "✔" indicates that making this change in the average American diet will reduce the risk for that disease. Source: Surgeon General's Report on Nutrition and Health, 1988.

After looking at this chart, it's plain to see how "eating less fat" became the most important dietary recommendation. There's a bonus in following this guideline, too. Eating less fat will also assist you in meeting the next recommendation — "control calories' — because "fat" has more than twice the calories per gram as carbohydrates and protein. High-fat foods, not surprisingly, tend to be high calorie foods.

Now, if you're ready, we'll proceed on to discuss each of America's three top health concerns individually (heart disease, obesity and dieting, and cancer). Then we will finish the chapter by making sense of all the various diet guidelines that have come out within the past decade —from the American Heart Association to the National Cancer Institute.

Heart Disease

Confused over cholesterol?

Can you say "NO cholesterol?" I knew you could, because most people can and do—quite often in an average day. This is one nutrition term America has down pat.

Oddly enough, so do the food companies who plaster "No Cholesterol" on their packages of potato chips, bottles of vegetable oils, or cans of vegetable shortening. I hate to break the news to everyone, but these foods never had cholesterol! But, they've always been (and still are) high in fat.

Then again, there are those products, such as egg noodles, mayonnaise, eggs, or ice cream, that normally do contain cholesterol and now have no cholesterol alternatives. Examples are "No Yolks" pasta or Mocha Mix, the second of which is still high in fat. So now that you're totally confused, how can we tell the difference between "Cholesterol" claims on products that never had cholesterol and products that really have been modified? And is this "No Cholesterol" stuff as important as everyone thinks it is?

There are actually two meanings for the word "cholesterol." Dietary cholesterol is the amount of cholesterol in the food we eat, and serum cholesterol is the amount of cholesterol-containing lipids (fats) swirling through our blood stream.

High serum cholesterol (the main contributor to the bad publicity on cholesterol) is one of the three most important controllable heart disease risk factors. The other two are cigarette smoking and high blood pressure. Dietary cholesterol is just one of the many food constituents that help dictate our serum cholesterol levels. The others are high amounts of total fat, saturated fat, and excess calories. And out of all of these, total fat is the main boogie man.

Experts agree that the major determinant of high serum cholesterol levels in otherwise normal people is the total amount of fat eaten. Thus, the most powerful way to reduce our serum cholesterol levels is to reduce the total amount of fat we eat—especially saturated fat. Plus by lowering the total amount of fat in our meal (and lowering our percent of calories from fat), we will most likely also lower the amount of saturated fat, excess calories, and dietary cholesterol.

Still, it's a good idea to make a point of limiting the other constituents, namely cholesterol and saturated fat. And, as luck would have it, where there's cholesterol, there's saturated fat. Interestingly, it's not necessarily vice versa: Sometimes there is saturated fat in non-cholesterol foods, such as hydrogenated vegetable oils and coconut and palm oil, which are two naturally saturated vegetable oils.

You'll find cholesterol in all animal foods (meats, dairy products, fish, and poultry) but egg yolks and organ meats have much more than their share. Just remember where there's animal fat, there tends to be cholesterol. As the fat content goes down in a product containing cholesterol, so does the cholesterol content. A cup of whole milk, for example, has 35 milligrams of cholesterol and is 51 percent of calories from fat, while nonfat milk has 5 milligrams of cholesterol and is 5 percent calories from fat.

It's true that we actually NEED cholesterol to form things like hormones and cell membranes in our bodies. But the human animal came prepared, and we actually produce this required cholesterol all by ourselves. So any cholesterol from the food we eat is extra.

What were our naturally "no cholesterol" options before food companies created no-cholesterol eggs or mayonnaise? Vegetables, fruits, breads, cereals, grains, and legumes. But we tend to pour cheese or butter sauces over our pure and innocent vegetables, plop whipped cream on our fruits, spread gobs of cream cheese or butter on our bread (you get the picture), all of which add fat and cholesterol. Take white or whole wheat flour. Knead it with butter and milk, and voila! You've got your basic croissant, with 60 milligrams of cholesterol each and around 50 percent of calories from fat!

What do we do about these other cholesterol-packed foods? First, keep in mind some are more packed than others. Obviously cholesterol-packed foods, such as egg yolks and organ meats, should be avoided or cut back when possible. And if you're going to reach into that egg carton, keep your hands off the sour cream, cheese, bacon, butter, etc.

Second, remember the bottom line is the total amount of fat (percent calories from fat).You'll find some foods, such as certain shellfish, are low in total fat but moderately high in cholesterol. Of what am I speaking? I'll save you the trouble (and boredom) of reading through your nearest food chart: The low-fat foods in the cholesterol hot seat are squid and shrimp.

In their defense, let me just add that, per ounce, these fishies have a much lower calorie and fat content than your average slice of beef or pork. The serving size is usually smaller (around 2 ounces) for these foods too, compared with the three-egg omelette or the 5-ounce T-bone.

So, let's review. What most of us have actually heard, from scientific sources, about lowering our serum cholesterol levels applies to eating a low-fat diet. Certainly eating less than 300 milligrams of cholesterol a day and limiting saturated fat is part of this low-fat way of eating. Just because something doesn't have cholesterol doesn't mean it's low in fat or good for you. Many of the non-dairy creamers, no-cholesterol ice cream or egg substitutes have just as much fat as the regular rich items.

Serum Cholesterol Tests

Heart disease usually strikes without warning. (Only 20 percent of heart attacks are preceded by chest pains or angina.) And even though being thin is seen as an "end-all" in our society, healthy arteries aren't necessarily part of the deal. Being thin doesn't automatically pardon you from having high blood pressure or high serum cholesterol.

And if you're young, congratulations are in order. You are at the BEST time in your life to start preventing heart disease! If you wait until you start feeling like a mere mortal, say around your 40s, some damage has probably already occurred. It's best to get a running start in the race against heart disease. Recent evidence shows a possible two-year lag period from the time serum cholesterol levels are lowered and the time there is an actual reduction in the risk of heart disease.

I know preventing heart disease isn't the most thrilling challenge to have. But if high drama is what you want, I've got plenty of morbidity and mortality statistics I can show you. Will you settle for one? "Total serum cholesterol" levels greater than 200 mg/dl are considered "incompatible with optimal cardiovascular health." This person is at moderate to high risk for heart disease, depending on how much above 200 the serum cholesterol levels are. Here's the scary part: More than half of all middle-aged Americans have serum cholesterol levels greater than 200 mg/dl.

Taking "The Test"

Are you waiting until your 40th birthday to have your serum cholesterol measured? If you have a family history of heart disease, that is if relatives have died at an early age (before 50) of stroke or heart attack, some experts are now recommending you be tested at age 20 and retested every three years. If you don't have heart disease in your family, first pat yourself on the back because you're rare. Then, take a cholesterol test when you're 30 and repeat the test every five years.

Now, for those of you hiding in your genes saying, "Either I'm born with it or I'm not," you should know that most of us are born with a serum cholesterol level of about 70 mg/dl. And between the ages of 1 and 17 our average serum cholesterol is about 150. This is the level for three-fourths of the world's adult population—who don't tend to get heart disease.

Many of the heart attacks in America strike people with a serum cholesterol level between 200 and 250 mg/dl. Still, some people in that group don't have heart attacks. Why? We have no absolute answers, but my guess is that it has to do with our lifestyles. Smoking, using alcohol or drugs, high blood pressure, and not eating the right food all play a role. Dr. William Castelli, one of the leading national experts on the subject, says, "Start with your diet." I couldn't agree more.

Several different serum cholesterol tests are available, some more indicative (and expensive) than others. You've got your basic "total serum cholesterol" test at around $24, or you have your complete "lipid profile" (which measure low-density lipoprotein, high-density lipoprotein, total serum cholesterol, and other components) at approximately $30. You can usually be tested at any private hospital, or you can call your local American Heart Association for a referral.

Good and Bad Serum Cholesterol

All cholesterol is not created equal. Low-density lipoproteins (LDL) are light in weight or "low in density" because they're mostly fat. They're better know as BAD cholesterol because high levels of LDLs in the blood usually mean high total serum cholesterol levels. These are associated with an increased risk of coronary heart disease because LDLs tend to deposit themselves on artery walls.

On the other hand, high-density lipoproteins (HDL) are heavy because they're mostly protein, and protein weighs more than water or fat. This provides more muscle to push bad cholesterol around and helps remove excess cholesterol from the artery wall. Higher levels of HDLs in the blood are associated with lower rates of heart disease.

The most accurate way to measure your heart disease risk is by looking at the ratio of either total serum cholesterol to HDL or LDL to HDL. These two ratios continue to predict risk on people older than 55 years, unlike the straight total serum cholesterol measurement. Let's look at RISK:

Total Serum Cholesterol Measurement

Age	Moderate Risk	High Risk
2-19	> 170	> 185
20-29	> 200	> 220
30-39	> 220	> 240
> 40	> 240	> 260

- Levels of 140 to 180 are associated with the lowest rates of coronary heart disease.
- Levels of 180 to 200 are associated with substantially lower heart disease incidence and favorable overall health status
- At 250 mg, you have twice the risk as at 200 mg.
- At 300 mg, your risk is four times higher than at 200 mg.

Total Serum Cholesterol to HDL Ratio

- A ratio of 5 reflects high risk
- 4.5 or higher is cause for concern (levels typical in affluent Western populations)
- At 3.5, risk is about half the standard (typical of levels found in countries with a low incidence of heart disease)

In general, pay attention to HDL levels of less than 40 mg.

LDL to HDL ratio in men 50 to 79 years of age.

- A ratio of 1.0 carries one-half the average risk.
- At 3.6 the risk is considered average.
- A ratio of 6.3 carries two times the average risk.
- At 8.0, the risk is three times average.

Allow me now to offer you some encouragement:

- Every 10 mg increase in HDL cholesterol is associated with a 50 percent decrease in heart disease risk.
- It is estimated that for every 1 percent you lower your serum cholesterol, your heart attack rate drops by 2 percent. More and more data show this is true for the young or older person.
- No environmental factor—smoking, exercise, stress reduction—has been shown to influence serum cholesterol and LDL-cholesterol more profoundly than DIET.

The Oat Bran Story

Within one year in recent history, oat bran sales skyrocketed by almost 800 percent! Ever wish you had stock in a particular product—after the fact? We definitely witnessed an oat bran boom. Newspapers and magazines constantly wrote about it. New food products featuring oat bran as an ingredient seem to squeeze their way onto the supermarket shelves daily. Dr. Dean Edel's TV show in San Francisco even featured members of the audience tasting various oat cereals last year. So what's going on? What's the real story on oat bran? The answer is a simple two words: Soluble fiber.

Oats contain a type of fiber that is soluble in water. When eaten in recommended amounts, this fiber reduces serum cholesterol levels. The soluble plant fiber found in oats (called beta glucangum) appears to form a gel in the intestines

and binds with bile acids. (Your body uses its stores of cholesterol to manufacture these digestive juices.) The undigestible
fiber and the bile acids attached to it (carrying the cholesterol)
pass right through your body. But this doesn't seem to be the
only oat bran benefit.

Another mechanism in the intestines (involving the production of short-chain fatty acids) may also have value for
lowering cholesterol. Unfortunately, we need more research
to understand this, but it's in the works.

Sounds pretty straight forward, right? All you have to do
is eat oat bran and your serum cholesterol will drop. Wrong!
Here's the catch. All the studies showing health benefits with
oats or oat bran were done as part of a low-cholesterol, low-fat
diet. One researcher even estimated that about a third of the
demonstrated reduction in serum cholesterol could be
attributed to the oat bran factor. He attributed the rest to the
infamous "Low-Fat Diet."

But don't get me wrong. Certainly all these studies are
telling us something. Oats and oat bran, as particularly great
sources of soluble fiber, can enhance the serum cholesterol
lowering effects of a diet low in fat and cholesterol.

At a time when boxes of oat bran remain scarce and
when mothers everywhere try to replace good old-fashioned
oatmeal with oat bran hot cereal, I'm thrilled to pass on some
truly liberating information. You don't have to eat "oat bran"
cereal to acquire the benefits of the soluble fiber in oats. You
can also eat plain old oats!

Because the bran part of the oat is particularly difficult
to extract without collecting quite a bit of oat starch with it,
there actually isn't a big difference between the amount of soluble fiber in oat bran versus regular oats. That's also why oat
bran contains some calories. The recommended daily dose of
oat bran is 2/3 cup (dry), which contributes 4 grams of water-
soluble fiber. One cup of dry oatmeal also offers you 4 grams
of water-soluble fiber. So for the people out there who have
been enjoying hot oatmeal for years, keep on enjoying it—
without added butter or cream, of course!

What about all the oat bran diehards? Should they buy
the finer or coarser (flakier) grinds? When first asked this

question, my instinct was to answer "coarser." (I must confess first that I do have a preference toward cooking with the coarser, flakier types.) Later it occurred to me that perhaps the finer, more granular types might blend with intestinal water and bile acids easier, therefore making itself more physiologically available and useful.

I frantically proceeded to fish around for some evidence one way or the other. My curiosity was captured. And the winner is . . . both! Currently, no specific information shows that one is better than the other. So my advice to you for now is to try them both and see which you like best.

Beyond Oat Bran

Oat bran has infiltrated supermarket shelves everywhere. From English muffins to frozen waffles, it's the star ingredient in many foods. You know you've made it when Mrs. Fields creates a cookie in your honor. (That's right! You can now buy oat bran cookies at Mrs. Fields.) What's next? Oat bran chips?

This may come as a shock to certain food companies, but oat bran does NOT have exclusive rights to "soluble fiber." (Remember soluble fibers, as a group, are thought to help reduce the bad cholesterol, LDL, in the blood. It's just that oat bran and oatmeal have particularly impressive amounts of this type of fiber.)

In fact, rice bran enthusiasts are eagerly trying to get their facts and figures together so they too can enter this profitable popularity contest. As we speak, studies are underway to test the beneficial effects of rice bran. But I can tell you right now, packaging and selling rice bran will be a bit more tricky than oat bran. Of the 78 calories or so per ounce of rice bran, 40 percent is from fat. With oat bran, only 10 percent of calories is from fat. With such a significant amount of fat, mostly UNsaturated, in rice bran, keeping the bran from turning rancid after a short time is a big challenge.

But before all of us start running around in search of the perfect bran, there is some more crucial information you should know. Many of the scientists conducting research on increasing the intake of water-soluble fiber suggested a VARI-

ETY of food sources for the fiber. I'm afraid this is one of those boring but true cases where "variety" is the key. No quick-fix, fancy solution, just your run-of-the-mill "balanced and varied" diet.

Where then are some of these other potential sources of soluble fiber? We can pick up some in the produce section, and we can buy it in a can. Certain beans—kidney, white, and pinto—in amounts of about 1/2 cup (canned), come close to matching the power of oats. That's what the *American Journal of Clinical Nutrition* reported recently. They also listed some fruits and vegetables. Specifically, 1/2 cup of broccoli, 1 small apple, 1/3 cup purple plums, 1 small orange, and 1/2 cup of carrots were shown to have 1/3 to 1/2 the water-soluble fiber found in 1/3 cup of oat bran.

The lesson here is that we will probably never find the perfect bran, since there are several different types of fiber. Each has specific physiological purposes and health benefits. Perfection, in this case, seems to come in the form of "variation."

Omega-3 Update: The Future for Fish Oils

It's been a while since Omega-3 fatty acids hit the press and airwaves as champions in the war against cholesterol build-up. (Sounds like a powerful bathroom cleanser, doesn't it?) Are these little fish oils going to swim out of the limelight as quickly as they swam in? I doubt it.

The Omega-3 fatty acids, which are polyunsaturated, by the way, apparently work by making it more difficult for blood to clot and by protecting blood vessel walls from cholesterol accumulation. For you and me, this means a reduced risk of artery blockage and heart attack. Fish oils somehow lower the levels of bad cholesterol and raise those for good cholesterol.

But it isn't as simple as it sounds. (Is it ever?) One study, in which people ate 7 ounces of fish every day, showed a decrease in serum triglycerides only. No change was seen in the LDL or HDL levels.

And the fish oil supplement studies aren't any help either. Even to meet the lower end of the dose scale (4 grams of EPA a day) used in these studies would require popping 35 to 100 high-priced pills every day! And speaking of fish oil supplements, I have just a few more gripes. Supplement companies have chosen not to list the amount of cholesterol and the exact part of the fish's body the oil comes from on their product labels.

Does that matter? In my opinion, yes it does. A typical dose, as used in these studies, may add around 300 milligrams of cholesterol to your diet each day. If the fish oils were taken from the liver of the fish, they may contain pesticides or other contaminants. Because Omega-3 fatty acids are easily oxidized (meaning they link up with oxygen molecules) they will most likely increase our need for anti-oxidants, such as vitamin E or selenium. (Anti-oxidants will link up with oxygen instead of the Omega-3 fatty acids.)

Work is still going on to test the various health attributes of the Omega-3's. But some studies suggest that a diet rich in fish oil can reduce levels of high blood fats. Omega-3's might also aid in keeping platelets in the blood from becoming less "sticky" and therefore less apt to form blood clots.

Stay tuned for new information over the next few years. In addition to their value in heart disease, Omega-3's are being studied in prevention of breast cancer, high blood pressure, migraine headaches, and rheumatoid arthritis. Nothing is conclusive yet. In fact, the long-term effects of fish oil supplements still are unknown. We do know Omega-3's affect each person differently, and it's impossible to prescribe a specific dosage at this point. Fish oil supplements, according to a recent Food and Drug Administration (FDA) ruling, should be classified as "drugs", forcing companies to prove their safety and value.

One company has already been ordered to stop marketing their products, and several similar cases are pending. What does the FDA say to fish oil supplements continually being promoted as beneficial to health? They say, "There is no general recognition by qualified experts to warrant these marketing claims at this time."

The word from experts on the best way to get your Omega-3's is still "EAT FISH!" Can a recommendation be so generic about fish? It certainly can. All seafood contains Omega-3 fatty acids. The fattier fish just have more.

How much fish? Moderation is still the key. Most experts are recommending 2 to 4 servings of fish each week, or an average of 9 ounces a week. Most Americans are still not measuring up. One source showed the average American has less than 20 ounces of fish a month—or less than 5 ounces a week. But that's nothing that a 4-ounce serving of salmon or sardines can't cure.

There's no magical oil or potion. And no getting around it, folks. America has to aim toward a diet lower in total fat and saturated fat. It's probably best that we "Westerners" think of this fish oil business in terms of trying to replace some of our overflowing amounts of saturated fat with Omega-3 foods—seafood, beans, nuts, and nut oils. Has a study been done from this angle? Glad you asked. A 16-year study was done in Seattle, where fish was substituted for meat three times a week. The control groups had four time the incidence of fatal heart attacks as the fish eaters.

Typically, we need more and better research before we can remove all doubts that Omega-3's were solely (there's a nifty pun) responsible for these results. What is clear is that benefits from Omega-3's last only as long as they are consumed, and there's no evidence so far that pre-existing heart disease can be reversed by consuming these fatty acids.

Non-fish sources of Omega-3's are listed on the next page, along with high Omega-3 and medium Omega-3 fish.

Non-Fish Omega-3 Foods

Food edible portion, raw	Grams of linolenic acid per 100 mg.
Linseed oil	53.3
Rapeseed oil (canola)	11.1
Soybean oil	6.8
Walnut oil	10.4
Wheatgerm oil	6.9
Beans, common, dry	0.6
Soybeans, dry	1.6
Beechnuts, dried	1.7
Butternuts, dried	8.7
Walnuts, English	6.8
Leeks, freeze-dried, raw	0.7
Seaweed, spirolina, dried	0.8
Soybeans, green, raw	3.2
Soybeans, mature seeds, cooked	2.1

High Omega-3 Fish

(Providing 1 to 2 gm. of Omega-3 fatty acids per 100 gm., edible portion, raw)

Salmon   Mackerel
Herring   Sardines
Sable Fish   Lake Trout
Fresh Tuna   Whitefish
Anchovies

Medium Omega-3 Fish

(Providing 0.5 to 0.9 gm. of Omega-3 fatty acids per 100 gm., edible portion, raw)

Halibut   Bluefish
Rockfish   Rainbow Trout
Sea Trout   Ocean Perch
Bass   Pollock
Oysters

Controlling High Blood Pressure

It seems the time has come to add "SALT" to our list of four letter words. But isn't it true (you might debate) SALT (also known as sodium chloride) is being cross-examined only because of its association with the mineral sodium? And shouldn't it really be SODIUM on trial?

Well, hear me out. One-third of the average American's sodium intake comes direct from the SALT he or she dutifully adds at the table or when cooking. And the average American's sodium intake totals around 5,000 mg per day. So, if this average American took the salt shaker off the table—or better yet, stuck it way behind the baking powder in some hard-to-reach cupboard—couldn't we expect to drop to the 1,000 to 3,000 mg per day limits recommended by the American Heart Association and the National Academy of Sciences? The prosecution rests.

Why all this fuss over salt and sodium? In a word, HYPERTENSION. Right at this moment, one of every four Americans have it—60 million people. About 95 percent of them are stuck with it for the rest of their lives because the cause is unknown. That's obviously the BAD news. The good news is there ARE several ways to help CONTROL HYPERTENSION.

Hypertension is a fancy name for high blood pressure. It's a major risk factor for the number one American killer, Heart Disease. It also is an underlying cause of America's number three cause of death, Stroke. It often develops when we reach age 30 or 40 without any symptoms. And it's difficult to predict who will be that one person in four to get it! More bad news. But I can tell you right now, if your parents have it or had it, there's a good chance you will too! Here are a few more facts about hypertension.

- The incidence of severely high blood pressure is three times higher for blacks than for whites.
- The older you get the higher your risk. (By age 74, half the U.S. population has hypertension.)
- If you're considered "obese", your risk is increased.
- If you're over 35, use oral contraceptives, and smoke, your risk is increased.
- If you have diabetes or kidney disease, your risk is high.

But no matter what, getting your blood pressure checked is the key. More than one-third of the 60 million people with hypertension don't even know they have it. And it's the high blood pressure that goes untreated that can lead to heart attack and stroke. If your blood pressure was normal the last time it was checked, be sure to get it rechecked every couple of years. And bring your kids with you. The National Heart Lung Blood Institute says, "High blood pressure in children represents a significant clinical problem."

High blood pressure treatment, other than medications, usually includes weight reduction if you're obese, limiting salt and sodium in your diet, controlling heavy drinking, and exercising. All of these are things we all should be doing for other reasons!

Some minerals, new on the hypertension scene, may help in the treatment and possibly the prevention of hypertension:

- *Magnesium:* Recent population studies suggest eating magnesium-packed foods, such as vegetables, fruits, whole grains, and low-fat dairy items, to ensure an adequate intake of magnesium.

- *Potassium:* The diet high in potassium may provide some protection in the arteries of people with high blood pressure. It may also lower blood pressure a little and protect the kidneys from related damage.

  Potassium is the mineral that made bananas the famous fruit it is. But potatoes, apricots, orange and grapefruit juice, and just about any kind of fruit and vegetable not cooked in water will add potassium to our diet. People with a history of kidney failure should check with their doctors before increasing their intake of these items.

  One researcher reported an increase of 10 millimoles of potassium in a retirement community—just one extra serving of fruit or vegetable—reduced the risk of stroke by 40 percent. Certainly, encouraging Americans to eat more fruits and vegetables is a good way to make sure we meet our Recommended Daily Allowance for potassium.

- *Calcium:* Just when you thought it was safe to avoid dairy products, evidence turns up linking decreases in systolic blood pressure and higher intakes of calcium or calcium supplements. It seems to work best for people with previous intake of calcium well below the RDA who have high systolic blood pressure readings. (Systolic is the top number in the blood pressure reading.)

A small number of people with hypertension may even have a rise in blood pressure with calcium supplements. And, of course, we're not able to detect who these people are beforehand. At this point, though, experts only recommend we take in the RDA for calcium (800 mg. per day, 1200 mg. per day for ages 11-24 and pregnant women). Very little evidence supports a need for more than this amount.

The Case Against Sodium

The learned taste for salt will take about two months to be unlearned. As you eat less and less salt, your taste buds become more aware of the salt and sodium that's there. You might ask, "Aren't only certain people sensitive to salt? (This refers to the people whose blood pressure rises from excessive sodium in their diet.)

Well, yes. But let me explain. We need to be concerned about two "salt sensitive" groups: those who already have high blood pressure and those who don't (yet). It has been estimated that 30 to 60 percent of people with essential hypertension (high blood pressure not caused by medications or other illnesses) can expect a significant drop in blood pressure (5 to 8 points) in response to salt restriction. Sometimes, after about 7 months of a mild sodium restricted diet, people can reduce or completely eliminate their blood pressure medication, which by the way, can have many side effects.

Obviously, if you add up the numbers (30 to 60 percent of a hypertensive group of possibly 15 percent of the total population, plus 25 percent in the remaining nonhypertensive category), it's far from 100 percent. Ah! There's the rub. Why then should everyone go out of the way to limit the criminal mineral sodium?

If reduced sodium will help protect even 20 percent of our population against potential stroke, heart attack, and kidney failure . . . and if we can still "taste saltiness" at these learned lower levels of salt and sodium . . . and as long as it is a reasonable reduction using basic steps like not salting food at the table and limiting heavily salted processed foods and not a severe restriction . . . the question isn't WHY, but WHY NOT?

Take soy sauce, or as I call it, "sodium sauce." You can buy the reduced-sodium soy sauce, cutting sodium in half without sacrificing flavor. At least I don't notice a difference, although I'm not really an expert on soy sauce.

Here are some sodium aliases, besides salt:

- Seasoning Salts (garlic salt, onion, salt, etc.)
- MSG (monosodium glutamate)
- soy sauce
- brine (salt and water)
- broth and bouillon
- sodium compounds:
  including sodium phosphate, sodium benzoate, sodium bicarbonate (baking soda), sodium hydroxide, sodium propionate, sodium sulfite, and baking powder
- AND any other compounds with the word "SODIUM" in them. (There are more than 70!)

Check the amount of sodium listed per serving on the label to truly know the combined effect of the sodium-containing ingredients.

If you tend to shake your salt . . .

Take the Salt Shaker Test

1. Cover a plate with wax paper or foil
2. Salt the make-believe plate of food as you would normally
3. Measure the salt into the appropriate size teaspoon:

   1/8 teaspoon of salt = 250 mg of sodium
   1/4 teaspoon of salt = 500 mg of sodium
   1/2 teaspoon of salt = 1,000 mg of sodium
   1 teaspoon of salt = 2,000 mg of sodium

   Now, multiply this amount by the number of times you grab the salt shaker in a day.

Obesity and Dieting

Like clockwork, the first few months in the new year and then the summer season simultaneously bring with them irritating commercials for countless weight loss programs. The profit-driven diet programs aren't dumb; they're capitalizing on the surge of good intentions and newly sworn goals (not to mention the fear of swimsuits) that typically accompany this time of year.

Americans can't seem to shake their attachment to two modern dieting criteria: We want whatever we do to be quick and painless. We know it—and the weight programs know it. The difference is they stand to make a profit every year because of it. And all we get is more frustrated, sometimes a bit heavier than we were, and of course, we get a bill.

The bottom line is these low calorie diets just don't take the fat off for good. Here's why:

#1. These diets are designed for quick "weight" loss, while losing body fat, which is what we really want, has to happen SLOWLY. In other words, if you're losing the pounds quickly, you can bet it isn't FAT you're losing. It could be body water, the breakdown of muscle tissue or essential carbohydrate stores. Keep in mind that in the best of circumstances you can only lose about two pounds of FAT a week; for some of us it might only be one pound a week.

#2. Many of these diets are too low in calories. Your brain alone requires 150 grams of glucose energy per day. Your body prefers to get its glucose energy from carbohydrates or, if it has to, from protein stores, also called lean body mass. So just to preserve our musculature and keep our brain happy and productive we need AT LEAST 600 calories in the form of mostly carbohydrates with about 1 gram of protein per kilogram of body weight (about 275 calories from protein for someone who weighs 150 pounds). But don't run off yet to check the calories on your diet shake. You also need some fat calories to balance your meals and contribute necessary fat-soluble vitamins, etc.

Which all means that most of us should never go on a diet that feeds us less than 1,000 calories a day. Not only is it counter-productive to losing the excess body fat that we're so anxious to lose (when we eat less than this our body starts conserving energy and actually burns and needs fewer calories than if we ate a little more), but we're risking our medical and nutritional safety as well.

#3. The whole philosophy of "dieting" works against long-term loss of body fat. These diets are programs that we learn to suffer through for a short period of time, when what obviously needs to happen is long-term life changes if we want the loss of body fat to also be for a lifetime. I know this isn't going to be a popular statement but someone has to say it. It's our lifestyle—the way we usually eat and exercise—that got us into this dieting dilemma. Eventually returning to the same high-fat, high-calorie, sedentary lifestyle isn't going to break the cycle permanently.

#4. Our suspicions should be raised by the very fact that most of these diet programs encourage you to depend on their particular products. Some even package their own salad dressings and vitamin supplements.

So how DO we lose weight safely and surely? First of all, we need to shift our focus from "a loss of pounds" to "a loss of body FAT." If scales were never invented, we would only have the way we feel and our appearance from which to judge, and isn't this what we should really be concerned about?

And you can encourage your body to use its extra fat by doing two things:

But I must warn you neither of these is easy or quick. They both involve pretty major changes in the way you've been doing business. And these changes should be permanent in order to keep your fat loss off for good.

#1. Start eating a low-fat diet.

#2. Make aerobic exercise a regular part of your life. (A special section at the end of this chapter on exercise will explain how this occurs.)

Rationale for Change

It has always made sense to me that the fat from food would be more likely to be deposited as fat in our bodies than carbohydrates, since the human body prefers to fuel itself with carbohydrate calories. Well, now I have some proof. It involves the Thermic Effect of Food (the "energy expended," or the caloric cost, of digestion, absorption, and storage of calories from fat, protein, and carbohydrate).

The body seems to handle the fat calories we eat more efficiently than equal calories from carbohydrates. This means it burns fewer calories taking care of the fat we just ingested than the carbohydrates. This is bad for us because we want the body to use as many calories as possible so we won't have unspent calories (so to speak) that will need to be "stored" as body fat. Don't underestimate how this might influence your weight control. The thermic effect of food accounts for approximately 10 percent of the calories we burn in a day.

Let's talk a bit more about why our body prefers to use carbohydrates as its main fuel and dietary fat for storage (energy for a rainy day). Well, for one thing it costs the body too much energy to convert dietary carbohydrate to stored fat. One researcher recently calculated the storage of fat from dietary fat (with a caloric cost of 7 percent) is greatly favored over the energy-intensive carbohydrate-to-fat conversion (costing 28 percent).

Putting it into simpler terms, new research is showing that adults gain weight much easier on a high-fat diet than on a diet consisting mostly of carbohydrate. Chalk one more up to the low-fat way of eating!

For many people, the fat loss process may be complicated by an internal control system—commonly referred to as the "set-point theory"—or a strong genetic influence that helps determine our basal metabolic rate (the amount of calories needed to sustain our bodies in a resting state) and how much fat each person carries and where. There are only two key lifestyle elements found to lower the theoretical "set point." Guess which two? Regular exercise and a low-fat diet.

I admit extremely overweight people may need some encouraging weight loss before they can collect the courage to face up to more effective and permanent lifestyle changes. Changing the way we eat and exercise requires extra personal motivation and external support. And that's where some of these commercial diet programs can help. The trick is finding a program that helps you with the behavioral aspects of your weight problem, teaches you the basics of eating a LOW-FAT diet, rich in essential nutrients for a lifetime, and includes an exercise component. They should also encourage you never to eat less than 1,000 calories a day.

Cancer and Diet

American is obsessed with cancer. Even Hollywood uses this disease to reach out to our emotions. Take, for example, the Academy Award winning film, "Terms of Endearment." I don't know about you, but I cried through the entire second half of this film.

But there is some new news about cancer—which happens to be good news: One-third of the cancer deaths in this country can be prevented through changes in our diet. If that hasn't impressed you, maybe this will. If America took to heart (and mouth) the dietary recommendations to prevent cancer—eating a diet low in fat, high in fiber with plenty of fruits and vegetables—200,000 lives would be saved each year!

How can we save those lives? Let's start by looking at two ways to prevent cancer through diet:

- Make sure you have plenty of the "good guys." (These are nutrients that help protect body cells from the "bad guys" or potential carcinogens.)
- Make sure you minimize your contact with these "bad guys" (These are substances that have a negative influence on your body's cells.)

Undoubtedly there are some people with their shoulders a shrugging or arms a waving who are declaring that "everything causes cancer!" "So, why bother?" I suggest these disbelievers re-read point #1 above.

Why not utilize the nutrients that help protect your body cells from the dangers of carcinogens? I think this is a winning strategy in the battle against cancer. Of course, if you're going out of your way to build up your body's defense against carcinogens, then it also makes sense to avoid close contact with the very enemies you're guarding yourself against (point #2).

So, okay, enough with the pep talk.

The Bad Guys

First, a rundown on some substances that are talked about in the media today. (At this point, however, no evidence is thought to exist proving these substances individually make a major contribution to cancer risk in the U.S.)

Nitrite: Sodium nitrite is a well-known additive (sometimes sodium nitrate is used) used mainly to "pinken" and preserve meat-like foods, such as hot dogs, ham, bologna, salami, sausage, corned beef, bacon, and cured fish. Nitrites can convert into carcinogenic nitrosamines. More nitrosamines can form from very hot charbroiling, barbequing, and frying—or in leftovers. So try to stay away from these on a daily basis.

Alflatoxins: These are formed by a certain type of mold that tends to grow on peanuts, corn, and cottonseed crops. Air-tight packaging and refrigeration help protect nuts and corn kernels from forming molds. Salt added to nut butter also will help. If you don't do anything else, be sure to throw out any moldy or abnormal looking nuts or corn kernels.

Natural Carcinogens: Mother nature creates carcinogenic substances too. They're found in produce such as mushrooms, potatoes, and rhubarb. But it isn't necessary, I repeat, isn't necessary, to stop eating these vegetables. Just inspect them closely for bad spots and sprouts, cutting them out to about an inch on all sides. And don't eat the spoiled one. (Although, you probably weren't going to do that anyway.)

Now, on to the biggest bad guy of them all—FAT.

In epidemiological (meaning the comparison of population groups) and animal studies, a high-fat diet was indeed associated with a higher risk of certain cancers (mainly colon, breast, and prostate cancers). Or looking at it in a more positive way, switching to a low-fat diet will likely decrease the risk of these cancers.

Some researchers might argue that the question of whether the amount of fat in our diet is related to certain cancers is, at this point, still considered a toss-up. But whenever anything is being "tossed up," I always say better safe than sorry. You better duck or be pretty well prepared to catch it!

There ARE indeed many studies that have suggested that a high-fat diet (no matter what type of fat) does increase your risk of these cancers. But whenever you study the effects of a diet high in fat, you're usually also—whether you want to or not—studying a diet high in total calories and protein. So far, it's been difficult to completely separate these factors and note their individual effect.

The Good Guys

I'll get right to the point. Diets high in plant foods (fruits, vegetables, legumes, and whole grain cereals), as part of a low-fat diet, are associated with a decrease in cancer of the lung, colon, esophagus, and stomach. There are several specific nutrients thought to be related to this protective effect.

Fiber

Fiber is thought to dilute potential cancer-forming substances by adding bulk that cannot be absorbed by the body. In addition, fiber decreases the time our intestinal wall is exposed to dangerous substances by escorting them quickly southward— if you know what I mean. It's suspected that the particularly insoluble fiber found in most whole grains and vegetables may protect the body against colon cancer. Other possible ways fiber protects the colon also have been proposed. Among them are: neutralizing various toxic metabolites by lowering the pH of the colonic lumen, binding with potential toxicants, which are then removed as waste along with the fiber.

Given there is still much to know and more research to be conducted about the different types of fiber (insoluble and soluble) and how one or more may aid in cancer prevention, experts recommend consuming a variety of fiber-containing foods.

What if I told you there was this great new high-fiber supplement you could inexpensively take several times a day that could increase your daily fiber total by 10 grams? Would you be willing to try it out? Would it help if I added that this

is half the amount of fiber recommended by the National
Cancer Institute (20 to 30 grams of fiber a day)?

What if I told you it wasn't a supplement at all, but a
common food we can easily buy in our supermarkets or order
in restaurants? Shouldn't you be even more interested in this
high-fiber food? What I'm asking you to do is take a fresh
look at "plain old fruits and vegetables."

Actually, there are quite a few different fruits and vegetables that give us as much fiber as a health food "fiber bar" or a
small scoop of bran. All fruits and vegetables, of course, contain some fiber and contribute to the "recommended daily
amount" of 20 to 30 grams.

Let's admit to one thing. Most of us don't sit down at the
end of the day and add up how many grams of fiber we ate
from whole grains and fruits and vegetables.

What would we do if our grand total was shy a few grams
anyway? (Maybe swallow down another scoop of bran?)

Keep reading for more information on fruits and vegetables and (for the first time) the actual number of servings recommended for the best health.

Antioxidants

Most of us already know about the fiber connection. Cereal
companies made sure of that. But which are the other body
protectors? In a word, produce.

Just as knights were in danger without their metal
armor, so a cell membrane should never leave home without
an antioxidant. These protectors block attacks, reducing or
neutralizing the effects of cancer-forming chemicals. Where
can we buy these coats of armor? Beta carotene (and vitamin
A), vitamins C and E, and the mineral selenium are your
potential antioxidants.

Beta carotene is thought to be particularly effective at
protecting against squamous-cell carcinoma (a common type
of lung cancer). One study showed people with low levels of
serum beta carotene were at least four times as likely to develop lung cancer as others.

How much is enough? The National Cancer Institute diet recommendations translate roughly into about 6 mg of beta carotene a day (about half a carrot). The typical American nibbles on only 1.5 mg a day. Popeye was on to something because spinach ranks number one in the top five beta carotene-rich foods, followed by carrots, broccoli, cantaloupe, and sweet potatoes. Not that I have anything against apples, but perhaps the saying should have been "a carrot a day . . ." Most of these foods also happen to be pretty good vitamin C providers, along with citrus fruits, of course. Vitamin C is the other antioxidant (when consumed in food) with some prospects of helping protect the body against some types of cancer.

Any Questions?

In the U.S. Surgeon General's report on Nutrition and Health released in 1987, fruits and vegetables as a group were listed as being associated with the prevention of lung, breast, colon, prostate, bladder, and stomach cancer. Specifically, fiber was listed as a fighter of breast and colon cancer.

Shortly after that, the National Academy of Sciences report on Diet and Health stressed that eating at least five servings of fruits and vegetables was an important disease preventing part of the highly recommended low-fat diet. "A serving" is 1/2 cup or 1 whole fruit (unless it's an exceptionally large fruit), or pure fruit juice or 1/4 cup of dried fruit.

In terms of the possible cancer prevention attributes of produce (fiber, vitamins A and C) some choices are better than others. The following lists are based on 1/2 cup servings or 1 whole fruit, unless otherwise noted.

Vitamin A rich fruits and vegetables

(These selections supply at least 50 percent of the RDA
for vitamin A.)

Cantaloupe	Bok choy
Carrots	Apricots (3 whole)
Greens	Winter squash
Sweet potatoes	

Spinach (1/2 cup cooked or 1 cup raw)

(These selections supply at least 25 percent of the RDA
for vitamin A.)

Nectarines	Papayas
Broccoli	Tomatoes

Romaine lettuce (1 cup fresh)
Loose leaf lettuce (1 cup fresh)

Vitamin C rich fruits and vegetables

(These selections supply at least 50 percent of the RDA for
vitamin C.)

Grapefruit (half)	Kiwi fruit
Oranges	Cantaloupe
Papaya	Strawberries
Orange juice	Broccoli
Brussels sprouts	Cauliflower
Green peppers	Green peas

(These selections supply at least 25 percent of the RDA
for vitamin C.)

Grapes (1 cup)	Honeydew
Raspberries	Grapefruit juice
Tomato juice	Asparagus
Spinach (1 cup raw)	Bok choy
Cabbage	Greens
Potatoes	Spinach, cooked
Tomatoes	

Fruits with 3 grams or more of fiber per serving:

1/2 cup raspberries	1 apple
1 grapefruit	1 orange
1 pear	2 dried figs
4 prunes	

Vegetables with 3 grams or more of fiber per serving:

1 potato	1/2 cup corn
1/2 cup Brussels sprouts	1/2 cup eggplant, cooked
1/2 cup peas	1/2 cup winter squash, mashed

* What about bananas or strawberries? Or carrots, broccoli, spinach and cauliflower? They'll give you at least 2 grams of fiber, so don't leave them off your list.

What Are Crucifers?

These are from the cabbage family. Indoles, chemical substances found in these vegetables, also enhance the body's cancer defense system. The American Cancer Society recommends we eat several servings a week. Some of the most common cruciferous vegetables are broccoli, cabbage, cauliflower, Brussels sprouts, kale, and turnips.

What it boils down to is basic good healthy eating. Boring but true. If we could just get Americans to eat more fruits, vegetables, and whole grains—as part of a low-fat diet. Ah! Wouldn't it be nice.

Diet Guidelines to Live By

It seems we have guidelines for almost everything—from safe sex to preventing disease through diet. Of course, I'm only going to talk about the latter.

Perhaps you haven't noticed, but the various leading health agencies and officials have spent the last few years coming up with their own packaged diet guidelines for the American public—some for preventing only heart disease, others for preventing some cancers, and still others for general good health.

The Leading DIETARY GUIDELINES

Title of document and organization	Total Fat	Saturated Fat	Polyunsaturated Fat	Cholesterol
Dietary Goals For The United States, 2nd ed. U.S. Senate Select Committee on Nutrition and Human Needs, 1977	Reduce to 27–33% of total Calories	Reduce to 8–12% of total Calories	Intake should be 8–12% of total Calories	Reduce to 250–350 mg per day
Dietary Guidelines for Healthy American Adults, American Heart Assoc.–Nutrition Committee, 1986	Less than 30% of total Calories	Less than 10% of total Calories	Less than 10% of total Calories	Reduce to 100 mg per 1000 Calories *not to exceed 300 mg/day
Recommended Dietary Allowances, Committee on Dietary Allowances, Food and Nutrition Board, National Research Council, National Academy of Sciences, 1980	Reduce to no more than 35% of total Calories		Reduce to 10% of total Calories	No more than 300 mg per day
Cholesterol Consensus Conference, National Institutes of Health, 1984	Less than 30% of Calories			250–300 mg per day
Year 2000 Dietary Objectives of NCI, National Cancer Institute, 1986	Less than 30% of total Calories			
National Cholesterol Education Program Adult Treatment Panel Report, 1987 — Step 1 of Dietary Treatment:	Should be less than 30% of Calories	Should be less than 10% of Calories		Should be less than 300 mg per day
National Cholesterol Education Program Adult Treatment Panel Report, 1987 — Step 2 of Dietary Treatment:	Should be less than 30% of Calories	Intake should be less than 7% of Calories	Should be less than 200 mg per day	
U.S. Surgeon General's Report "Nutrition and Health," 1988	Reduce consumption of Fat (especially saturated fat) and cholesterol			
National Academy of Sciences "Diet and Health—Implications for Reducing Chronic Disease Risk," 1989	Reduce total fat to 30% or less of Calories	Reduce to less than 10% of Calories		Reduce to less than 300 mg per day

Complex Carbohydrates	Fiber	Sugar	Sodium	Calcium
Increase complex carbohydrates and naturally occurring sugar to 45–51% of total Calories	Increase	Reduce to 8–12% of total Calories		
Increase to 50–55% or more of total Calories, with emphasis on increased complex carbohydrates			Reduce to 1 Gram per 1000 Calories, not to exceed 3 Grams	
		Reduce intake	Safe and adequate range of sodium is about 1100 –3300 mg/day	800 mg the Recommended Daily Allowance
Several servings daily of: • vitamin A rich fruits & vegetables • vitamin C rich fruits & vegetables Several servings weekly of: • cruciferous vegetables	Increase to 20–30 Grams per day			
Increase consumption of whole grain foods and cereal products, vegetables (including beans & peas), and fruits		Those vulnerable to dental cavities should limit their consumption and frequency of use of sugar	Reduce intake of sodium	Adolescent girls and adult women should increase intake of calcium, including low-fat dairy products
Eat greater amounts of complex carbohydrates			Limit daily salt to 6 Grams or less	Maintain adequate calcium intake

This surge in diet guidelines is rather bittersweet for me. While I'm thrilled they're finally paying tribute to the relationship between diet and disease, there now seems to be too many guidelines for the health-conscious consumer to sort through. There are just too many diet guidelines telling us to do too many different things pertaining to too many diseases!

So I decided to end this guideline quandry here and now by organizing the assorted guidelines in a table. I then selected the most rigid or specific guideline for each nutrient (better safe than sorry) and . . . ta da! A new set of guidelines, the "bottom line" guidelines were born, with only one rule to follow for fat, one for cholesterol, sodium, etc. These are the guidelines that are considered in the remainder of the book as far as recipes, restaurant suggestions, etc.

Bottom Line Guides:

- Reduce total fat to 30% or less of calories
- Reduce saturated fat to less than 10% of calories
- Reduce polyunsaturated fat to less than 10% of calories
- Reduce dietary cholesterol to 250 to 300 mg per day
- Increase carbohydrates to 50 to 55% or more of total calories with emphasis on increased complex carbohydrates (fruits, vegetables, starches, grain products, beans)
- Eat at least five servings of fruits and vegetables every day

AND for specific fruit and vegetable guidelines:
- Several servings daily of
  - vitamin A rich fruits and vegetables
  - vitamin C rich fruits and vegetables
- Several servings weekly of cruciferous vegetables
- Increase fiber to 20 to 30 grams per day
- Reduce sugar (refined carbohydrate) to 8 to 12% of total calories
- Limit sodium to the safe and adequate range of about 1,100 to 3,300 mg per day
- Maintain adequate calcium intake. The recommended daily allowance is 800 mg (1,200 mg for ages 11-24 and pregnant women)

But the greatest of all these is FAT. Always remember the guideline to eat a diet low in fat is the common denominator between the diet recommendations to prevent heart disease, obesity, and those for cancer and the link to all the other diet recommendations (except possibly sodium and calcium).

For example, if someone is eating a diet low in fat (less than 30% of calories from fat) they are most likely also eating a diet low in saturated fat and cholesterol as well, since saturated fat and cholesterol are usually found together in fatty foods.

And the reduction in fat is considered much more significant for the American public in the prevention of disease than the others, such as reducing sugar and sodium. For example, the only disease that excessive sugar in the diet directly causes is dental caries! So please keep all this in perspective. I though it was vital you be given all the guidelines so you could finally see them all together and how they really fit. For instance, there are at least seven different guidelines out for fat, but they are all pretty much saying the same thing. Eat less than 30% of calories from fat.

When fat is being reduced in the diet, some type of food will need to be increased. What's the missing piece to this puzzle? This is where the guidelines for increasing complex carbohydrates, fruits, and vegetables, and fiber fits in to complete the whole low-fat eating picture.

More Words on Exercise

There is an unspoken decree between some exercise and nutrition professionals to say a few qualifying words about the importance of exercise when good nutrition is being discussed, and vice versa. Well, the time has come for this nutritionist to progress beyond her simplified declaration that "aerobic exercise also is an essential part of a healthful (disease preventing) lifestyle."

Far from what movies such as *Pumping Iron* or *Perfect* might lead you to believe, there IS more to exercise than flashing your favorite muscle groups, "toning," or feeling "the burn." In fact, there are so many wonderful health benefits to exercise (other than feeling more invigorated), that I can ask you confidently, "How many really good reasons do you need to start exercising regularly and aerobically for your health? What? Three at least? All right, I'll name four, but you drive a hard bargain."

But first, let me mention that the operative concept here is "AEROBIC exercise," which is a fancy way of saying exercise that requires oxygen. Aerobic exercise is character-ized by unfluctuating type exercise with consistent breathing such as running, bicycling, swimming, walking fast, etc., and not so much stop and start as in baseball or tennis. So in order to prevent visions of leotards jumping up and down from interfering with your reading enjoyment, from here until the end of this chapter, when I write "exercise" I'm referring to "aerobic exercise."

Reason #1:
Increasing "Good Blood Cholesterol"

We've all heard about "bad cholesterol" and what we can do to help lower it. Well, here's blood cholesterol's better half—HDL (high-density lipoprotein) or "good cholesterol."

Increased levels of HDL in the blood have been associat-ed with a decrease in your risk of coronary heart disease.

There are only a couple of things that have been shown to increase our circulating HDLs, besides certain medications. These are body fat loss in overweight people and aerobic exer-cise. Recent studies have shown that exercise and weight loss (in the overweight) together will increase HDLs the most.

Reason #2:
Loss of Body Fat (Weight Loss)

Weight loss is such a common result of exercise that it is almost impossible for people in research studies involving reg-ular exercise NOT to lose weight in a big way. Some people would rather take their chances on the latest "diet" than exer-cise regularly.

When you compare lost pound to lost pound, exercise has a more powerful effect on increasing HDLs than "dieting" alone. And body fat lost through exercise is more likely to stay off, too! But here's the catch. It usually takes a little longer to lose a pound through exercise.

There are no definite answers as to why all these wonderful things occur as a result of exercise, but I can tell you that a certain enzyme called lipoprotein lipase (an enzyme involved in forming and converting lipoproteins, the fat carriers in the blood) is being carefully watched by researchers. They have already discovered that exercise causes a greater change in levels of this enzyme than does "dieting" alone.

Most of these research "diets" have only been lower in calories with no consideration of fat content. But alas, a study has just been completed using a lower fat diet with an exercise program (the ideal combination) to measure what effect it might have on HDL levels, and the results will soon be available.

Reason #3:
Decreased Triglyceride Levels in the Blood

High triglycerides (one type of fat particle circulating in the blood) are currently thought to be a risk factor for heart disease when serum cholesterol levels are also high. According to the authors of a study published recently in the American Heart Association journal, *Circulation*, exercise may encourage a decrease in blood triglycerides (after a meal) by removing triglyceride-rich fatty particles from the blood faster and possibly helping to reduce the risk of heart disease.

Reason #4:
Decreased Blood Pressure

In research where people start on regular exercise programs there seems to be a significant decrease in their blood pressure that could be advantageous if blood pressure started off on the high side. But again, it's difficult to ascertain whether this is a consequence of the exercise or the loss in body fat that usually results from the exercise.

So there are four great reasons to think twice about enhancing your new low-fat way of eating by making exercise a regular (and enjoyable) part of your life!

CHAPTER

3

Shopping Savvy

Every time you step into a supermarket, thousands of products confront you, hundreds of exhausting buying decisions await you. Misleading packaging ads accost you at every corner. The supermarket—why, it's a jungle in there!

The answer is shopping savvy. Years ago the simple wisdom was "Shop the perimeter of the store and you'll avoid all the bad foods." That's unfortunately not possible. We've got to penetrate the dreaded "center" of the store—unless we are willing to exist without vitals such as flour, cereal, and even toilet paper. (I thought you would see it my way.)

Next, we must become "food label literate." This also involves developing a keen critical eye through which we view food advertisements so we aren't so easy to impress. You'll see what I mean when we go over some examples of deceptive advertising.

Label Literacy

Food companies use all sorts of alluring nutrition terms to help sell their products. These terms often deceive shoppers by suggesting a product is more healthy than it actually is.

Exhibit A

Take your average potato chip. The potato chip has always been and always will be a high-fat, high-sodium snack. Because vegetable oils and shortening are typically used to make them, they happen to NOT CONTAIN CHOLESTEROL.

So what, pray tell, do you see plastered across some potato chip bags? "No Cholesterol" of course. In isolation, this is a good thing, but it certainly doesn't cancel out the fact that the chip oozes with fat and sodium. (The "No Cholesterol" banner also advertises vegetable oils and shortenings—as if they ever had cholesterol!)

Exhibit B

"All Natural" or "100 PERCENT NATURAL" doesn't mean a whole lot in dietary guideline terms. After all, lard, salt, sugar, and butter are all perfectly "natural," but that doesn't mean you should sit down to a big bowl of sugary fat!

Then there's the "95 Percent Fat-Free" advertising claim you'll find on everything from turkey bologna to ice cream. Food advertisers are definitely faithfully following the "if you can't say anything nice" rule here. Because they could label it the other way—as 5 percent fat by weight.

Don't let this fool you, though. This doesn't tell you anything about its PERCENT OF CALORIES FROM FAT, which is a more accurate way of judging fat content.

Many of the processed meats awarded this "95 Percent Fat-Free" status have, in fact, over half of their calories from fat! How can this be? When in doubt, check out the label. In most cases you'll find the second ingredient is something that carries weight without calories (such as water), helping fat out in terms of its weight percentage but not the percentage that really counts—the percent of calories from fat.

Case closed? Before we go on, there are some words you should get acquainted with.

The Label Literacy Glossary

Low Calorie: 40 calories or less per serving and no more than 0.4 calories per gram. Foods naturally low in calories cannot be labeled low calorie. The FDA monitors whether the "serving size" chosen by the food company is reasonable.

Reduced Calorie: Must contain one-third less calories than the food it replaces and must include a comparison on the label.

Low Cholesterol: 20 milligrams or less per serving.

Reduced Cholesterol: Cannot contain more than one-fourth the cholesterol of the food it replaces.

No Cholesterol: No cholesterol is detectable by present analytical methods. (NOTE: These food items can still be high in fat!)

Cholesterol Free: Less than 2 milligrams cholesterol per serving. (Proposed by FDA.)

Diet or Dietetic: Same requirements as low or reduced calorie.

Enriched: This means that some, although not necessarily all, of the nutrients lost in food processing have been added back into the product.

Low Fat: Dairy products must contain between 0.5 and 2 percent milk fat to be labeled low-fat. Low-fat meat can be no more than 10 percent fat by weight.

Fortified: This means additional vitamins and minerals have been added during processing, such as vitamin D added to milk.

Hydrogenation: A process of adding hydrogen molecules to monounsaturated or polyunsaturated fatty acids. As a result, liquid oils chemically become more saturated (with hydrogen) and physically change from liquid to semisolid forms.

Imitation: Not the "real thing" and nutritionally inferior in that it is lower in protein, vitamins, or minerals.

"Lite" in general: Same definition as "low calorie" when "lite" refers to caloric content. (Companies can use the word "light" in advertising to refer to color or weight or whatever they want it to refer to.)

"Lite" and "Lean" (referring to red meat and poultry): "Lean"

and "low-fat": Contains no more than 10 percent fat by weight—not percent of calories from fat.

Extra lean: Contains no more than 5 percent fat.

Lower in fat: Has at least a 25 percent reduction in fat.

Light or Lite: Has a 25 percent reduction of specific ingredients, such as fat, calories, or salt.

Natural or Organic: There is NO LEGAL DEFINITION, and there are no future plans by the FTC, FDA, or USDA to develop any*. Years ago these agencies met on this issue. FTC agreed to take primary responsibility, but in 1983, they gave up on the task, saying they couldn't come up with a "suitable" definition. Suitable to whom, I wonder.

Salt-free, Unsalted: No salt was added to the product during processing, but it could contain significant sodium levels naturally or from other ingredients.

Very Low Sodium: 35 milligrams or less per serving.

Low Sodium: 140 Milligrams or less per serving.

Reduced Sodium: The amount of sodium in the regular product is reduced by 75 percent.

Substitute: Not the "real thing" but nutritionally equivalent to the food it is imitating.

Sugar Free or Sugarless: These foods cannot contain sucrose (table sugar) but can have other sweeteners, including honey, corn syrup, fructose, sorbitol, etc.

The Ingredient Label

Under Federal law, all food products must list the ingredients starting with the ingredient added in the largest quantity (by weight) and continuing in descending order.

So if you want a general idea of what you'll be eating, check out the first three or four ingredients. Since this is a

*Guess which state managed to come up with its very own definition in 1981 for "organic" and "organically grown?" California, of course! Through the California Sherman Food, Drug, and Cosmetic Law of the Department of Health Services.

"lesson," how about a little quiz? Come on. It'll be fun! I'll list the first four ingredients of a popular food and you guess what it is.

Quiz: Would you put this in your mouth?

1. Carbonated water, high fructose corn syrup and/or sucrose, caramel color, phosphoric acid.
2. Soybean oil, partially hydrogenated soybean oil, whole eggs, vinegar.
3. Sugar, enriched wheat flour, vegetable and animal shortening (partially hydrogenated soybean oil, hydrogenated cottonseed oil, lard), cocoa.
4. Water, corn syrup, hydrogenated coconut and palm kernel oils, sugar.
5. Milk chocolate (sugar, milk, cocoa butter, chocolate, lecithin, vanillin—an artificial flavor), peanuts, corn syrup, sugar.
6. Sugar, citric acid, potassium citrate (regulates tartness).
7. Soybean oil, water, sugar.
8. Sugar, partially hydrogenated animal and/or vegetable shortening, enriched flour.
9. Milled and flaked corn, salt, sugar.
10. Enriched corn meal, vegetable oil (contains 1 or more of the following: Cottonseed oil, corn oil, peanut oil, partially hydrogenated cottonseed oil, partially hydrogenated soybean oil, partially hydrogenated sunflower oil or palm oil), whey.
11. Corn syrup, brown sugar, peanut butter.
12. Pork snouts, cured pork tongues, water.
13. Water, sugar and corn syrups, fruit juices and purees.

Answers:

1. Coke, 2. Mayonnaise, 3. Oreo Cookies, 4. Cool Whip, 5. Snickers Candy Bar, 6. Tang, 7. Kraft Thousand Island Dressing, 8. HoHo Snack Cakes, 9. Shake & Bake, pork flavor, 10. Chee-tos Cheese Twists, 11. Tiger's Milk Nutrition Bar (original protein-rich flavor), 12. Head cheese cold cut, 13. Hawaiian Punch (in ready-to-drink boxes)

Some foods have standard ingredients, such as jellies, jams, ketchup, ice cream, mayonnaise, peanut butter, cheeses, and milk, and are not required to list the ingredients. Unfortunately, sometimes these products can contain ingredients some people could be allergic to, but they still don't need to be listed. When these foods are made "lighter," you'll notice they usually get called something else such as "sandwich spread" instead of mayonnaise or "Light Dessert" instead of ice cream.

Label Literacy Lesson #2

The Nutrition Information Label is not required by law unless a nutrient is added to the product (such as in enriched breads, pastas, etc.) or if a nutritional claim is made about the product either on the label or in an advertisement (as with "lite" salad dressings, low-sodium crackers, etc.).

Today more than half of all food products feature nutrition information on the labels, which gives you an idea of just how many products have nutritional claims in their name or on their packaging!

The Nutrient Information Label tells you:

• **The serving size.** This could be misleading, so read it carefully. For example, the serving size on the label might be 1/2 a bar of candy (when most people would eat the whole thing) or 1 ounce of potato chips when the small package contains 2 ounces.
• **Servings per container.**
• **The nutrient analysis per serving of:**
    protein (in grams)
    carbohydrate (in grams)
    fat (in grams)
    sodium* (in milligrams), which became a requirement as of July, 1986.

- **Percent of the U.S. RDA per serving for:**
  Protein, Vitamin A, Vitamin C, Vitamin B^1 (thiamin),
  Vitamin B^2 (riboflavin), Vitamin B^3 (niacin),
  Calcium, and Iron.

What it doesn't tell you is:

- **the percent calories from fat**
- **the percent calories from saturated fat** (or even grams of saturated fat for that matter)
- **the cholesterol content,** unless a specific claim is made concerning the amount of cholesterol fiber (in grams)

Sometimes two columns appear on the nutrient information label, especially with packaged mixes that require the addition of other ingredients. The first column usually lists information about the package contents only, and the second includes the ingredients the instructions tell you to add at home.

For practice, let's look at the nutrient information label on Aunt Jemima's Buckwheat Pancake and Waffle Mix.

Nutrition Information Per Serving

Dri Mix Pancakes*

Serving Size	1/4 cup (1.1 ounce)	Three 4-inch pancakes
Servings per container	29	29
Calories	110	200
Protein	4 gm	7 gm
Carbohydrate	21 gm	24 gm
Fat	1 gm	8 gm
Sodium	490 mg	520 mg
Potassium	95 mg	20 mg

* Prepared with egg, milk, and oil as the package directs.

Percentage of U.S. Recommended Daily Allowances (Percent U.S. RDA)

	Per 1.1 ounce Mix	Per Three 4-inch pancakes
Protein	4	10
Vitamin B1	*	4
Vitamin C	*	*
Thiamine	10	
Riboflavin	4	10
Niacin	6	6
Calcium	10	
Iron	8	8
Vitamin D	*	10
Phosphorus	25	

*Contains less than 2 percent of the U.S. RDA for this nutrient.

Label Literacy Lesson #3

• Beware of Ingredients That Are What They Don't Appear To Be

Sometimes we think we can outsmart the food companies by reading our labels solely for that nasty word "sugar." But remember, those guys make it their business (and a big profit-making business at that) to always stay a few steps ahead of the consumer. SO, let's get ahead of the game.

Sugar (refined carbohydrate, processed sugar, etc.) goes by many names, none significantly better than the others. The aliases include:

Sucrose	Dextrose
Fructose	Honey
Brown sugar	High fructose corn syrup
Maltose	Molasses
Invert sugar	

Syrups (for example, corn or maple syrup)
"Sweeteners" (for example, corn sweeteners)

Sodium in disguise

Hard to imagine, but more than 70 sodium-containing substances are added to foods today. Salt (sodium chloride) leads the pack. "Sodium" and "salt" are used interchangeably. Here are some of the sodium-containing criminals:

Salt (sodium chloride), the major sodium contributor in the American diet. Salt is 40 percent sodium.
MSG (monosodium glutamate)
Soy sauce
Brine (salt and water)
Broth and bouillon
Sodium compounds:
    Sodium phosphate
    Sodium benzoate
    Sodium bicarbonate (baking soda)
    Sodium hydroxide

Sodium propionate
Sodium sulfite
Baking powder
And any other compounds with the word "sodium" in them.

FATS also come in disguises:

Butter
All oils, such as vegetable, coconut, palm kernel, etc.
Shortening, vegetable or animal
Hydrogenated fats or oils
Animal fats, such as bacon or pork fat, beef fat, lard,
        suet, chicken or turkey fat
Mono- or diglycerides
Glycerolesters
Cocoa butter, chocolate, or milk chocolate
Cream
Egg and egg-yolk solids
Whole-milk solids

Taking a Tour Through Your Supermarket

Picture yourself sandwiched between a shopping cart and a conglomeration of salad dressing bottles. Which dressing do you grab? You want to reduce the fat in your diet, but you don't even know where to start. Where's a nutritionist when you need one?

Similar problems can strike as you cruise the cracker aisle or face countless fancy-named entrees in the frozen food section. You can't even buy cat food these days without dealing with a cloud of brands and flavors—most, for some reason, with fancier names than people food.

So if I can't accompany you on a trip through your supermarket, you can tag along through mine, as I hopefully answer some of your questions. (I won't even attempt to answer cat food questions. But then we all know who really "chooses" the flavor and brand anyway.)

The Frozen Food Aisles

Given the invitation to give up half my refrigerator space for an equal amount of expansion in the freezer compartment, I would gladly accept. I attribute this love for freezer space not only to my over-reliance on freezing individualized portions of leftovers in plastic containers but also to several fabulous frozen foods I've found over the years.

Frozen Bagels

Sounds simple, I know, but you might reconsider their value one morning when you only have two minutes to fix your breakfast. This is exactly the amount of time it takes to split your frozen bagel in half, pop it in the toaster, prepare the filling for when the bagel pops up, wrap it in a napkin, and go! Bagels, by themselves, are low in fat so they can be a great snack or breakfast on the run.

Egg Substitutes

While we're on the subject of breakfast, I'll mention another favorite frozen food find—frozen eggs. But not just any frozen eggs—Fleischmann's Egg Beaters. Other egg substitutes may not have cholesterol, but they do have about 45 percent of their calories from FAT (and up to 60 calories per 1/4 cup). Egg Beaters is 99 percent egg white (remember all the fat and cholesterol in eggs are in the yolk), which explains why it has almost no fat (about 4 calories from fat) and very few calories (25 per 1/4 cup). It looks like scrambled eggs so you can use it in omelettes, quiche, etc.

What About Frozen Breakfast Foods?

You can now buy everything from breakfast muffins to a complete egg, sausage, and hash browns breakfast in the frozen food section. The egg and sausage type selections don't even come close to meeting my diet guidelines, and neither do the croissant varieties, no matter how whole-wheaty and "au naturel" they make them sound.

Ms. Sara Lee, for example, labels her "Healthy Fruit Muffins" as FIBER RICH, but she's not telling just how much fiber these little babies actually contain. This isn't surprising considering sugar ranks as the first ingredient in this product.

If you're a frozen pancake lover and you've joined the wave of microwave users, you can choose from several different brands. Pillsbury makes microwave original and buttermilk pancakes while Krusteaz makes them in blueberry (with imitation "blueberry nuggets") or buttermilk, all with less than 20 percent calories from fat. But do check the ingredient list for possible sugars.

I know you frozen waffle lovers are out there too. Unfortunately, only one brand in my supermarket passed the fat test, and there are now a few boxes of them stacked in my freezer: Aunt Jemima's Buttermilk and Original Waffles. (Auntie Jemima also now freezes her French toast.)

All the breakfast-type products that meet the guidelines are listed below:

Brand Name	Calories	Percent from FAT	Calories Sodium (mg)
Pancakes: (3 pieces per serving)			
Pillsbury			
Microwave Original	240	15%	550
Microwave Buttermilk	260	14%	590
Krusteaz			
Microwave Blueberry	332	14%	328
Microwave Buttermilk	305	5%	1328*
Waffles (2 per serving)			
Aunt Jemima			
Buttermilk	190	28%	600
Original	190	28%	630
French Toast			
Aunt Jemima	170	26%	——

Now that you've bought a frozen breakfast that meets the guidelines and you're heating it up, are you going to add gobs of butter or whipped cream? Absolutely not! But you can add whatever fruit you want, such as sliced or baked apples, peaches, or frozen berries. Any fresh fruit will go great on top of a waffle, pancake or slice of french toast. A modest amount (2 tablespoons on a stack of three pancakes) of "lite" or flavored syrups can also be added.

Frozen Entrees

Dinner recipes have a tough challenge ahead—it's not enough anymore simply to taste good or to be "gourmet." Dinner recipes today compete head on with meals that can be popped in the microwave and ready to eat in eight to ten minutes. Americans everywhere have enthusiastically discovered the "frozen entree."

In the next few pages, though, we're only going to talk about the "light" entrees, since they're the only ones that have nutrition information on the packaging. Remember, when a company makes a nutritional claim about their product, such as saying it's "lite" or "low calorie," legally the nutrition information must be on the label along with the mandatory list of ingredients.

The distinguished list of contenders includes Le Menu, Light Style, Healthy Choice by Con Agra, Tyson-Gourmet Slim Selects, Lean Cuisine, and Weight Watchers. Notice the buzz words "slim," "lean," "weight." All these enticing descriptors are based solely on calories—not FAT. This falsely impressive "low-calorie" status is not accomplished through anything terribly magical or scientific. This is an exercise in good old-fashioned portion control! The smaller the portion, the lower the calories.

For our purposes—for fighting FAT—we won't be judging frozen entrees merely on their caloric contributions. We're going to up the ante and factor in fat, following these five rules for healthy eating.

Rule #1:
No Info, No Purchase

If you can't find the number of calories and grams of fat printed on the package, don't buy it! You need to know this information before making a decision about whether to eat this unknown food.

Rule #2:
The 25 Percent Solution

Make sure you start out with an entree that contains 25 percent or less calories from fat. Most entree labels will list the calories per serving and grams of fat. From this you will need to figure out the percent of calories from fat. To do this, multiply grams of fat per serving by 9—the number of calories per gram of fat. Then convert this to a percentage by dividing by the number of calories per serving and multiplying by 100.

Next time you stock up on frozen entrees, bring a calculator with you. That way you can calculate the percent of calories from fat as you walk down the aisle deciding which ones to try. Here's a list of the entrees I found with less than 26 percent of calories from FAT:

	Calories	Fat (gm)	% Fat Calories	Sodium (mg)
Classic Lite				
Seafood Natural Herbs	250	6	22%	1240
Bay Shrimp in Sherried Cream Sauce	280	8	26%	- -
Chicken Oriental	250	6	22%	- -
Benihana Oriental Lites				
Oriental Style Shrimp with Rice	250	4	14%	1200
Chicken in Peking Sauce	270	6	20%	- -
Seafood Supreme	260	6	21%	1470
Shrimp Chow Mein	220	2	8%	1140
Chicken in Spicy Garlic Sauce	280	6	19%	940
Oriental Glazed Chicken	250	3	11%	880
Shrimp and Cashews	260	7	24%	1110
Lean Cuisine				
Chicken a l'Orange	270	5	17%	400
Chicken & Vegetables with Vermicelli	270	7	23%	1120
Linguini with Clam Sauce	260	7	24%	800
Zucchini Lasagna	260	7	24%	975
Chicken Chow Mein	250	5	18%	1030
Spaghetti with Beef and Mushroom Sauce	280	7	23%	1140
Breast of Chicken Marsala	190	5	24%	850

	Calories	Fat (gm)	% Fat Calories	Sodium (mg)
Oriental Beef	250	7	25%	1150
Weight Watchers				
Imperial Chicken	230	4	16%	980
Spaghetti with Meat Sauce	290	7	25%	900
Sweet and Sour Chicken Tenders	250	2	7%	600
Chicken Fajitas	260	3	10%	640
Chicken Divan Baked Potato	300	6	18%	840
Broccoli & Cheese Baked Potato	280	7	23%	700
Pasta Rigati	290	8	25%	800
Chicken Cacciatore	300	6	18%	670
Filet of Fish Au Gratin	220	6	25%	660
Candle Lite by Weight Watchers				
Stuffed Fillet of Sole	280	7	23%	1180
Budget Gourmet Slim-Line				
Oriental Beef	260	6	21%	850
Mandarin Chicken	290	6	19%	690
Chicken Chow Mein	290	4	12%	1230
Glazed Turkey	270	5	17%	760
Cheese Ravioli	260	7	24%	960
Great Escapes—Lite Dinners				
Chicken with BBQ Sauce	290	4	12%	1610
Great Escapes—Lite Entrees				
Glazed Chicken	260	4	14%	1270
Spaghetti with Beef & Mushrooms	270	3	10%	1540
Legume				
Sweet n' Sour Tofu	270	3	10%	600
Le Menu—Light Style				
Chicken Cannelloni	250	5	18%	600
Veal Marsala	260	6	20%	800
Herb Roasted Chicken	220	6	25%	610
Healthy Choice (Con Agra)				
Sweet & Sour Chicken	260	2	7%	260
Chicken Parmigiana	290	5	16%	320
Breast of Turkey	270	5	17%	450
Oriental Pepper Steak	270	5	17%	530
Sirloin Tips	280	6	19%	320
Salisbury Steak	300	7	21%	560
Armour Dinner Classics Lite				
Chicken Burgundy	210	2	9%	1360

Maybe you already have a favorite frozen entree—one you salivate over while driving home from work. Even though they have diet-like names, you still need to process the nutrient data for yourself. Some of these innocent looking and sounding entrees are actually way over 30 percent of calories from fat.

Rule #3:
Cutting the FAT

If that favorite entree of yours is more than 25 percent calories from fat but less than 30 percent, relax. You can still work it out. Just add complex carbohydrate foods to bring down the total meal to less than 25 percent calories from fat.

For example, if you took the Weight Watchers Lasagna with Meat and added a cup of steamed zucchini and a roll (sorry, no butter), it turns into a 23 percent calories from fat meal. Some other workable entrees I found are:

Lean Cuisine
Oriental Beef with Vegetables and Rice
Filet of Fish Divan
Glazed Chicken with Vegetables and Rice
Tune Lasagna

Weight Watchers
Lasagna with Meat

Rule #4:
Finding the Missing Carbohydrates

Check the entree for missing complex carbohydrates by running through the complex carbohydrate roll call: Vegetables, fruits, grains, starches, cereals. Work these foods into the meal. If the entree doesn't come with a vegetable, add some to it. Sometimes you can just stir them right into the entree, like with Chicken a l'Orange or Oriental Style Shrimp with Rice.

Using frozen entrees may require a teeny bit of planning. You may need to prepare or bring along whatever complex carbohydrate you need to complete the meal. Two examples are:

- If you bring a Zucchini Lasagna (Lean Cuisine) to work for lunch, pack an orange or apple and a roll with it in the morning.
- If you have Filet of Fish Divan for dinner, boil some rice or noodles while your entree is cooking. (It already has broccoli.) Cut up some melon or strawberries to add the missing complex carbohydrates.

Rule #5:
Hide the Salt Shaker

Salt has already been added—in massive amounts, I might add—to your frozen entrees. So adding MORE salt at the table is a major no-no.

Ice Cream, You Scream

I'm one of those people who, if given a nudge or two, could eat ice cream every day. Double chocolate fudge, strawberry delight, virtuous vanilla—it doesn't really matter which, as long as it's ice cream. This wonderful multi-season treat addicts people with its "light yet creamy" feeling, comes in oh-so-many-fun flavors, and tops a meal or warm Sunday afternoon like no other.

You might think I'm setting you up with images of ice cream just to let you down with healthful horror stories. Would a fellow ice cream lover do that? Actually, I'm happy to announce that lower fat selections in the frozen dessert aisle have never looked better. Gone are the days of only chocolate or vanilla ice milk. Say hello to mint chocolate chip, mocha nut sundae, or strawberry cheesecake—and that's just the first couple rows!

I took the ice cream section with clipboard and calculator in hand, writing down only those items with less than 30 percent of calories from fat—which usually means 8 grams or less of fat per 1-cup serving. But to help you truly appreciate the significance of these great lower fat options, let's review what the regular rich ice creams would add. The standard store brand ice cream has around 300 calories per cup, 48 percent from fat, and the fancy rich types can add from 400 to 600 calories per cup, with up to 60 percent of calories from fat. Even sherbets have up to 300 calories per cup because the calories they don't have from cream are present in sugar. A better choice would be the fruit sorbets, sweetened with mostly fruit juice instead of plain old sugar.

Now for the good news:

The following items contain no more than 25 percent calories from fat, 2 grams or less fat per 3-ounce serving, and do not have sucrose or other sugars listed as the first or second ingredient (besides water).

Rhapsody Farms Frozen Yogurt—Strawberry Cheesecake, Mocha Almond, Marble Fudge, Dutch Chocolate, Vanilla, Peanut Butter & Chocolate
Rhapsody Farms Frozen Yogurt—Nonfat All flavors
Breyers Frozen Yogurt Inspirations—All flavors
Sunnyside Lite Icemilk—All flavors
Sunnyside Lite Frozen Yogurt—All flavors
Knudsen Nice N' Light—Strawberry, Double Blueberry Swirl, Chocolate, Vanilla, and Neopolitan
Knudsen Push-Ups—All flavors

Lower Fat Dairy Products

*Pass the Low-Fat Milk, Please!**

Where would most meals and beverages be without milk. It's still the best thing for lightening your coffee—better than cream and nondairy creamers. (Most of the latter still have the same amount of FAT as cream—just not the cholesterol.) We need milk to keep our cereal company, wet our pancake batters, and on and on. But along with bringing all these attributes to our table, it brings fat calories and cholesterol.

*This information applies only to people over the age of two. Children under age two need the fat and fat soluble vitamins of whole milk because of their rapid growth, etc.

The great thing about milk, though, is you can "skim" some (low-fat milk) or most (non-fat milk) of the fat away and still have a milk that, for the most part, does all the things you want it to do. And the other amazing trick with milk is as the fat calories decrease, so does the cholesterol. Actually this is true of most foods with fat, since cholesterol goes where the fat is. As you remove the fat you are also removing the cholesterol.

They say seeing is believing. Listed below are the average nutrient values from the assorted ways to buy your milk, starting with the lowest in fat, and moving to the highest. Remember to watch the cholesterol go up, too.

Per 1 Cup	Calories	% Fat Calories	Fat (gm)	Cholesterol (milligrams)
Skim milk	86	5	0.4	5
Buttermilk	99	20	2.0	7
Low-fat milk (1% milkfat)	102	22	2.5	14
Low-fat milk (2% milkfat)	121	35	4.8	22
Whole milk (3.3% milkfat)	150	49	8.0	34

Yelling for Yogurt

You can get it plain or flavored, sweetened with fruit on the bottom or swirled throughout. These days you can even get it with granola sprinkled on top. Welcome to the wonderful world of yogurt.

Yogurt was one of the popular products that came of age in the 80's. People started taking it to lunch, having it for dessert, even basing their weight-reducing diets around it. Just count how many different yogurt brands and flavors you can buy in your supermarket. You could say that in the last decade, yogurt underwent a metamorphosis from a caterpillar into a big-business butterfly.

Sales rose from less than one pound per person per year in 1970 to 4.6 pounds per person in 1987. Some might ask why? Aside from the fact that some people like the way it tastes, there are certain health attributes that have been advertised on yogurt's behalf over the years.

Mainly, yogurt is known as a member of the dairy family, giving it high calcium and complete protein status. An 8-ounce serving contains anywhere from 30 to 40 percent of the U.S. RDA (1,000 mg) for calcium, actually offering more than an 8-ounce glass of milk. This is due to a secret ingredient added by manufacturers to give a custard-like feel to it—non-fat dry milk. One of the highest is Dannon nonfat and low-fat plain yogurt with 430 mg. per 8-ounce cup. And let's not forget, an 8-ounce serving pumps you with 9 grams of protein (approximately 20 percent of the U.S. RDA for adults.)

Lately, plain yogurt has been enjoying some free publicity as a lower fat substitute for sour cream. This healthful replacement idea is, of course, poo-pooed by real sour cream lovers. But others can easily learn to top their potato or enchilada with it or make dips and spreads with it.

When choosing your yogurt, though, there are a few things that help you distinguish the better choices: The FAT content of the milk or cream used to make the yogurt, the amount of sugar added, and the container size.

- "Container size?" you ask. "Isn't that a little obvious?" The way some of the individual-sized containers are packaged with 4, 6, or 8 ounces, it is rather difficult to note the difference. There are a couple brands boasting "only 150 calories per serving" that use 6-ounce containers. In that case, you would be better off buying Weight Watchers at 150 calories per 8-ounce container.

- The fat content is fairly straight forward. The ones called nonfat yogurt have less than 0.5 percent milk fat, low-fat yogurts contain between 0.5 and 2 percent milk fat, and whole milk types contain 3.25 percent milk fat or more. So the percentage of calories from fat for nonfat types is around zero and low-fat plain around 25 percent, with low-fat flavored totalling about 16 percent. This brings us to the third point.

- The more sugar and sweetened fruit mixture added, the lower the percentage of calories from fat. The sugar and fruit add carbohydrate calories, which reduce the proportion (or percentage) of the total calories from fat.

So some of the highly sweetened yogurts may mislead you to believe they are low in fat—because the percentage of calories from fat is low. The best way to judge the sugar content of the various flavored yogurts is to compare the calories per 8-ounce serving. Remember, as sugar is added, the calories will increase. So far, I've found that Weight Watchers brand (regular types, not "a la Francais") has the lowest sugar content at 150 calories per 8-ounce serving.

There are all kinds of nonfat yogurt brands and flavors in the supermarket today. Listed below are the ones with no artificial sweeteners.

Nonfat Yogurt, Plain:	Calories	Sodium
Weight Watchers, 1 cup	90	135
Continental, 1 cup	140	—
Dannon, 1 cup	110	—

Nonfat Yogurt, Flavored:

Weight Watchers-Regular	150	120
8-ounce containers		
Lemon, Raspberry, Strawberry, Peach, Vanilla, Black Cherry		
Weight Watchers, A La Francais		
per 8-ounce serving	199	160
Black Cherry, Peach, Strawberry, Raspberry, Lemon, Strawberry-Banana		
Alta-Dena, European Style		
per 8-ounce serving	173	128
Mixed Berry, Peach, Raspberry, Strawberry Black Cherry, Pina Colada		
Continental		
8-ounce containers	200	105
Wild Berries, Honey Nut Crunch, Strawberries, Boysenberry, Peach, Raspberry, Capuccino		
Yoplait 150		
per 8-ounce serving	200	126
Blueberry, Strawberry, Mixed Berry, Raspberry, Peach, Strawberry-Banana, Cherry		

Cottage Cheese

Low-fat cottage cheese is certainly not one of the more glamorous dairy products in the market today. But it quite possibly could have the most promising future amidst the rising low-fat furor in America.

I'm asking you to look beyond the "diet food" stereotype that has haunted cottage cheese over the years. You know the one—the torturous diet plate featuring a boring white mound of cottage cheese sitting on a pineapple ring (and if you're lucky, a cherry on top).

No, what I've got in store for cottage cheese today and beyond is a whole lot more exciting. Fancy cottage cheese whipped with Philadelphia Light Cream Cheese with a bit of pesto layered on top for a tasty colorful spread. Picture whipped cottage cheese as an extender for your favorite frosting. Imagine a cup of cottage cheese whipped with only a couple tablespoons of reduced-calorie mayonnaise to make a creamy potato or pasta salad. And that's only the beginning!

I've been experimenting with cottage cheese lately and am finding out the only limit to composing new uses for cottage cheese is my own imagination. I mean, what could I have been thinking when I mixed half the usual amount of vanilla frosting with the same amount of whipped nonfat cottage cheese? (You can "whip" cottage cheese and smooth out the lumps by using a food processor or blender.) But you know, it actually worked. People didn't even notice the difference! I've even started using half cottage cheese (whipped) and half light cream cheese to make a lower fat cheesecake.

If low-fat cottage cheese isn't low-fat enough for you, progress has already visited the cottage cheese case. Knudsen just introduced NONFAT cottage cheese as part of their new "Nice N' Light" line.

When cottage cheese is whipped in a food processor or blender it transforms into something with more of a ricotta cheese resemblance. And today's low and nonfat cottage cheese options make it a lower fat filler to your favorite pasta dishes, a lower fat thickener for creamy sauces, and the major ingredient of choice for dips and creamy dressings.

Just so you can appreciate the value of this truly momentous dairy discovery, we've listed calories, fat, and cholesterol content of the new nonfat cottage cheese alongside the fattier ingredients it can replace in the following table:

	Calories	Percent Calories from Fat	Choles-terol (mg)	Sodium (mg)
1/2 cup (about 4 oz.)				
Knudsen Nonfat Cottage Cheese	70	>5%	6	420
Low-fat Cottage Cheese (2% fat)	102	20%	10	459
Part-Skim Ricotta Cheese	170	53%	40	154
Regular Sour Cream	247	36%	64	57
Knudsen Light Sour Cream	180	60%	Not listed	100
Best Foods Light Reduced Calorie Mayonnaise	400	91%	40	920
Regular Mayonnaise	788	98%	78	624
Regular Cream Cheese	396	88%	124	336
Light Philadelphia (tub)	240	75%	Not listed	160

Say "Cheese"

One of our favorite foods is cheese. Whether it sits on a cracker, tops our tortilla, or is layered in our lasagna, let's face it, we love cheese! Unfortunately, cheeses are "fat city." You can cut your fat per ounce almost in half by buying the reduced fat (part skim type) cheeses. Who can refuse an offer like that?

To be considered "reduced fat," cheeses must have no more than 5 gram of fat per ounce. To be considered "reduced sodium" they must have no more than 100 milligrams of sodium per ounce. Try these cheeses next time:

Per ounce	Calories	Fat (gm)	% Calories from Fat	Sodium (mg)
Lifetime:				
Mozzarella	45	2	40%	75
Mild Cheddar	55	3	49%	85
Monterey Jack	55	3	40%	75
Weight Watchers:				
Cheddar Chunk	80	5	56%	150
Natural Jack	80	5	56%	150
Laughing Cow:				
Reduced Calorie	52	2.6	52%	305
Polly-O Lite:				
Part-skim Mozzarella	45	4	51%	200
Heidi Ann-Thinline				
Muenster-style	85	5	53%	53
Galaxy Cheese Co.:				
Formagg	70	5	64%	140
Kraft-Light Naturals (Reduced Fat):				
Mild Cheddar Cheese	80	5	58%	210
Sonoma Lite Reduced Fat:				
Hot Pepper, Jack	80	6	58%	95
Reduced Fat, Jack	80	6	58%	95
Garlic, Jack	80	6	58%	95
Part-Skim Mozzarella (various brands)	80	6	58%	150

**Other cheese products with at least one-third less fat than
the regular items:**

Per ounce	Calories	Fat (gm)	% Calories from Fat	Sodium (mg)
Cream Cheese				
Light Philadelphia Cream Cheese (in tub)	60	5	75%	160
Ricotta Cheese—Part skim				
Precious Part Skim	42	2.5	54%	37
Precious "Lite"	40	2	45%	20
Polly-O Lite	40	2	45%	32

Lunch Meats and Other Processed Meat Items

I went on a processed meats section expedition over a year
ago in search of healthful items and found almost nothing
worth mentioning. But now, a whole year later, I could even
buy a lower fat hot dog! Now, that's progress. After this year's
investigation (reading labels), I was so excited about the positive changes I had seen that I took home some Butterball
"Less Fat" turkey franks and surprised my husband that night
with hot dogs and fries (they were low-fat fries, of course). He
thought he was in the wrong house.

The following are the lunch meats I found that are actually
"low in fat," having less than 30 percent of their calories from fat:

Per ounce	Calories	Fat (gm)	% Calories from Fat	Sodium (mg)
Jubilee Ham Slice	30	1	30%	350
Oscar Mayer Baked Cooked Ham	27	1	20%	333
Rose's Canadian Style Bacon	35	1	326%	NA

Per ounce	Calories	Fat (gm)	% Calories from Fat	Sodium (mg)
Butterball Turkey Pastrami	30	1	30%	290
Oscar Mayer Pastrami	27	<1	<25%	366!
Zacky Hickory Smoked Turkey Breast	35	<1	<26%	250
Butterball Honey Roasted Breast of Turkey	35	1	26%	230
Louis Rich Oven Roasted Turkey Breast	35	1	26%	340!
Butterball Oven Roasted Turkey Breast	30	1	30%	230
Butterball Honey Roasted Turkey Breast	35	1	26%	220
Butterball Smoked Turkey Breast	30	1	30%	220
Oscar Mayer Smoked Turkey Breast	27	<1	<20%	404!
Oscar Mayer Smoked Chicken Breast	25	<1	<20%	410!

Now for the surprises that had at least a third less FAT than the regular products but didn't qualify for the "less than 30 percent of calories from FAT" category above:

1. Regular hot dogs usually have 15 grams of fat per 2-ounce frank. So for another hot dog to have a third less fat, it needs to have 11 grams or less per 2-ounce frank. Of the various brands now advertising "less fat," this is the only one that made it:

    • Butterball Turkey Frank

2-ounce serving has 140 calories and 11 grams of fat. (Sodium information was not on the label.)

2. Your regular old slice of fatty bologna (beef/pork) usually has 8 grams of fat per 1-ounce slice. So for other bologna look-alikes to have a third less fat, they need to have 5.3 grams or less of fat per 1-ounce slice. A couple actually made it! Here they are:

- Louis Rich Original Turkey Bologna

1-ounce slice has 60 calories, 5 grams of fat, and 260 milligrams of sodium

  - Butterball Turkey Bologna

1-ounce slice has 67 calories, 5.3 grams of fat, and 373 milligrams of sodium.

3. Regular run-of-the-mill Kielbasa sausage has around 90 calories per ounce and 7.7 grams of fat (77 percent of calories from fat). So for an alternative to have "less fat" it should have less than 5 grams of fat per ounce. And here one is:

  - Louis Rich Turkey Polska Kielbasa Sausage

1 ounce uncooked has 50 calories, 3 grams of fat (54 percent of calories from fat) and 270 milligrams of sodium

CAUTION: The above "less fat" items still have more than 30 percent of their calories from fat, so make sure you serve them with ample complex carbohydrates and very little additional fat. This means sliding the above turkey frank into a hot dog bun with mustard or catsup (no mayo), with all the onions and tomato you want. Get the picture?

Other Boxes, Bottles, and Cans

Cereal

Most of us ate it for the first time long before our first birthday. And some of us, now deep into adulthood, remain faithful cereal eaters. Whether you prefer it hot, wet, or dry, most everyone likes some type of cereal. And we all eat it our own special way—letting the cereal sit in the milk for just the right amount of time, munching it right out of the box, etc.

We develop our own little cereal rituals because we've had so much practice. (Only after eating the last marshmallow "lucky charm," for example, would I turn to the wheaty loops.) If you figure that most of us, as children, ate cereal at least 5 times a week, that means we sat down to a bowl of cereal about 2,400 times in 10 years!

The word "cereal" traces back to the antique word "Ceres," the ancient goddess of agriculture and corn. However, the story goes, the word "cereal" sprang forth from humble grainy beginnings. But long after the Roman empire, assorted goddesses, and ancient crops of wheat, rye, and corn, cereal became a big American business. Breakfast grains are now processed, colored, sugar coated (sometimes sliced with oil), packaged, and then promoted. Some are touted by Tigers named Tony, others by serious sounding people relaying serious quotes from the National Cancer Institute.

Considering the small amount of talent and time it takes to prepare a bowl of cereal, you can bet the cereal market isn't going anywhere but up. It then becomes extra important to buy the box that will contribute to good health—rather than threaten it.

As any of you cereal lovers, or parents of cereal lovers, can attest, the cereal aisle is full of colors, confusion, and what seems like hundreds of choices. The good news is the nutrition information provided on cereal labels have improved greatly. Today, in most cases, the grams of dietary fiber along with the carbohydrate grams from "sucrose and other sugars" are listed per serving.

To find out what percentage of the calories are from sucrose and other sugars, follow these steps:

Step 1: Multiply the grams listed for "Sucrose and Other Sugars" per serving by 4. (You will always multiply this number by 4 because there are 4 calories per gram of carbohydrate.)

Step 2: Divide this new number by the total calories listed per serving.

Step 3: Multiply by 100 to get the percent.

Just so the suspense doesn't keep you up tonight and ruin tomorrow's breakfast, here's what I deduced after my last journey through the cereal jungle.

Cereals with No Added Sugars and Less than 20 percent Calories from Fat

Cereal	Percent Calories from Fat	Percent Calories from Sugar	Sodium (mg)	Fiber (gm)
Sunflakes, 1 oz. (Ralston Purina)	9	0	240	3
Shredded Wheat, 5/6 oz (Nabisco)	10	0	0	3
Shredded Wheat 'N Bran (Nabisco) 1 oz.	0	0	0	4
Spoon Size Shredded Wheat (Nabisco) 1 oz.	0	0	0	3
All Bran with Extra Fiber (Kelloggs) 1 oz.	18	0	140	14
Puffed Rice, 1/2 oz. (Quaker)	0	0	0	NA
Puffed Wheat, 1/2 oz. (Quaker)	0	0	0	NA
NutriGrain Biscuits 1 oz. (Kelloggs)	0	0	0	4
Uncle Sam, 1 oz. (U.S. Mills)	8	0	65	7

Cereals with Less than 10 Percent Calories from Fat and Less than 10 Percent Calories from "Sucrose and Other Sugars"

Cereals	Percent Calories from Fat	Percent Calories from Sugar	Sodium (mg)	Fiber (gm)
Rice Chex, 1 oz.	0	7	280	2
Wheat Chex, 1 oz. (Ralston Purina)	0	8	200	2
Corn Flakes, 1 oz.	0	8	290	1
NutriGrain Nuggets, 1 oz.	0	4*	110	4
NutriGrain Corn, 1 oz. (Kelloggs)	9	8*	170	3
Total Corn Flakes, 1 oz. (General Mills)	8	7	280	NA

NA = information not available on label
 * = "Maltose and other sugars", * = "added sugar"

Cereals with Less than 20 Percent Calories from Fat and Less Than 20 Percent Calories from "Sucrose and Other Sugars"

Cereals	Percent Calories from Fat	Percent Calories from Sugar	Sodium (mg)	Fiber (gm)
Rice Krispies, 1 oz	0	11	290	NA
Special K, 1 oz	0	11	230	NA
Crispix, 1 oz	0	11	220	NA
Product 19, 1 oz	0	12	320	1
Nut & Honey Crunch Biscuits, 1 oz	9	20	5	3
Common Sense Oat Bran, 1 oz	9	20	270	3
NutriGrain, 1.4 oz almond/raisin/walnuts (Kelloggs)	13	20	220	3
Crispy Critters, 1 oz	0	11	230	1
Grape Nuts, 1 oz	0	11	170	2
Grape Nuts Flakes, 1 oz	9	20	160	2
Fruit & Fibre, 1 oz peaches/raisins/ almonds	10	18	170	4
Fruit & Fibre, 1 oz dates/raisins/ walnuts (Post)	10	18	150	5
Total Whole Wheat, 1 oz	9	12	240	3
Fiber One, 1 oz	15	7	135	13
Cheerios, 1 oz	16	4	290	2
Oatmeal Raisin Crisp, 1oz (General Mills)	16	18**	140	NA
Muesli, 1.45 oz raisins/almonds/dates	13	11	95	3
Muesli, 1.45 oz raisins/peaches/pecans	18	13	95	3
Oat Bran Options, 1.45 oz (Ralston Purina)	7	18	150	NA
Life, 1 oz	15	20	180	NA
Oat Squares, 1 oz (Quaker)	18	20	160	2

NA = information not available on label
 * = "maltose and other sugars"
** = "added sugar"

See, that's not so bad, is it? If you want to know the calories per serving or if you are wondering why your favorite cereal isn't on these lists, check the nutrition label on the box. Some cereals could have been left off because they're too new or not available in Northern California, where I read my labels.

Cereal box reading could become your new hobby. You might discover some of the real healthy sounding cereals have over a third of their calories from sugars, and there are certain words to stay away from, such as "frosted" or "fruity." I also found that when some perfectly great bran or grain cereals make a new variation like "cinnamon" or "with raisins" they end up adding other items (namely sugars or more fat). Guess where all this put Tony the Tiger and Trix the Rabbit. In the dog house!

Crackers

Most of us know that crackers tend to be loaded down with fat and salt. But that doesn't mean we never find ourselves buying crackers. A lot of the spreads we cover our crackers with are also high in fat, sodium, and who knows what else. So we want to make sure that at least we start out with a low-fat (less than 30 percent of calories from fat), low-salt cracker, right?

And the final contestants for the "Low-Fat" (sometimes "Lower Sodium") Crackers category are:

Cracker	Per 1/2 ounces		
	Calories	**% Calories from Fat**	**Sodium (mg)**
Crisp Bread— Whole Grain	49	0%	.8
Crisp Bread— Fiber with Sesame Seeds	46	0%	154
Thin Crisp Bread—Extra (ideal)	50	0%	124
Crokine	58	0%	110
Finn Crisp Dark	49	0%	166
Finn Crisp Dark with Caraway	49	0%	166
Kavli Norwegian Crisp Bread			
Thick Style	53	6%	47
Thin Style	57	6%	46
Krispy Original Saltines	60	15%	210
Krispy Unsalted Tops	60	15%	120
Krispy Whole Wheat (Sunshine)	60	15%	210
Matzo (Manischewitz)	55	2%	2
Melba Toast—Rye	50	<18%	130
Melba Toast—White	50	<18%	130
Melba-Sesame Rounds	60	30%	160
Melba Toast—Garlic (Old London)	60	30%	130
Pepperidge Farms— English Water Biscuits	60	13%	77
Royal Lunch—Milk Crackers	60	30%	80
Ry Krisp, Natural	40	0%	100
Ry Krisp-Seasoned	45	20%	140
Wasa-Golden Rye	47	0%	74
Wasa-Breakfast	51	18%	66
Wasa-Fiber Plus	46	26%	65
Wasa-Savory Sesame	43	30%	57
Wasa-Lite Rye	43	0%	69
Wasa-Hearty Rye	41	0%	110
Wasa-Extra Crisp	50	10%	91
Zwieback Teething Toast (Nabisco)	60	15%	20

Jams, Jellies, and Preserves—
An Alternative to Fats

Many of us have said no to jams and jellies for years because we know they're usually laced with sugar or corn syrup—most of the time with only a little more fruit than sugar. But let me try and make a case for the fine preserves out there.

When do we usually dip into that jar of jam? How about just after we've toasted an English muffin or bagel? Okay. So what could we coat our bread with instead? Remember, butter, cream cheese, etc., are all high in calories and the percentage of calories from fat.

Let's put it this way. Say you toast an English muffin and instead of margarine, you grab the Smucker's low sugar boysenberry spread. Your snack just became respectable. It went from 237 calories to 150 and from 47 percent of calories from fat to 6 percent of calories from fat.

All right, so maybe you're not into nooks and crannies. Maybe you're more the bagel type—slicing an ounce or two of cream cheese in the middle. Using 2 tablespoons of a low-sugar type of jam or preserve instead will save you about 50 calories and will transform your fatty breakfast from 39 percent of calories from fat to 6 percent! And that's just switching to a reduced-sugar preserve. There are all types of NO sugar preserves in your market, too. (Once you open the jar, these tend to spoil faster. So if you're the only jam eater in your house, you might want to buy the smaller-sized jars.)

	Calories	Percent Calories from Fat	Protein	Carbo-hydrate
English Muffin with 1 tablespoon margarine	237	47%	8%	45%
English Muffin with 1 tablespoon Smuckers Low Sugar Spread	159	6%	11%	83%
Bagel with 1 ounce (2 tablespoons) cream cheese	262	39%	12%	49%
Bagel with 2 tablespoons Smuckers low-sugar spread	211	6%	11%	83%

Sufficiently impressed? I have just one more argument for low- or no-sugar preserves. The calorie difference (which in the land of preserves usually also means the sugar difference) between regular jams and jellies and the "no sugar added" (juice sweetened) types is worth mentioning.

- Regular jams, jellies, and preserves 1 tablespoon = 55 calories
- Smuckers Low-Sugar Boysenberry Spread 1 tablespoon = 24 calories
- Fruit juice sweetened brands 1 tablespoon = 6 calories (averages)

If you use a couple tablespoons of preserves every day on your toast, this adds up to a savings of around 700 calories a week if you choose fruit juice sweetened preserves versus full strength sugar types. (And you can bet those are 700 refined sugar calories you're saving yourself from.)

Soups Can Be Good Food

Soup. So delicious, especially on a cold winter day, yet quite a project to make from scratch. The way I see it, we have a couple options. Buy canned or packaged soups, but only those low in fat and not too terribly high in sodium or make a big pot of soup, freezing several containers full for future quick and warm meals.

The key to low-fat soups, whether at home or from a can, is to choose the clear broth types most of the time and leave the creamy and cheesy types for those special occasions. Campbell's Creamy Chicken Mushroom Soup & Sauce has 60 percent of its calories from fat. Campbell's Cheddar Cheese Soup has 55 percent of calories from fat. See what I mean? Campbell's Zesty Tomato, on the other hand, has 10 percent of its calories from fat, while Campbell's Home Cookin' Country Vegetable has 15 percent.

Now sodium, that's another story. Sodium doesn't discriminate between the clear and the creamy soup types. High amounts can be found in both. Campbell's has a "Special Request" line out on the shelves with one-third less salt. Even these selections have around 550 milligrams of sodium per 1-cup serving. Look at enough cans and packages of soup and you can even see numbers in the low one-thousands.

After paying the soup aisle a little visit, I was amazed at the vast assortment of flavors lining shelf after shelf, in cans where you add water or milk, in one serving envelopes or plastic tubs, now even in 10 3/4-ounce ready to serve cans. Soup isn't just the chicken noodle variety of yesteryear. Today soup is Lipton's Minestrone (9 percent calories from fat) or Lemon Chicken from Lipton's "lite" line (less than 20 percent of calories from fat).

Before I leave the subject of soup for the duration of the book, I'll share with you the "something new" I learned the other day while walking through the soup section. If you add 4 ounces of skim milk to 4 ounces of condensed Campbell's Creamy Natural Broccoli Soup, it transforms into a 26 percent calories from fat soup instead of using whole milk.

Let's take a look at the better soups I found in my supermarket that had less than 30 percent of calories from fat and less than 600 milligrams of sodium.

	Calories	% of Calories from Fat	Sodium (mg)
Campbell's Ready to Serve, Low Sodium (10 3/4oz serving)			
Split Pea	240	19%	25
Chicken with Noodles	160	28%	85
Tomato with Tomato Pieces	180	25%	40
Chunky Vegetable Beef	170	26%	60
Hain Naturals— No Salt Added (9 1/2 oz serving)			
Minestrone	160	22.5%	35
Lentil	160	22.5%	50
Campbell's Special Request— 1/3 less salt (8 oz prepared)			
Tomato	90	20%	430
Vegetable	80	22.5%	520
Vegetable Beef	70	26%	480
Chicken Noodle	70	26%	580
Health Valley			
Vegetable	100	9%	460
Tomato	100	27%	450
Minestrone	120	22.5%	490
Vegetable (No Salt Added)	100	9%	40

Bottled Sauces

I keep a bottle of spaghetti sauce in my refrigerator at all times. (I won't leave the supermarket without it.) In a pinch, it can substitute for pizza sauce, sauce for a quick quasadilla, pasta sauce (add non- or low-fat milk for a creamy variation), or topping for a 5-minute microwave potato—along with part-skim cheese, of course.

But the lesson here is to stock up only on spaghetti sauces that are themselves low in fat. That way if you add them to low-fat foods (pasta noodles, potatoes, rice, corn tortillas) you are sure to produce a low-fat meal. And here they are:

- *Enrico's All Natural Spaghetti Sauce*
  4 ounces has 60 calories (15 percent of calories from fat)
  and 345 milligrams of sodium
- *Enrico's All Natural Spaghetti Sauce* (No Salt Added)
  4 ounces has 60 calories (15 percent of calories from fat)
  and 35 milligrams of sodium
- *Ragu Chunky Gardenstyle*
  4 ounces has 80 calories (22 percent of calories from fat)
  and 400 milligrams of sodium
- *Ragu Homestyle*
  4 ounces has 70 calories (26 percent of calories from fat)
  and 390 milligrams of sodium

The next two come so close (they are slightly over 30 percent of calories from fat) that I thought I should mention them:

- *Ragu with Leaner Ground Beef—Thick & Hearty*
  4 ounces has 140 calories (32 percent of calories from fat) and 530 milligrams of sodium
- *Prego Spaghetti Sauce with Fresh Mushrooms*
  4 ounces has 140 calories (32 percent of calories from fat) and 640 milligrams of sodium

Undressing Your Salad

You're staring down at an innocent bed of salad greens, thinking to yourself, "Boy, this must be good for me! Look at all those cucumber slices, tomato wedges, red cabbage strips." Meanwhile you're tipping a bottle of creamy dressing over and around your bowl of salad, ruining its healthful effect. Are salads healthful? Let's take a closer look at a generic bowl of salad—and especially that bottle of salad dressing.

Your basic 2 cups of shredded romaine lettuce topped with 1/4 of a medium cucumber, 1 medium tomato, and 1/4 cup of shredded red cabbage is indeed a low-calorie, low-fat, low-sodium dish—at least until you dress it. It has a total of 70 calories, 10 percent of them from fat, and a grand total of 25 milligrams of sodium. Pretty impressive? But what does the typical American do to this garden-fresh masterpiece?

If you use regular salad dressings, even a little bit, it is almost impossible to keep the percent of calories from fat in your salad decent. The calories will start to pour out real quick, too. Salad dressings typically have 70 to 100 calories per tablespoon. Some people pour about 1/4 cup (4 tablespoons!) to 1/2 cup (8 tablespoons!) onto their once low-fat and low-calorie lettuce and vegetables.

This means if you add 1/4 cup of dressing, your salad has just become a 350 calorie dish, with 85 percent of those calories from FAT! And the ante for sodium has just been upped to around 475 milligrams.

So what's a health-conscious, salad-loving person to do? First of all, trade in your measuring cup for a tablespoon measure, and try to keep your pouring down to 2 tablespoons. Then, start sampling some of the lower calorie (thus lower fat) dressing alternatives. These days "reduced calorie" salad dressings come in all types of brands and flavors. Those salad dressings lower in anything worth mentioning are listed here. Unfortunately, it seems that no one offers reduced sodium in a salad dressing—at least not yet. The sodium is up there (they're all over 100 milligrams per tablespoon) so don't even think about grabbing that salt shaker.

Salad dressings with 3 grams or less of fat and less than 300 milligrams of sodium per tablespoon:

Per Tablespoon	Calories	Grams of Fat	Sodium (mg)
Pritikin:			
French Style	10	0	0
Ranch	18	0	0
Vinaigrette	10	0	0
Italian	6	0	0
Weight Watchers:			
French Style	10	0	170
Tomato Vinaigrette	8	0	170
Caesar Salad	4	0	200
Richard Simmons Salad Spray:			
Dijon Vinaigrette	14	1	160
Roma Cheese	14	1	170
Oriental	14	1	105
Italian	14	1	160
French Style	14	1	90
Walden Farms Low-fat Reduced Calorie:			
Thousand Island	24	<3	132
Ranch	35	2	165
Blue Cheese	27	<3	270
Bernstein's Reduced Calorie:			
Italian	14	1	150
Italian with Cheese	12	1	270
Wish Bone Lite:			
Dijon Vinaigrette	25	2	190
French	30	2	70
Russian	25	<1	140
Italian	6	<1	210
Kraft Reduced Calorie:			
Thousand Island	30	2	150
Catalina	16	0	120
Creamy Cucumber	25	2	220
Zesty Italian	20	2	230

Some of these salad dressings make great low-fat pasta vinaigrettes or meat or vegetable marinades!

So, say you're now pouring two tablespoons of Bernstein's Italian with Cheese (low calorie) dressing over your generic salad. Your salad now contains about 82 calories and a little more than 10 percent of calories from fat. Sounds a little better, doesn't it? Hopefully something we can all live with, because if not, we'll have to start calling salad a dessert!

Make Way for the Mayo

One of the supermarket sections that has undergone a face lift lately is the mayonnaise shelf. My advice as a nutritionist used to be quite simple: "Hold the mayo." Now things are a little more complicated. Many varieties of reduced calorie (which also means reduced fat) mayonnaise are now available on most supermarket shelves.

Regular mayonnaise has an average of 98 calories per tablespoon. (Think of that when you're dipping into the gallon-sized jug of mayonnaise.) And that mayo has 11 grams of fat! For the mayonnaise look-alikes to have half the fat, they should have 5 or fewer grams of fat per tablespoon. Well, guess what? Several of them do! Here they are:

- *Miracle Whip Light Cholesterol Free*, 435 calories, 4 gm fat, 0 mg cholesterol, 115 mg sodium
- *Kraft Light Cholesterol Free*, 45 calories, 5 gm fat, 0 mg cholesterol, 100 mg sodium
- *Weight Watchers Whipped Reduced Calorie*, 35 calories, 3 gm fat, 4 mg cholesterol, 80 mg sodium
- *Weight Watchers Reduced Calorie*, 40 calories, 4 gm fat, 5 mg cholesterol, 80 mg sodium
- *Best Foods Light*, 50 calories, 5 gm fat, 5 mg cholesterol, 115 mg sodium
- *Best Foods Cholesterol-Free Reduced Calorie*, 50 calories, 5 gm fat, 0 mg cholesterol, 80 mg sodium
- *Nucoa, Heart Beat Reduced Calorie*, 40 calories, 4 gm fat, 0 mg cholesterol, 110 mg sodium

What about the "cholesterol-free" types versus the others? Well, as you can see from the list, once the fat has been cut down to size (making it reduced calorie), the cholesterol also goes way down. The ones above WITH cholesterol only have around 5 measly milligrams per tablespoon. So I say, go with the one you like the best . . . the one that will tempt you away from using regular fatty mayonnaise the most. (As long as it's lower in fat.)

4

Big Fat Mac Attack: Cutting the Fat at the Top Fast Food Chains

So there you sit, in the middle of nowhere. Your stomach has growled at least three times, so you get off at the next exit where you recognize a fast food chain. You already thought about, visualized, and salivated over what to order. That's one of the best things about fast food chains—reliability. You know what to expect whether you're in L.A., London, or Nebraska. You never quite know with the "Dick's Diner" or the "Alice's Grill" types—except if their parking lot is empty, you know to stay away!

Or say you're running errands on your lunch hour, with 15 minutes to grab something to eat on your way back to the office. Where else can you get a meal in minutes? (If there's a drive-in window, you don't even have to leave your car if you don't want to.) That's the other great thing about fast food; it really is fast!

But I don't have to remind you about the advantages of fast food. America obviously already has them down pat. The problems start when it comes to ordering.

Five Rules for Feeding in the Fast Lane

Rule #1.
Learn to Limit Total Fat

Start off by ordering a sandwich or entree with close to or less than 35 percent of calories from fat. Then, when you order other items with much less fat, you can be sure the total fast food meal will be under 30 percent of calories from fat. Only those choices that qualify are listed below in the table.

Best Bets for Fast Food

	Calories	% Calories from Fat	Sodium (mg)
Arby's			
Baked potato, plain	290	2	12
French dip roast beef sandwich	386	28	1111
Sub (no dressing)	484	30	1354
French fries	211	34	30
Junior roast beef	218	33	345
Roasted chicken breast	254	35	930
King roast beef	467	37	765
Regular roast beef	353	38	590
Hot ham 'n cheese	353	38	1655
Baked potato stuffed with mushroom & cheese*	<506	<39	<653
Baked potato stuffed taco	<619	<39	<1065

* Ask for 1/2 of the usual amount of stuffing
< = less than this amount

	Calories	% Calories from Fat	Sodium (mg)
Burger King			
Hamburger	275	39	509
Whopper (without mayonnaise)	482	39	773
Whopper Junior (without mayonnaise)	274	39	450
Whaler fish (without tartar sauce)	354	33	390
Ham & Cheese specialty sandwich (without mayo)	374	31	1463
Chicken specialty sandwich (without mayo)	494	36	1281

	Calories	% Calories from Fat	Sodium (mg)
Breakfast bagel sandwich	387	33	780
Breakfast bagel with ham	418	32	1130
Low-fat Milk (2%)	121	37	122
Orange Juice	82	----	2
Chicken Salad (not including dressing)	140	26	440
Chicken salad with 1 packet reduced-calorie Italian dressing	170	32	1310
Salad Bar: Typical serving of vegetables only (5.2 oz no dressing)*	28	----	23
Reduced calorie Italian dressing, 1 packet	30	60	870

*A typical serving of salad (iceburg lettuce, tomatoes, mushrooms, cucumber, bell pepper, broccoli, cauliflower, spinach) according to the Produce Marketing Association.

Carl Junior

	Calories	% Calories from Fat	Sodium (mg)
Lite potato	250	1	35
Broccoli & cheese potato	470	32	690
Sour cream & chive potato	350	33	140
California roast beef 'N swiss	360	20	1070
Charbroiler BBQ chicken	320	14	955
Happy Star hamburger	220	33	445
Old Time Star hamburger	400	38	760
Old fashioned chicken English muffin with margarine	180	30	275
Hot cakes with margarine (no syrup)	360	30	1190
Blueberry muffin	256	25	360
Bran muffin	220	25	300
Low-fat milk, 10 oz	175	31	181
Orange juice, small	94	9	2
Noodle soup	80	11	605
To-go salads (not including dressing)			
Chicken salad-to-go	206	35	453
Chef salad-to-go	180	35	581
Reduced calorie French dressing (1 oz serving)	38	47	292

	Calories	% Calories from Fat	Sodium (mg)
Domino's Pizza			
12" Cheese pizza, 2 slices	340	16	660
16" Cheese pizza, 2 slices	400	18	800
12" Pepperoni pizza, 2 slices	380	28	880
16" Pepperoni pizza, 2 slices	440	29	1080
Hardee's			
Orange juice, 6 oz.	81	0	0
Side salad, no dressing	21	4	42
Biscuit with jelly	324	36	653
Hot ham 'n cheese	376	36	1067
Roast beef sandwich	312	36	826
Cheeseburger	309	37	825
Jack-in-the-Box			
Breakfast Jack	307	38	871
Hamburger	267	37	556
Chicken fajita pita	292	25	703
(no guacamole or sour cream)			
Beef fajita pita	333	38	635
(no guacamole or sour cream)			
Grilled chicken fillet	408	37	1130
Pancake platter (includes syrup)	612	32	888
Low-fat milk	122	----	122
Orange juice (1 serving)	80	----	------
Ice tea (12 oz)	3	----	4.5
Reduced-calorie French dressing, 1 oz	70	41	240
Sweet & sour sauce, 1 oz	40	----	160
Seafood cocktail sauce, 1 oz	32	----	206
Salsa (0.9 oz)			
Kentucky Fried Chicken			
Mashed potatoes	59	9	228
Mashed potatoes with gravy	62	20	297
Corn on the cob	176	16	10
Baked beans	105	10	387

	Calories	% Calories from Fat	Sodium (mg)
Long John Silver			
Corn on the cob	176	20	----
Ocean chef salad	229	31	986
Clam chowder, 6.6 oz.	128	35	611
McDonald's			
Orange juice, 6 oz.	80	0	2
Grapefruit juice, 6 oz.	80	0	0
Skim milk (0.5% fat), 8 oz.	90	6	130
English muffin with butter	170	24	270
Chicken salad Oriental (with 1 oz. Oriental dressing)*	188	17	590

*Note: the salad dressing packages they give you contain 2 oz.

	Calories	% Calories from Fat	Sodium (mg)
Fillet-O-Fish (without tartar sauce)	300	32	<800
Low-fat milk, 8 oz.	120	35	130
Hamburger	268	35	510
*Meals:			
Hot cakes with syrup and butter	410	20	640
2 English muffins with butter and low-fat milk	460	27	670
Roy Rogers			
Baked potato, plain	211	1	trace
Orange juice, 7 oz.	99	2	2
Orange juice, 10 oz.	136	2	3
Potato with margarine	274	24	161
Roast beef sandwich	317	29	785
Large roast beef sandwich	360	30	1044
Taco Bell			
Bean burrito with red or green sauce	357	26	888
Combo burrito	375	33	833
Chicken fajita	226	41	619
Beef fajita	234	42	485
Tostada with red sauce	243	41	596
Pintos & cheese	184	42	518

	Calories	% Calories from Fat	Sodium (mg)
Wendy's			
Baked potato, plain	250	7	trace
Potato with chicken a la king	350	13	820
Chicken breast fillet (ordered without mayonnaise)	340	24	645
New chili, 9 oz	230	35	960
Baked potato with chili and cheese*	510	35	610

*If you order it without the cheese sauce, it's 370 calories, 19 percent from fat!

	Calories	% Calories from Fat	Sodium (mg)
Small hamburger	260	31	510
Orange juice, 6 oz	80	0	0
Low-fat milk	110	33	115
Reduced-calorie Italian dressing, 2 tbsp.	50	72	360
Reduced-calorie bacon & tomato dressing, 2 tbsp.	90	80	380
Picante sauce, 2 oz	18	<10	5

Selective salad bar items (1.4 cup servings):

	Calories	% Calories from Fat	Sodium (mg)
Old fashioned corn relish	35	----	205
Deluxe three-bean salad	60	7	15
Pasta deli salad	35	<9	120
Broccoli	6	----	3
Red cabbage	4	----	5
Carrots	10	----	15
Cauliflower	6	----	3
Green peppers	8	----	5
Fresh mushrooms	4	----	----
Pineapple chunks	35	----	----

Think back over your fast food travels this past year. Which chains did you frequent? Drive through the list above and find your favorite stopping places. Circle at least one of the healthier choices listed that you would be willing to order next time.

*If you eat big (or a lot) and one of those smaller (less fatty) hamburgers isn't enough, order two. You'll still be way ahead of the fat game. If you don't believe me, see for yourself:

McDonald's

2 hamburgers = 520 calories, 33 percent of calories from fat, 1000 mg
of sodium

McDLT = 580 calories, 58 percent of calories from fat, 990 mg. of
sodium

Burger King

2 hamburgers = 550 calories, 39 percent of calories from fat, 1018 mg.
sodium

Whopper with cheese = 711 calories, 54 percent from fat, 1164 mg
sodium

---

*Try having it "your way" by ordering your sandwich or burger
without mayonnaise or other sauces. Mustard or catsup is okay.

This rule rescues the Fillet-O-Fish at McDonald's and Burger King's
Whaler sandwich from being banished from the prestigious "Best
Bets Table" because by taking their sauces off, you shave fat. Note the
before and after shots of these sandwiches:

Fillet-O-Fish (McDonald's)

Before: (Dressed in tartar sauce) 435 calories, 50% from fat
After: (Undressed) 296 calories, 32% from fat

Whaler Sandwich (Burger King)

Before: 488 calories, 50% fat
After: 354 calories, 33 % fat

Chicken Specialty Sandwich (Burger King)

Before: 688 calories, 52% from fat
After: 494 calories, 36% from fat

Now I'm going to list fast food choices which, although popular, are
among your "Worst Bets" because they have half their calories from
fat. If just reading the names makes you start to salivate, quickly turn
back to "Best Bets Table" and fixate on one of the healthier choices
instead.

Worst Bets

	Calories	Gms of Fat	% of Calories from Fat	Sodium (mg)
Burger King				
Whopper hamburger	628	36	51	880
Whopper with cheese	711	43	54	1164
Bacon Double				
Whaler fish with tartar sauce	488	27	50	592
Chicken specialty with mayo	688	40	52	1423
Onion rings	274	16	52	665
French fries (lightly salted)	227	13	51	160
Breakfast Croissan'wich:				
Eggs & Cheese	304	19	56	637
with bacon	355	24	61	762
with sausage	538	41	69	1042
with ham	335	20	54	987
Scrambled egg platter	468	30	57	808
(eggs, croissant, hash browns)				
Scrambled egg platter with sausage	702	52	67	1213
Scrambled egg platter with bacon	536	36	60	975
French toast sticks	499	29	52	498
Great Danish	500	36	64	288
Whole milk	157	9	52	119
Carl's Jr.				
Famous Star hamburger	590	36	55	890
Super Sar hamburger	770	50	58	990
Double western bacon cheeseburger	890	53	54	1620
Sunrise with sausage	500	32	58	990
Hashed brown potato, 1 patty	180	13	65	370
Scrambled eggs with 1 sausage patty	310	26	75	380
Scrambled eggs with 2 strips bacon	170	13	69	305
Soups: Boston clam chowder	140	8	51	861
Hardee's				
Big deluxe hamburger	503	29	52	903
Bacon cheeseburger	556	33	53	888
1/4 pounder with cheese	511	28	50	1112
Hot dog	346	22	57	768
Chef salad	277	16	52	517

	Calories	Gms of Fat	% of Calories from Fat	Sodium (mg)
Jack-in-the Box				
Supreme crescent	547	40	65	1053
Sausage crescent	584	43	66	1012
Canadian crescent	452	31	62	851
Scrambled egg platter	662	40	54	1188
Jumbo Jack	584	34	52	733
Jumbo with cheese	677	40	53	1090
Swiss 7 bacon burger	678	47	62	1458
Bacon cheeseburger	705	39	50	1127
Chicken supreme	575	36	56	1525
Fish supreme	554	32	52	1047
Ultimate cheeseburger	942	69	66	1176
Taco	191	11	52	406
Super taco	288	17	53	765
Cheese nachos	571	35	55	1154
Supreme nachos	639	36	51	2187
Jumbo fries	442	24	54	328
Onion rings	382	23	54	407
Hot apple turnover	410	24	53	350
Cheesecake	309	17.5	51	208
*Salad values are without added dressing				
Chef salad	295	18	55	812
Side salad	51	3	53	84
Taco salad	503	31	55	N/A
Dressing	181	18	89	347
Thousand Island dressing	156	15	86	350

Kentucky Fried Chicken:

	Calories	Gms of Fat	% of Calories from Fat	Sodium (mg)
Original Recipe:				
Wing	181	12	61	387
Side Breast	276	17	56	654
Drumstick	147	9	54	269
Thigh	278	19	62	517
Extra Crispy:				
Wing	218	15	64	437
Side Breast	354	23.7	60	797
Drumstick	173	11	57	346

	Calories	Gms of Fat	% of Calories from Fat	Sodium (mg)
Thigh	371	26.3	64	766
Kentucky Nuggets,	276	17.3	56	840
6 pieces without sauce				
Cole slaw	103	5.7	50	171
Potato salad	141	9.3	59	396

McDonald's

Sausage McMuffin with egg	440	26.8	55	980
Hash brown potatoes	130	7.3	51	270
Scrambled eggs	140	9.8	63	290
Pork Sausage	180	16.3	81	350
Biscuit with sausage	440	29	59	1180
Biscuit with sausage and egg	520	34.5	60	1250
Biscuit with bacon, egg, and cheese	440	26.4	54	1230
Quarter pounder with cheese	520	29.2	51	1150
Big Mac	560	32.4	52	950
McDLT	580	36.8	57	990
McChicken	490	29	52	780
Fillet-O-Fish	440	26	53	1030
Chicken McNuggets without sauce	290	16.3	51	520
Chef salad without dressing	230	13.3	52	490
Garden salad without dressing	110	6.6	54	160
Dressings: 1 packet (2 oz.)				
Ranch	330	34	94	520
French	114	10.3	81	340

Taco Bell

Cinnamon Crispas	259	15	53	127
Taco	183	11	53	276
Soft taco supreme	275	16	53	516
Taco light	410	29	63	594
Taco salad with salsa	941	61	59	1662
Taco salad without shell	502	31	56	1056
Mexican pizza	575	37	58	1031
Taco BelGrande	355	23	58	472
Super combo taco	286	16	50	462
Maxi melt	266	15	52	689

	Calories	Gms of Fat	% of Calories from Fat	Sodium (mg)
Wendy's				
Big classic	580	34	53	1015
Big classic with cheese	640	40	56	1310
Single cheese with everything	490	28	51	1100
Bacon swiss burger	710	44	56	1390
Breakfast potatoes	360	22	55	745
Ham & Cheese Omelet*	290	21	65	570
Ham, mushroom, and cheese omelet	250	17	61	405
Cheese, onion, and green pepper omelet	280	19	61	485
Mushroom, green pepper, and onion omelet	210	15	64	200
Taco salad	660	37	50	1110
Cheese potato	590	34	52	450
Crispy chicken nuggets (6-piece order)	290	21	65	615

*The omelets have a range of 360 to 530 mg of cholesterol!

Exceptions to Rule #1: How to Dilute Total Fat

A friend of mine, after hearing about my fast food rules, said, "Just tell me what I need to order so I don't have to give up my French fries." My sister had a similar reaction. "You might succeed in getting me off the quarter pounder with cheese and onto the little cheeseburgers, but I'm not ordering the plain hamburgers—no matter how much healthier they are."

I realize we all have our fast food obsessions (although I'm never telling what mine is). It's important to take them into account. After all, if you set unrealistic goals for yourself, you'll never be able to stick with the program. Maybe you've even found the loophole in Regulation #1. If no, I'll let you in on it.

The bottom line to Rule #1 is to make sure your total fast food meal is less than 30 percent of calories from fat. Theoretically, you could order a sandwich or side order that was somewhere in the 40 percent range, adding the necessary carbo calories such as orange juice or salad with vegetables (with low-calorie dressing of course), bringing the percent of calories from fat for the meal down to an acceptable level.

So let's try to solve the "gotta have the French fries" or "cheese on the burger" blues.

The French Fry Obsession:

1. Start by placing Carl's Jr. French fries (for example) at the top of your list

   French fries = 360 calories (42 percent from fat), or 17 grams of fat.

   Remember: You can calculate grams of fat from the percent of calories from fat by first multiplying the calories per serving by the percent of calories from fat divided by 100.

   Then, divide this number by 9 (the number of calories in each gram of fat).

2. Add on the lower fat sandwiches or side orders, such as Carl's Charbroiler Chicken sandwich, with 320 calories, 14 percent of them from fat, and 5 grams of fat.

   (I calculated this by multiplying 320 calories by 14 (percent of calories from fat) divided by 100. Then I divided this number by 9. My answer is 5 grams of fat.

3. Let's see how much orange juice you need to drink to get down to 30 percent of total calories from fat:

   Each small glass of orange juice at Carl's has 94 calories and 1 gram of fat.

   If you can manage to guzzle just one small orange juice with your fries and sandwich, for a total of 774 calories, you'll have brought the percentage of fat calories down to 27%. So the fries will work —provided you're not on a weight reduction plan that limits calories as well as fat.

The Cheese on the Burger Obsession

1. Start with your cheeseburger from McDonald's at 318 calories, with 45 percent of those calories from fat and 16 grams of fat.

2. Add some carbohydrate calories, such as a sack of carrot sticks. (You probably have to bring these from home.) 1 cup of carrots = 40 calories and 0.3 grams of fat.

3. Buy 2 grapefruit juice containers, each with 6 oz and 80 calories, with no grams of fat, or some orange juice. Voila! You've got your cheese on the burger and a fairly healthful meal to boot, with 518 total calories, 28 percent of which are from fat.

Rule #2.
Zip-Lock Carbohydrates

Have you heard the game "Find the missing complex carbohydrates"? (This is very popular in nutrition circles.) I'll give you a hint. With fast food this usually refers to fruits and vegetables. The purpose of the game isn't just to find them but to then plan them into your fast food meal.

If you're lucky, some chains sell orange juice or let you make your own vegetable-packed salad. If not, you should plan to bring your own. "Bring vegetables and fruits with me?" you ask. I know this might take some getting used to. Your co-workers might laugh a little—maybe a lot—when you pull your Zip-Lock bag filled with broccoli or carrot sticks and your apple or orange out of your briefcase or purse. But you'll probably only have to explain the first time. Maybe they'll even start to tote their carbohydrates with them, too.

Practice Scenario #1:

You've decided to go to Wendy's for lunch. You're going to order the chicken breast sandwich and go to the salad bar, adding only 2 tablespoons of reduced-calorie dressing. (By the way, you're going to have to carry a measuring spoon with you, because what you think a tablespoons is and what it really is can be two very different animals.) In this case, only your fruit carbohydrate is missing. You can either order an orange juice or bring some fruit with you. Buy a bottle of juice or a piece of fruit at the market on the way, or bring it from home.

Practice Scenario #2:

There you sit in 5 o'clock traffic. You're tired, frustrated, and worst of all, starving to the point of food fantasizing. Just then you spot a yellow Taco Bell in the distance.

You decide to order the combo burrito. Okay, so let's go through nutrition roll call: The tortilla definitely counts as the bread/starch group; it might be pushing it a bit, but you could consider the chopped tomatoes as part of your fruit serving (tomatoes really are fruit). But where's the vegetable: Looks like some carrot sticks are in order, and maybe a bottle of juice or a piece of fruit from home.

Rule #3.
Dress Your Food Yourself

You may need to come equipped with some toppings. If the fast food chain you patronize doesn't offer a low-calorie salad dressing, you still have these options:

- You can measure a couple of tablespoons of your low-calorie dressing from home into a small container and bring it with you.
- If you typically munch your fast food meal back at work, you can bring a bottle of low-cal dressing to the office and keep it in the refrigerator for a fat-reducing salad.

How to Avoid Those Slabs of Butter

If you order a plain baked potato, you can add your own non- or low-fat yogurt or grated part-skim mozzarella cheese.

- Buy a small container of yogurt on the way to the fast food place.
- Bring yogurt or cheese from home, keeping it in the refrigerator at work.

Rule #4.
Beware of Fast Food Liquids!

I know, I know, it's convenient and tempting to order your drink there. But fast food chains typically don't sell you a drink free from fat, sugar, or artificial sweeteners.

Nonfat milk, mineral water, and juices, as well as fruits and vegetables (and I'm not talking about the slice of tomato or leaf of lettuce on your hamburger) are simply not the common fare at fast food chains, at least not yet. So be ready to make a pit stop for them on the way or bring them from home.

Rule #5.
Once is Enough

Eat fast food a maximum of once a day. Most fast food items are loaded with sodium, and if you're trying to stay within the health guidelines (less than 4 grams of sodium per day), two large fast food meals might push you way over the edge.

Before you even start your work day you could be half way to your sodium limit. A pancake platter (with ham, syrup, and butter) at Roy Rogers totals 1,264 milligrams of sodium. Now onto lunch—an Arby's Sub Sandwich (no dressing) by itself has 1,655 milligrams of sodium. Or a Ham & Cheese Specialty Sandwich (without mayo) ordered with a salad totals 2,000 milligrams of sodium. And these are from the "Best Bets Table"!

Needless to say, don't even think about salting your fast food at the table. Leave those salt packets alone. Believe me, the salt's already in there.

Other Tips for Fast Lane Food

1. Cut the Cream

    Wipe off the mayonnaise or tartar sauce (all the creamy type sauces) on your sandwiches, or order them "your way" without sauces. Just try spreading a little catsup or mustard instead. It make a BIG difference—fat and calories-wise.

    Fast food companies supposedly test and retest their recipes based on what the average consumer wants. It's hard for me to believe the average American really wants two tablespoons of gloppy tartar sauce on a Fillet-O-Fish Sandwich. Evidently McDonald's does. Or that a Chicken

Specialty Sandwich "needs" two tablespoons of mayonnaise. Still that's how much Burger King squirts on.

2. Double Your Pleasure, Double Your Fat

   Avoid the "deluxe" or "double this, double that" type of burgers, and you'll rescue yourself from a whopping amount of fat and calories. Here are some examples:

   • Jack-In-The-Box Ultimate Cheeseburger (942 calories, 66 percent from fat)
   • McDonald's Big Mac (570 calories, 55 percent from fat)
   • Carl's Jr. Double Western Bacon Cheeseburger (890 calories, 54 percent from fat)

3. Fatty Fryers

   Avoid the fried chicken and fried chicken pieces. Are those six itsy bitsy bite size nuggets really worth 323 calories, especially when 56 percent of those calories are from fat?And that's before dipping them.

4. Pizza To Go, Hold the Fat

   When ordering pizza, stick with ordering vegetables on top. Skipping the pepperoni, salami, or sausage will save you from much extra calories and fat.

Salad Bar Minefield

When in the salad bar, remember to keep your distance from cheese, chow mein noodles, cole slaw, croutons, eggs, pasta salad, and mayonnaise-loaded salads, such as macaroni and egg. Instead, load up on the greens, raw vegetables, and beans and use the low-calorie dressings or bring them from home.

Blowing the Whistle on Some Fast Food Frauds

The "Light" Taco?

Taco Bell came out with a "Taco Light" a few years ago. The word "light" must have been referring to the color of the taco shell, because one Taco Light has 410 calories, compared with 183 in a regular taco. Worse yet, 63 percent of the total calories are from FAT. The regular taco has 53 percent and the soft taco 47 percent of calories from fat.

To Eat or Not to Eat the Shell?

Taco Bell has a taco salad that comes in a deep fried (very attractive) flour tortilla shell. And everyone who orders it, I'm sure, ponders whether or not to crunch the shell into bite size pieces and mix it into the salad, bite off chunks, or toss it, quickly, into the nearest trash can. Well, ponder no more. They must really be deep frying those babies extra long—each has about 400 calories, with 67 percent from fat. That's a high price to pay for "cute."

Does Kentucky Really "Do Chicken Right"?

Only if you like GREASE! What does the Colonel "do" to a normally low-fat chicken breast? An original recipe chicken breast is 270 calories, 48 to 52 percent from fat. Extra Crispy, which is really extra fatty, is 354 calories, with 53 to 60 percent from fat. For comparison sake (or shock value), a regular unadulterated broiled chicken breast (without the skin) is 140 calories, 21 percent from fat.

The Criminal—Mr. Mayo

It's bad enough that fast food chicken and fish patties are deep fried in grease, but squirting mayonnaise or tartar sauce (Mr. Mayo's daughter) on top is absolutely criminal. Take Burger King's Chicken Specialty Sandwich (which comes with a chicken patty, bun, mayonnaise, and lettuce) with a total of 688 calories, 52 percent of them from fat. Scrape off the mayo—or order it "your way" without mayo—and suddenly we're talking about a 495-calorie sandwich, with only 36 percent of calories from fat. That's good enough to qualify for a "Best Bet."

Big Mac (Heart) Attack

Bite into a Big Mac and you bite into some big calories—and fat calories at that. One Big Mac has 570 calories, 55 percent from fat, along with 980 milligrams of sodium.

What is it about the Big Mac that makes it such a fat snack? Could it be the slices of processed cheese? Or the heaping tablespoons of thousand island-like dressing? (Of course they call it their "special sauce.") Or maybe it's the two hamburger patties with only the three slices of bun?

If you find the "stacked-up" look attractive in the Big Mac, why don't you order two regular (little) hamburgers and place one on top of the other before eating. Oh, and don't think you'll do any better with the Mc DLT ("Mc Fat LT"). It has 680 calories, with 58 percent from fat, and 1,030 milligrams of sodium.

5

Five Star Dining

Eating Out is America's favorite pastime. Often, even when we're "eating in", we're really "eating out" by buying take-out food to eat at home. I don't know about you, but when I'm dining in a restaurant my mind automatically snaps into its "splurge" mode. This may be because when I was growing up, eating out, even at McDonald's, was usually a special occasion.

Don't get me wrong. I'm not against the occasional "what the heck, this time I'm going to order what I really want, and then I'm going to order dessert" approach. But with eating out becoming a daily ritual for some of us, this splurging stuff can get way out of hand. So to help you (and me) out of this splurge rut, I put together nine tips to help us keep FAT calories in line when eating out, except for those rare and truly "special" occasions.

1. The Before Dinner Ditties

The bread sitting pretty in that basket on the table is usually fine. It's the clumps of chilled butter that can get you into some major calories from fat before dinner is even served. One slice of French bread has 70 calories, about 10 percent from fat. A small pat of butter (1 teaspoon) has 36 calories — all of them from fat. Put them together and what have you got? A fairly fatty appetizer. If buttering your bread is non-negotiable, then try to keep the butter to a half teaspoon per slice, which totals around 88 calories with the slice of bread, with 31 percent of calories from fat, or less.

When it comes to soups, order the clear, broth-type soups, such as chicken noodle, bean, beef-vegetable or tomato-based, instead of the creamy-type soups. (One exception is the clear broth-like French onion soup, which has only 100 calories per cup but is 70 percent fat calories.) For example, beef barley soup has about 195 calories per cup, with 6 percent of calories from fat. Cream of cauliflower soup, on the other hand, has 280 calories and is 71 percent calories from fat.

And you usually can't get into too much trouble with a shrimp or crab cocktail. Half a cup has about 65 calories (10 percent from fat) and a tablespoon of cocktail sauce only adds about 15 calories.

Then there's always the raw vegetable platters, which can be a fresh, crisp and low-fat way to work in your daily dose of vegetables, as long as you make sure the creamy dip is on the side and that you really do "dip" and not "scoop." Better yet, use a small spoon to scoop out about half a tablespoon onto your plate and use only that amount to dress your veggies.

1. Watch out for anything described as "creamy," "breaded" or "fried." Also watch for anything dressed with mayonnaise. (Remember mayo is made from egg yolks and oil.) It's wise to beware of cole slaw, potato, or macaroni salad.

2. Avoid ordering meat, poultry, or seafood portions larger than about 4 ounces cooked (6 ounces raw) or take the excess home for tomorrow's sandwich.

3. Order your meat, poultry, or seafood grilled or broiled (without added butter or fats) or poached.

5. If your entree is ordinarily "sauteed" or "simmered" in cream or butter, ask that it be simmered in wine instead.

4. Most sauces and dressings can quickly get you into fat calories Big Time, so order them on the side so you know how much you're adding. If, for example, you want some melted butter with your steamed clams or prawns but you want to keep the meal low in fat, take your small spoon and dip it in the butter and pour that onto a portion of

your plate. This way you will only be adding a teaspoon or so of butter to your shellfish.

5. When visiting your friendly neighborhood deli, avoid selecting the corned beef, pastrami, sausage, liverwurst, bologna, meatloaf, or luncheon meat sandwich (or mayo-drenched shrimp, tuna, or egg salad sandwiches). Choose instead sandwiches filled with chicken or turkey breast, cheese, or roast beef, and try to wet the bread with mustard or a teeny bit of mayo (about 1/2 a teaspoon).

6. On the side, load up on complex carbohydrates, such as rice pilaf, veggies, beans, boiled or baked potatoes.

7. What about the tempting dessert tray? Of course, being satisfied with a bowl of fresh fruit would be great, but is it realistic all the time? If the fruit comes complete with whipped cream, ask them to dab a little dollop on top (not plop a pile all over it). For those times when you just can't hold yourself back from the Chocolate Whiskey Cake or Hot Apple Pie, order one slice and share it with the table. Keep in mind most pies and pastries are actually higher in fat than cakes (except cakes with extra thick layers of filling or frosting). Angel food cake is the lowest fat cake of all.

For Better or for Worse: Menu Selections

So many choices—Chinese or Japanese, basic Italian or just pizza, should we go Mexican and Margueritas or French and red wine. And once you choose "where" to go, you still have to decide "what" to order.

For example, most people don't picture 650 calories (77 percent from fat) alongside the vision of one slice of Quiche Lorraine dancing in their heads as they drive to their favorite French restaurant.

And if you're an avid lover of Fettucine Alfredo, sorry Charlie, but it's time to cut the courtship. Alfredo, dressed in the typical Italian fare, is carrying a bit of excess fat with him, to say the least. He has 720 calories per serving, with 81 percent from fat. No cause for panic though. You can still make it a lower fat (and still delicious) way at home.

Let's take an up-close and personal look at some international favorites, as well as a couple more American options.

French

While thumbing through my *Mastering the Art of French Cooking* cookbook by Julia Child, I couldn't help but notice that if you have to describe the "art of French cooking" in four words or less, they would be "eggs, butter, cream, and salt." They're in almost every recipe. It seems the only way to get away from them is to move to another country or cuisine.

We might all expect the standard light and fluffy cheese souffle to be loaded with fat and cholesterol (a two-cup serving has about 600 calories, 70 percent from fat and almost 500 milligrams of cholesterol). But what about a seemingly innocent menu item described as "scallops with wine, garlic, and herbs"? In this case, the menu failed to inform the eater it also contains butter, olive oil, and cheese. And don't let those elegant names sidetrack you, such as lobster thermidor, which happens to be laced with butter and whipping cream.

So enough of the bad news. The key to eating healthful but still eating French is "Watch Your Sauces." You can start off with a lean chicken breast or fish fillet, but given a chance the French will smother it in a heavy sauce like Hollandaise or Bearnaise (made with egg yolks and butter), which has about 450 calories per half cup (98 percent from fat), 250 milligrams of cholesterol, and about 750 milligrams of sodium. Bechamel sauce (made with milk, butter, and flour) has 228 calories per half cup, with 74 percent from fat, and 57 milligrams of cholesterol plus about 900 milligrams of sodium.

You can either ask that only one tablespoon of these sauces be added to your fish or chicken or you can order (or cook) your entree with a Bordelaise sauce (wine sauce), which has about 155 calories per half cup. About 76 percent of the calories are from fat, and Bordelaise sauce has only about 10 milligrams of cholesterol and 400 milligrams of sodium.

There are unadulterated French recipes that actually come to your table already pretty low in fat, such as steamed mussels or fish fillets poached in white wine. The latter has

227 calories per serving, with 26 percent of calories from fat, 125 milligrams of cholesterol, and about 220 milligrams of sodium.

What about crepes? Well, I confess, I'm a crepe lover from way back. Just remember before you decide what to fill it or top it with, one crepe (all by itself) already starts off with 150 calories, 40 percent from fat, and 100 milligrams of cholesterol.

Italian

If I could eat my way through any country, it would be Italy, no question. Mostly because of the two "P" words—Pizza and Pasta. (I don't care what the food critics say. In my book, pasta is still "IN.")

I know, pizza is different over there. Actually it's probably lower in fat because they like their pizza dough with only a little cheese on it (unlike us Americans who like our cheese with only a little pizza bread under it). But even if you have it the American way, when you order the vegetarian special or cheese only versions (no extra cheese), you're still dealing with a comparatively low-fat entree (28 to 32 percent of calories from fat).

In the pasta department, one of your best choices is mushroom spaghetti. Even the stand-by spaghetti and meatballs isn't too bad—with 38 percent of calories from fat. If you're going to cover your noodles or ravioli with something, choose the Marsala, made with wine, or Marinara, made with tomatoes, onions, and garlic. It's the pesto and cream type sauces that are the trouble makers. Mix your fettucini noodles with a pesto cream sauce and suddenly you're looking at a 67 percent calories from fat dish.

If it's a must-have situation, you could order or serve your pasta with half the original amount of sauce. This will cut the fat and calories way down.

Then comes a dilemma I know I've faced in a few Italian restaurants: Manicotti or cannelloni, which should it be?

Well, the answer is neither — at least not the way they're traditionally made. Both have about 800 calories a serving (namely, two manicotti or cannelloni rolls), with 65 percent of calories from fat and from 300 to 600 milligrams of cholesterol. But you could order or serve them covered with a Marinara sauce and just a sprinkle of cheese—instead of the creamy sauces and blankets of cheese usually topping them.

You will get less stuffing and more pasta for your money when you stuff a ravioli or tortellini instead of a cannelloni — one of the best ways I know to lower the percent of fat calories. A large serving of meat-filled ravioli with a tomato sauce and a generous amount of cheese has around 700 calories, with 42 percent from fat.

With a last name like Moquette, my European bias toward food may come as no surprise. Still, I do love foods from the South and East as well. First, we'll look at some Mexican cuisine.

Mexican

The first choice confronting anyone planning a Tex-Mex type meal is flour versus corn tortillas. They are different in more ways than just color. The flour-type has the four-letter "L" word in it—LARD.

Flour tortillas have up to 150 calories each, compared with corn tortillas with about 50 calories. The flour types have 34 percent of calories from fat, compared with 10 percent for corn tortillas. Flour tortillas have about 140 milligrams of sodium, while corn tortillas have just one milligram of sodium each. Deep fry either one, though, and it doesn't matter which you've chosen. They'll both come up loaded with grease and calories.

So it's best to leave those entrees with fried tortillas where they belong—on the menu! The second major consideration, especially when dining out, is whether to reach into that basket of tortilla chips or to hold on until dinner. One innocent handful of chips adds about 140 calories, half of which are from fat. And dip them into the salsa or chili sauces? One-fourth cup contains around 900 milligrams of sodium!

If you have a thing for that chili-flavored sausage, chorizo, try and forget about it. A small 2-ounce serving has about 430 calories, 83 percent from fat, and 85 milligrams of cholesterol. And, speaking of fat and cholesterol, a typical recipe of Huevos

Rancheros has 530 milligrams of cholesterol—480 calories, 50 percent from fat, and about 2,000 milligrams of sodium. You're already way past your daily cholesterol target of 300 milligrams a day and darn near your sodium limit of 3,000 milligrams. And you haven't even left the breakfast table!

So what can you order or cook up? Believe it or not, that side of rice and beans, even the refried type, is a good place to start. Even though the secret "refried" ingredient is usually lard (they have cans of "vegetarian refried beans" that add vegetable oil instead), a typical 3/4 cup side serving with a sprinkle of melted Jack cheese on top is still between 25 and 35 percent of calories from fat—around 300 calories, with 20 milligrams of cholesterol, 100 milligrams of sodium, and an impressive 15 grams of fiber!! Not bad!

The distinctively Mexican tomato-colored rice has about 240 calories per 3/4 cup serving, with 22 percent of calories from fat. Depending on the recipe, the rice can have up to 600 milligrams of sodium.

For possible entrees, I'll give it to you straight:

- Try to order them without the sour cream and guacamole. Per 1/4 cup dollop, sour cream has 125 calories, 86 percent from fat, and 32 milligrams of cholesterol. Guacamole has almost 100 calories per 1/4 cup, with 79 percent from fat (but no cholesterol).
- If you absolutely have to have the taco or tostada, order chicken instead of beef and ask if you can have it with a baked or steamed tortilla instead of fried. (Don't tell yourself "it's the best part," because it isn't. And even if you think it is, it's not worth all the extra fat and calories.)
- Chicken tends to be the lowest fat enchilada (about 35 percent of calories from fat and around 240 calories each, 30 milligrams of cholesterol, and 200 milligrams of sodium).
- If you're a burrito person:

    Bean burritos are always a safe bet (about 30 percent fat calories from a total of 340 calories, 7.5 grams of fiber, 7 milligrams of cholesterol, and 270 milligrams of sodium).

    The beef and bean combos (about 36 percent calories from fat) are usually better choices than the all-beef types.

    Those fresh, regular-sized vegetarian burritos (where

they, or you, fill a steamed tortilla with whole beans, rice, mild salsa, and some cheese) are an excellent choice. I indulge in these at least once a week. One, which is usually more than plenty for me, has about 500 calories, 20 percent from fat, 11 grams of fiber, and 26 milligrams of cholesterol. Sodium values can get up around 1,300 milligrams, depending on the chili sauce and how much you or they add. The one with chicken but no cheese is still a great choice. It has about the same calories, percent of fat calories, and fiber as the vegetarian—but twice the cholesterol.

• What's the secret to these soft, yummy cornmeal tamale exteriors? They're held together with lots of LARD! (There's that word again!) So don't be shocked that half the calories are from fat. The chicken ones are pretty low in calories (around 300 for two small tamales), so technically you could probably have a low-fat meal if you ate some rice and enough fruit or something to bring down the percentage of calories from fat. The same goes for chicken tacos. Two have about 300 calories, 40 percent from fat.

• And here's my last word on eating Mexican. Think twice— or even three times—before opting for a cheesy chili relleno. One dinky relleno has 500 calories, 62 percent of calories from fat, 185 milligrams of cholesterol, and up to 1,550 milligrams of sodium.

Chinese

Let's start off by listing some of the more obvious no-no's: Fried wontons, fried noodles, fried egg rolls, Egg Foo Young (66 percent of calories from fat and 400 milligrams of cholesterol per serving), too much soy sauce or teriyaki sauce (a mere 1/4 teaspoon of soy sauce has 100 milligrams of sodium). And if you're in a restaurant, ask if your food can be made without monosodium glutamate.

Not So Obvious No-No's

Lobster sauce, which contains egg yolks, fried rice, which typically adds up to 400 calories a cup, with 45 percent of calories from fat, Peking duck, crispy fish (which is crispy because it's fried), batter dipped and fried shrimp or chicken, and fried dim sum appetizers.

Before we go any further, I have just three words to emphasize. Eat your rice. Rice is your salvation from ordering high- or moderately high-fat stir fry dishes. You see, rice has a glorious 237 calories per cup—almost all complex carbohydrate calories (91 percent) and only 2 percent fat calories. Can't beat those numbers!

So say you order green pepper beef or Mongolian beef (where the mixture is mostly beef strips). How much rice are we talking about? A good rule to follow if your entree is mostly meat is to add about twice as much rice as your meat dish. I'll show you how it works. Say you're looking down at 3/4 cup green pepper beef (at 285 calories, 68 percent from fat). If you add or mix it with one and a half cups rice, the meal is now 28 percent calories from fat.

If you're dealing with a mixture that is about half chicken, tofu, or meat and the other half vegetables, you'll only need to add the same amount of rice as your stir-fry dish. Take broccoli with chicken (a 1 1/4 cup serving has 267 calories, 47 percent from fat), plop it over 1 1/4 cup rice, and suddenly it's a 23 percent calories from fat meal, with 563 total calories. You would follow this rule whether you chose shrimp in black bean sauce, tofu with veggies, chicken in snow peas, or whatever, as long as part of the dish was definitely vegetables.

Well, thanks for listening. You may have undergone a shock or two. But if it makes you feel any better, I underwent one of my own. I had no idea Mu Shu Pork (you know the wonderful dish with mushrooms, scrambled egg, etc., all wrapped up in a cute little Chinese crepe-like pancake with hoisin sauce and green onion strips) was so high in percent of calories from fat (about 46 percent)! It's reasonably low in calories (2 pancakes stuffed have about 275 calories), so it's possible to make it "part" of a low-fat meal. Still, that 46 percent was a shock!

Japanese

Just because the food comes to us from across the Pacific doesn't mean the same rules don't apply. Once again, when you choose Japanese, stay away from the deep-fried dishes such as tempura, tonkatsu (deep fried pork), torikatsu (deep fried chicken), and katsudon (deep fried pork, onion, and egg). And keep the high sodium sauces to a minimum. In fact, ask for them on the side. Just three teaspoons of Teriyaki sauce adds 700 milligrams of sodium—but zero fat and only 15 calories.

The key words on a Japanese menu are "yakimono" which means "broiled" with little fat added and "rice", your low-fat, go-with-anything, carbohydrate-rich filler.

Speaking of rice, are we voting "yes" on sushi? (This new taste sensation, although not new to the Japanese, is vinegared rice rolled up several different ways, including with seaweed, and combined with raw fish or vegetables or both.) Yes. Yes. And triple yes. There is no added fat involved in sushi making. Even when an oily raw fish is used, it's more as a decoration, such as a strip of fish acting as a center in a seaweed roll or a thin fillet laying atop a bed of rice.

Tofu is a great meat alternative, if you're into those, with 4 ounces (about 1/2 cup) totalling 81 calories, 40 percent from protein, and no cholesterol. It is 48 percent calories from fat, but at 81 calories, you won't do much damage to your percentage from fat for the meal. If we were talking about the same amount of relatively lean beef (2 1/2 ounces), for example, we would be dealing instead with about 53 percent of calories from fat and 185 added calories.

Greek

What can I say. The Greeks like their meat, olive oil, butter, and creamy dressings. What I remember clearest of this Greek restaurant I went to in Holland (which I figured was "more authentic" than the ones I had gone to here, since the Dutch and the Greeks at least share the same continent) was that I have never seen as much cooked meat on one plate before in my entire life. They literally "piled" it on. So the first suggestion I have is to keep your meat portion modest. There is an ancient proverb (that I just made up) that says: "The meat you take home tonight could fill tomorrow's sandwich."

I also recall a smaller, creamier pile lying conveniently next to the meat pile and resembling mayonnaise. Remember,

1/4 cup is equal to 400 calories, 98 percent from fat! A yogurt dressing (there is a type mixed with garlic and cucumbers called Tzatziki) would cost you fewer calories, but since it's probably made from whole milk it would still be at least 47 percent calories from fat. If you're making it at home, use the nonfat or low-fat plain yogurts.

Also keep the anchovies, olives, and feta cheese in perspective. All three are high in percent of calories from fat and in sodium. (Six olives contain 50 calories, 93 percent from fat, plus 230 milligrams of sodium. Three anchovies equal 25 calories, 54 percent of them from fat. Two ounces of feta cheese have 150 calories, 71 percent from fat, and 632 milligrams of sodium.)

One Greek taste treat rates in the "very high-fat" category—probably the richest dessert cake ever created, *baklava*. Before you take that first bite, just promise me you'll think about the pound of butter (4 sticks!), 2 pounds of naturally fat nuts, 2 cups of honey, and 2 cups of sugar that went into the baklava.

Hang in there. I'm almost finished with the "bad" list. Avoid ordering babaganoosh (an eggplant appetizer made with fat), Kibbeh (lamb and butter), and those two wonderfully fatty pies, tyropita and spanokopita.

So, what's left? The forever famous shish kabob, where lamb and assorted vegetables are broiled on a spit, or plaki, fish cooked with tomatoes, onions, and garlic. And you can have plenty of pilaf, rice, and bread— as long as you're going extremely easy on the butter.

Deli Delights

Sandwiches—the one common noon hour notion that often makes its way onto our dinner plates and into our picnic baskets. Not to worry though, sandwiches can be a healthful alternative to greasy fast food, frozen entrees, or the usual picnic munchies such as fried chicken or barbequed hot dogs. You just have to know what to fill them with and how to dress them up.

There's a huge difference healthwise between a French dip steak sandwich with mayo dripping down the sides and a breast of turkey sandwich on wheat with spicy mustard and juicy tomato slices. And it's much better to eat a chicken BREAST sandwich with no mayonnaise or butter (about 16 percent of calories from fat) than a chicken SALAD sandwich (about 48 percent of calories from fat). See what I mean? So on to the sandwich suggestions.

Suggestion #1

Start with a low-fat bread—preferably something high in fiber.

Choose the whole wheat or whole grain types, or even sourdough, but leave the croissants, crescent rolls, or other fancy fatty breads for someone else.

Suggestion #2

Choose a lower fat filling.

The more desirable fillers are: turkey or chicken breast slices (about 19 percent of calories from fat), roast beef slices (24 percent of calories from fat), or tuna, chicken, shrimp, and crab salad made with yogurt or small amounts of reduced-calorie mayonnaise. The world's worst fillers are: salami (75 percent of calories from fat), polish sausage or liverwurst (80 percent fat calories), bologna (82 percent fat calories), and chicken, tuna, and egg salad with regular mayonnaise (71, 76, and 87 percent of calories from fat, respectively).

Suggestion #3

Add all the lettuce leaves, tomato slices, and onion rings you want. They'll add no more than 10 calories each. I must confess, avocado and turkey is one of my favorite sandwiches, so it is with great pain that I announce to you that one-third of an avocado adds about 110 calories (79 percent from fat).

Suggestion #4

Lay off the mayonnaise.

In case you hadn't heard, just one tablespoon of mayonnaise (which is about the amount that globs onto your knife after you pull it from the jar) adds 100 calories, 98 percent of which are from fat. This, of course, can make or break your sandwich's goal of "no more than 30 percent of calories from fat." Try adding some color instead—yellow or red. One teaspoon of mustard adds less than 5 calories and 65 milligrams of sodium, while one tablespoon of catsup adds about 18 calories and 170 milligrams of sodium.

Suggestion #5

Pass up the mayonnaise-coated potato salads and cole slaws.

One cup of standard potato salad has almost 400 calories (67 percent from fat) and 190 milligrams of cholesterol. One cup of cole slaw has 150 calories , with 63 percent from fat. Keep your sandwich company with a fruit or vegetable salad or a green salad with reduced fat dressing.

Suggestion #6

Skip the chips.

When you grab each little bag of chips (about 2 ounces), you're buying about 325 extra calories (with 62 percent from fat) and 350 milligrams of sodium.

I hope these suggestions haven't taken the fun out of fixing or ordering yourself a sandwich.

Salad Bar Savvy

We opt for the salad bar, thinking to ourselves I'll be "good" today. Or we drag others to the best salad bar in town instead of Hamburger Heaven, promptly explaining that we're "on a diet" or that we're "watching it."

What we don't realize is that when we confidently line up at that salad bar, we're really skipping through a virtual fat and calorie minefield.

I'm going to describe a typical salad bar meal, and you tell me whether it comes close to your salad bar expectations.

You start out with about 2 cups of crisp and crunchy lettuce. (You try to pick out the real green leaves, but there are usually only a few left.) Then you grab a few cherry tomatoes and some sliced cucumber, a spoon of chopped egg and bacon, several strips of ham, maybe a scoop (about 1/4 cup) of grated cheddar cheese, and two small ladles or about 1/4 cup total of dressing. (A lot of people use twice this amount!)

Then, just when you thought there was no possible way you could fit one more thing in your salad bowl, you spot the chunky potato salad and the creamy macaroni salad. So you manage to balance about 1/3 cup of each side of the bowl. You've just walked away from the salad bar carrying a total of 775 calories—75 percent from FAT. Sound like a diet plate to you?

The point is you CAN eat a wonderfully low-fat, high-fiber, tasty meal at a salad bar. You just have to have some savvy. You have to know what to sprinkle on top of your salad and what to skip. You need to learn which spoons to keep your hand off and which to use freely. As a guide, take a look for yourself at the accompanying chart.

Choose the Most Healthful Salad Ingredients

Salad Ingredients	% Calories from Fat	Calories	Fiber (gm)
(1/8 cup portions unless otherwise noted)			
cauliflower, 1/3 cup		4	.5
carrot, grated		5	.5
strawberries/pineapple, 1/3 cup		15–50	1
melon pieces, 1/3 cup	less than 10%	20	.5
kidney beans		27	2
green peas		12	2
tomato, 1/2 whole		12	1
cucumber, 6 slices		2	--
broccoli, 1/3 cup		8	2
green pepper		4	--
crab meat and shrimp, 1/3 cup		40–60	--
mushrooms	less than 20%	2	.5
garbanzo beans		30	1.3
turkey/chicken breast, 1/3 cup		70–80	--

Maximize these

lean ham, 1/3 cup diced	37%	68	--
fried noodles, croutons	43%	28–?	--
coleslaw, 1/3 cup	55%	120	.5
Parmesan cheese	60%	44	--
chopped egg	65%	26	--
potato salad, 1/3 cup	67%	128	1
sunflower seeds	71%	97	1
macaroni salad, 1/3 cup	74%	118	--
cheddar cheese, grated	74%	55	--
bacon, crumbled, 1 Tbsp	78%	18	--
avocado, 1/4 whole	79%	81	1.5
black olives	93%	25	1

(left margin: Maximize these)

Dress for Success Tips:

- Too much of any dressing defeats the purpose of a healthy salad. Try to dress your salad with only 2–3 tablespoons.
- Fruit juices, vinegars, and herbs make dressings flavorful without adding fat or salt.
- For guilt-free creamy dressings, use buttermilk or lower fat yogurt and add reduced calorie mayonnaise sparingly to thicken it.
- For a tangy fruit salad topping, try low-fat yogurt such as vanilla or lemon.

Dressings: (2 Tablespoons)*	% Calories from Fat	Calories
non-fat yogurt, plain	3%	16
low-fat yogurt, flavored	9%	29
low-fat yogurt, plain	22%	18
light sour cream	60%	45
reduced calorie mayo-type salad dressing	73%	70
thousand island	83%	118
French	84%	134
Russian	90%	151
Italian	91%	137
blue cheese	91%	154
ranch	92%	109

*average values

The first thing you can do for yourself is pick the right head of lettuce. Spinach has more than four times the fiber and vitamin A and three times the vitamin C of all the other types of lettuce. Your best choice after that is Romaine and leaf lettuce, which have more vitamin A, C, and calcium than the others.

Then, when you've got the nutrient-rich bed of lettuce ready, you don't want to ruin it by adding all sorts of fat, cholesterol, and sodium. That means skipping the crocks of chopped egg, bacon, croutons, fried noodles, grated cheese, sliced olives, avocado, and creamy salads, such as potato salad and macaroni salads.

Instead, dip all you want into the green peas, beets, sliced mushrooms, kidney and garbanzo beans, tomato, sliced cucumber, green pepper strips, grated carrot, broccoli, and cauliflower. You can usually get away with a tablespoon or so of grated Parmesan or cheddar cheese and you can add some shrimp, crab meat, or turkey. Lay low on the sliced ham. It's usually higher in fat and sodium than the others.

Just by adding 1/8 cup each of peas, kidney beans, and broccoli, the fiber in your salad is up 6 grams. You're also well on your way to meeting the recommended daily requirement for certain vitamins and minerals. For example, just by adding 1/3 cup of broccoli, you're already halfway to your vitamin C requirement.

Now that you've carefully constructed a perfectly healthful salad, you must choose a dressing and how much of that dressing just as judiciously. Somewhere between French and Thousand Island, Italian dressing deceitfully became the lower fat dressing of choice. As you can see from the evidence in the accompanying table, they're all pretty much the same. Italian dressing has just as much fat and just as many calories as the others.

The only way to be able to add more than a few drops of dressing to your mound of foliage is to use the reduced-calorie types. Wishbone Reduced Calorie Lite Ranch has 40 calories per tablespoon with 3 grams of fat, compared with the regular Ranch, which has 80 calories and twice as much fat. Bernstein's Reduced Calorie Italian with Cheese dressing has only 8 calories per tablespoon with less than a gram of fat.

But don't get too crazy with the reduced-calorie types. The ones with 40 calories per tablespoon can add up quickly and the others with about 10 calories per tablespoon come with quite a bit of sodium.

On a salad with 2 cups of spinach or Romaine leaves, a few cherry tomatoes, 1/3 cup broccoli and crab and 1/8 cup of sliced mushrooms, garbanzo beans, and green pepper, for example, if you drizzle 1 tablespoons of reduced calorie ranch dressing, you'll end up with a 195 calorie salad, with 36 percent of calories from fat. If you use Bernstein's Italian Dressing, it's a 125 calorie salad, with 13 percent of calories from fat.

If the salad bar is your entire meal, obviously less than 200 calories isn't going to cut it. So load up on the items like beans, peas, shrimp, or turkey, broccoli and cauliflower, etc. And don't forget the fresh fruit that some salad bars offer—for dessert.

The All-American Diner and Coffee Shop

Wherever you are in the United States, there's one type of restaurant you'll find just about everywhere—the American style diner and coffee shop. It could be Lou's Diner or the Pennsylvania Pancake House. But no matter what it's called, you will usually find fixings such as pancakes, waffles, potatoes, and eggs served during the morning hours and burgers, grilled cheese sandwiches, and steaks served until closing.

Even at the diner in your town, or the town you're passing through, there are lower fat choices awaiting you.

Better Breakfast Selections

- Two pieces of toast or one English muffin with 1 teaspoon of butter = 200 calories, 25 percent from fat, 11 milligrams of cholesterol, and 400 milligrams of sodium.
- Two pieces of toast or one English muffin with 1 teaspoon butter and 1 tablespoon of jam and preserves = 250 calories, 20 percent from fat, 11 milligrams of cholesterol, and 400 milligrams of sodium.

- One medium-sized biscuit made from a mix, with 2 teaspoons of jam or preserves = 180 calories, 27 percent from fat, 54 milligrams of cholesterol and 375 milligrams of sodium.

- Hot or cold cereal (see cereal section for listing of low-fat choices in "Supermarket Savvy" chapter). Ask for skim or low-fat milk. These are sometimes served with fresh fruit, too!

- Full stack (3) of pancakes with 2 tablespoons of syrup = 280 calories, 18 percent from fat, with 60 milligrams of cholesterol and 265 milligrams of sodium.

- French toast (2 pieces and 2 tablespoons of syrup) = 370 calories, 22 percent from fat (33 percent without syrup), 145 milligrams of cholesterol, and 400 milligrams of sodium.

- Three pancakes with 2 tablespoons syrup and 2 slices of bacon = 355 calories, 28 percent from fat, 70 milligrams of cholesterol, and 570 milligrams of sodium.

The "You Could Order Worse" Breakfast Selections

- Strawberry waffle with 1/4 cup whipped cream = 495 calories, 33 percent from fat, 95 milligrams cholesterol, and 370 milligrams of sodium.

- Pigs in a blanket (3 pancakes, 3 sausage links, and 2 tablespoons syrup, but no butter) = 425 calories, 37 percent from fat, 90 milligrams cholesterol, and 870 milligrams of sodium.

- Three strawberry pancakes with 1/4 cup whipped cream = 465 calories, 31 percent from fat, 95 milligrams cholesterol, and 360 milligrams of sodium.

- One medium blueberry muffin = 225 calories, 30 percent from fat, 40 milligrams cholesterol, and 350 milligrams sodium.

- One medium bran muffin = 210 calories, 30 percent from fat, 42 milligrams cholesterol, and 355 milligrams sodium.

Better Lunch/Dinner Selections

(For sandwich selections, refer back to the Deli Delights section.)

- One medium baked potato with 1 teaspoon butter = 180 calories, 20 percent from fat, 10 milligrams cholesterol, and 45 milligrams sodium.

  OR

  One medium baked potato with 2 tablespoons sour cream = 205 calories, 25 percent from fat, 15 milligrams cholesterol, and 20 milligrams sodium.

  OR

  One medium baked potato with 1 teaspoon butter and 1 tablespoon sour cream = 210 calories, 29 percent from fat, 20 milligrams cholesterol, and 50 milligrams sodium.

- One cup of chili with beans (no cheese) and a slice of French bread (no butter) = 400 calories, 34 percent from fat, 38 milligrams cholesterol, and up to 1,300 milligrams of sodium, depending on whether it's canned.

- A quarter-pound hamburger on a large bun with no mayonnaise or cheese added (catsup or mustard optional) = 400 calories, about 40 percent from fat, 75 milligrams cholesterol, and 470 milligrams sodium.

- Choice sirloin steak (9 1/2-oz raw) with 2 slices of French bread (1 teaspoon butter) and 1 cup of vegetables = 660 calories, 30 percent from fat, 195 milligrams cholesterol, and 530 milligrams sodium—if no salt is added to steak.

Some Items That Might Surprise You

- Huevos Rancheros (flour tortilla with ground beef and beans, scrambled eggs, cheese, and salsa) = 650 calories, 60 percent from fat, 600 milligrams cholesterol, and more than 1,000 milligrams of sodium.

- One hot dog or corn dog with mustard = 325 calories, 56 percent from fat, 35 milligrams of cholesterol, and 1,050 to 1,250 milligrams of sodium.

- One slice apple pie (1/6 of a 9-inch pie) = 400 calories, 38 percent from fat, 475 milligrams of sodium.
- Bacon versus sausage "on the side"
  - One strip of bacon has 35 calories, 56 percent from fat, 5 milligrams of cholesterol, and 100 milligrams of sodium.
  - One link of sausage has 48 calories, 77 percent from fat, 10 milligrams of cholesterol and 170 milligrams of sodium.
- Grilled cheese sandwich = 400 calories, 55 percent from fat, 55 milligrams of cholesterol and 1150 milligrams of sodium.

The lesson here is that it IS indeed possible to eat out in restaurants and maintain a low-fat diet. Of course, each restaurant will be preparing their items in their own special way. Some chefs might have a heavier hand when it comes to pouring oil or cream, for example. But for the purposes of this chapter, customary recipes were used for the computer analysis and should encompass most establishments today.

Before we leave this subject though, I want to remind you that the survival of any restaurant depends on whether or not they have customers to serve. And whether or not customers return to a restaurant depends on how pleased they were with their meal and eating experience. You hold all the cards. If you want your fish broiled without added butter, if you want your sandwich prepared without mayonnaise, then it's in the restaurant's best business interest to serve it to you that way. So don't be afraid to ask how something is prepared or to request that it be prepared a little differently just for you.

CHAPTER

6

Grab a Bite and Run

The great part about "eating in" is that YOU get to be chef! "Great," you say, "I never asked to be chef." But think about it: It's the chef and only the chef who controls "what" and "how much" is added to make the meal. When you eat in, YOU choose whether yogurt or sour cream is added to your chicken enchilada, whether your fish fillet is simmered in wine or butter, whether you shake basil and pepper onto your pasta instead of salt. YOU choose whether to follow a diet that meets disease prevention guidelines.

The Fighting Fat Basics — A Survival Course

We've talked about how to cut the fat in foods that others prepare (fast food, food companies, restaurants, etc.) But what about foods that we have no one to blame but ourselves, where WE actually perform the act of cutting the butter or pouring the oil? There are basically six steps to successfully cut the fat at home:

131

#1. *Beware of Mixers.* I'm referring to products we use to mix or dip other foods, such as mayonnaise, salad dressings, and sour cream.

#2. *Pay Attention to Naturally Fat Foods.* These foods are mostly fat themselves, such as cheese or some red meat. This doesn't mean they're "bad" foods. We just have to start treating them with some respect. You might begin by using smaller quantities, such as "sprinkling" cheese instead of "slicing" it in chunks.

#3. *Try Not to Eat Two Naturally Fat Foods Together.* This means not adding cheese to a high-fat cracker or ham sandwich or butter to a croissant, tartar sauce or mayonnaise to a fried fish fillet, etc.

#4. *Use Less Fat in the Preparation of Food.* Bake, oven broil (draining off any fat), boil, stew (skimming fat off), poach, stir fry (without a lot of oil), simmer, or steam. Use non-stick cookware to avoid adding cooking fat. Substitute low-fat liquids, such as broth, tomato juice, lemon juice or wine, for grease in cooking.

#5. *Add Less Fat at the Table.* Be aware of these "table fats" and how much they're costing you. For example, next time you're staring down at that bare potato, remember sour cream is about 85 percent calories from fat and 26 calories per tablespoon, while nonfat plain yogurt is only about 3 percent calories from fat and 8 calories per tablespoon.

#6. *Add Fruits, Vegetables, and Grains.* Pasta and breads somehow have developed the reputation for being "fattening." But if you look at the facts—or fats—, it isn't the complex carbohydrates at all but what we ADD to them that can quickly boost the calories from fat. One full cup of boiled noodles only has about 170 calories and is 10 percent calories from fat. Olive oil is 100 percent calories from fat, and two tablespoons will add 238 calories. A typical thick white sauce is 71 percent calories from fat, and 1/2 cup will add 262 calories.

You can even add a layer of pasta or vegetables to your main dish instead of other more fat-filled items. For example, use a layer of pasta instead of one of the layers of cheese for your lasagna, or cut the amount of meat used to make a spaghetti sauce or casserole in half by adding vegetables instead.

Equipment you might not have:

#1. Can you say "Teflon?" Save yourself from all the grease and shortening you usually need to coat your frypan or baking tins to keep your food from sticking. Try non-stick Teflon. I know I sound like a commercial again, but honest, I don't own any stock in Teflon companies!

What I do own are quality, nonstick frying pans (one large and one small), bundt pans, a cookie sheet, loaf pans, muffin pans and casserole dishes. Nonstick pans are wonderful for all kinds of foods, from pizza crust (without olive oil) to cakes (without shortening). But buy the best quality, bonded versus the spray-on types, so the surface doesn't wear off easily. Some are easy to scratch, too, so it's wise to use only plastic utensils. (And only use a plastic scrubber.)

#2. This next piece of equipment is going to cost a bit more— La Food Processor. Trust me, you'll be more likely to make meals and snacks from scratch with "Oscar" (or any other food processor) on your team.

For example, when whipping the Almost Fat-Free Dip/Dressing in Chapter 9, a food processor will work best. And to make the incredibly colorful and tasty Creamy Carrot Sauce in Chapter 8, not only will it make the grating carrots step easier, but it's essential for the puree part. Not to mention the delicious pasta or crepe filling recipe also found in Chapter 8, "Chicken, Basil, and Baby Carrot Filling," which definitely requires the pureeing advantages of a food processor.

#3. The novelty of the 80's , the Microwave, is the necessity of the 90's.

How else can you cook potatoes in eight minutes flat? Low-fat leftovers are more likely to be eaten, at work or at home, when a microwave is present. Vegetables can be cooked a few minutes before your main dish is ready. Items can be defrosted at the last minute using a microwave. I even use the microwave to make the Two-Minute Cheese Sauce in Chapter 7.

Ten Kitchen Staples for Fighting Fat

While filling my shopping cart last week, I couldn't help but notice I definitely favor a particular group of food items. Not so coincidentally, they all happen to be staples for waging war against fat in the diet.

I call this select group "staples" because I make sure these items can be found at any one time in my kitchen—and for good reason. I use some of them regularly to replace fat in recipes (i.e., Herb-Ox Low Sodium Chicken Broth) and others are lower fat alternatives to usually fat foods that I happen to love, along with most of America (i.e., Kraft Light Monterey Jack Cheese, Bernstein's Reduced Calorie Italian Dressing).

You may recognize a couple of these if you've glanced at the recipes in the next several chapters because I tend to use them over and over again when creating new low-fat recipes. So without further ado, allow me to introduce you to the Ten Fighting Fat Staples:

#1. *Ragu Garden Style or Homestyle Spaghetti Sauce.* This is the current lowest fat winner in the bottled spaghetti sauce category—and a distinguished category it is. I always have a jar in my refrigerator to spread on pizza crust, pour over pasta or eggplant Parmesan, baked potatoes, etc., or to mix with chili powder or salsa to make a quick Mexican-style sauce for enchiladas or quesadillas.

Are you ready to be impressed? Most bottled spaghetti sauces have up to 9 grams of fat per 1/2 cup, or 49 percent of calories from fat, compared with Ragu Gardenstyle, with 2 grams of fat per 1/2 cup and 24 percent of calories from fat. I found this out while I was desperately trying to find my Ragu Homestyle in a Lake Tahoe supermarket—to no avail. So I started looking at the nutrition information labels of the other bottled spaghetti sauces and none of them came close to being as low in fat as Ragu Gardenstyle.

In case you were wondering if this story had a happy ending, I did finally find a jar of Ragu Gardenstyle and so my ski trip was indeed off to a proper start with a high complex carbohydrate, low-fat spaghetti dinner.

#2. *Bernstein's Low-Calorie Italian Dressing (or other reduced-calorie Italian dressings, equally as tasty and low in fat).* I don't know who "Bernstein" is but he or she sure makes a tasteful low-calorie salad dressing. You can drizzle 2 tablespoons gloriously guilt-free over your pasta, vegetables, tuna, chicken, or shrimp salad, over your grilled chicken breast or fish, or even on your traditional green salad. A 2-tablespoon serving only costs you 12 calories and less than 1 gram of fat, a small price to pay for a versatile, delicious dressing. (Be careful, though. The sodium is still high at 275 milligrams per tablespoon.)

#3. *Herb-Ox Low Sodium Chicken Broth (or other low-sodium chicken broths).* How can chicken broth be a staple? Well, chicken broth is to me what vegetable oil or olive oil is to other people. I use it to stir fry, saute vegetables, pan simmer fish or chicken fillets, boil and flavor rice, etc.

The broth comes in individual serving packets. You can make 1 cup at a time, which is great for people living alone or in pairs. One packet, or 1 cup of made-up broth, only adds 5 milligrams of sodium, while your run-of-the-mill broth or bouillon cube adds 800 milligrams.

#4. *Part-Skim Ricotta Cheese.* This is a new staple for me. I've recently been discovering all sorts of wonderful ways to use it. I add it to Marinara sauce to make the sauce thicker and creamier. I use it as a base for my low-fat garlic spread on bread and for my low-fat cheese sauce. The cheese sauce can be used in casseroles, to perk up pasta, to top a potato, etc.

#5. *Aunt Jemima's Buttermilk, Whole Wheat or Buckwheat Pancake and Waffle Mix (the "incomplete" mixes).* I couldn't talk about staples without talking about dear old Aunt Jemima. I mix her incomplete (which means you add the eggs, milk, and oil) buttermilk mix with her buckwheat mix to make semi-wheaty, fluffy pancakes or waffles. Don't follow the directions on the box though.

Just add egg whites and skim or low-fat milk. You don't
need to add any oil or egg yolks.

#6. *Part-Skim Cheeses.* If I'm not adding an ounce of part-skim
cheese to my toasted bagel in the morning, I'm grating
some into my enchilada or pasta at dinner time. By
grating Kraft Light Monterey Jack instead of regular
cheeses, for example, I cut the fat by two thirds! Most
cheeses have about 9 grams of fat per ounce; others calling
themselves "reduced fat" cheeses may have 7 or 8 grams of
fat per ounce (check those labels). Those "part skim"
mozzarella balls have around 5 grams of fat per ounce,
and they definitely help bring down the fat. But Kraft's
Light Monterey Jack, as well as their cheddar, has 3 grams
of fat per ounce.

#7. *Skim Milk.* Aside from its more typical reputation as a
beverage, skim milk is a savvy substitute for many of the
fatty ingredients usually called for in recipes, namely
cream and whole milk. I add skim milk to make my "Very
Berry Smoothie," or Salad Bar Quiche. It even teams up
with part-skim ricotta cheese to make a low-fat cheese
sauce or plain nonfat yogurt to make an almost fat-free
ranch dressing and dip.

#8. *Wine.* Ever wonder what you are possibly going to do
with the bottles of wine that were "such a good deal, you
had to buy them" yet tend not to use? Well start wiping
the dust off because wine is a nice substitute for cooking
fats and oils. I use wine to simmer mushrooms and
onions in instead of butter, margarine, or oils. I would
say saute instead of simmer, but this particular word
specifically denotes the use of fat. However, where it says
"saute in butter or oil" in recipes, you can go ahead and
use a nonfat ingredient such as wine.

#9. *Naturally Butter Flavored Sprinkles.* For a butter lover
such as myself, items like Molly McButter, Best O' Butter,
or Butter Buds, where they extract the natural butter
flavor and mix it with starch to create sprinkles, come in
handy. I admit I have a hard time eating corn without a
little butter, but the butter flavored sprinkles help me
keep the calories in a reasonable range. For example, I
use it to add some rich flavor to my favorite garlic spread

recipe. You still need to watch the amount you add because 1/2 teaspoon may only add about 60 milligrams of sodium, but a tablespoon will add almost 400!

#10. *Crackermeal.* Cracker who? You may not have heard of or noticed this product on your supermarket shelf. But it's a staple in my kitchen because it's the "no fat added," "no salt added" substitute for bread crumbs. Crackermeal can be used as coating for your oven roasted chicken breast or fish fillet, filler for your low-fat meatloaf or meatballs, and topping for your low-fat fruit crisps and casseroles.

You didn't know breadcrumbs even had fat? If you read the label, you'll find most bread crumbs have a fat listed as the second ingredient and salt as the third!

A Few Words on Two Favorite Fatty Ingredients (Cheese and Beef)

The Big Cheese

All those in favor of cheese say "aye", all opposed? It's no secret, Americans definitely love their cheese, and lots of it. Sheets of cheese cover America's hamburgers, sandwiches, and hotdogs. Gobs of cheese sauce drip over piles of nacho chips and vegetables.

Me? Well, it's hard for me personally to imagine life without cheese. It's an irreplaceable ingredient on two of my favorite foods—pizza and lasagne. Where would eggplant be without Parmesan, burger without cheese, quiche without Lorraine? What would happen if enchiladas suddenly stopped being smothered by Monterey Jack? Basically, where would America be without the big cheese? But isn't it time we all put cheese in perspective?

I've lost count of the people I've talked with who have looked at me with longing and torment in their eyes as they said, "I love cheese but I gave it up" or "but cheese is BAD, isn't it?"

The good news for cheese lovers is that cheese does have nutritional attributes. It's a complete protein, it's a great source of calcium (200 mg per ounce) and other vitamins and minerals. But the bad news is that cheese is a high-fat animal product. Not only is it high in fat (usually around 73 percent of calories from fat) but a large portion of that fat is saturated. Then there's the issue of cholesterol. One ounce has about 28 milligrams of cholesterol.

Like many things, though, Americans seem to have exaggerated this whole cheese concept. Where else in the world do they take cheese strips (already having about 73 percent of calories from fat) and deep fry them and call them appetizers? Where else do they offer "extra cheese" as an added topping on pizza? And how often at a party have you resisted saying, "Excuse me, sir, but would you like some cracker with your cheese?"

So take it from a veteran cheese lover. We don't have to cut the big cheese out of our lives forever in order to eat a low-fat diet. We just have to start putting it into perspective. We can do this by following the "Say Cheese Guidelines":

#1. *Don't eat cheese all alone.* (I'm talking to those of you, and you know who you are, who open the refrigerator and automatically cut off a good-sized chunk of cheese and call it a "snack," or those of you who when grating cheese for a recipe, end up saving about half of it from the grater by rescuing it into your mouth!) Remember. Cheese "all alone" has about 73 percent of its calories from fat and about 28 milligrams of cholesterol per ounce.

What "eating a low-fat diet" means is eating "meals" that are low in fat (making sure the percentage of calories from fat for the meal is less than 30 percent). So theoretically you can still eat high-fat items, such as butter and cheese, as long as the total meal stays under 30 percent of calories from fat. Which brings us to the next guidelines.

#2. *Only add cheese to low-fat foods—not other already high-fat foods.* This way the percentage of calories from fat for the meal has a chance of staying low overall. In other words, don't add cheese to something already high in fat, and don't add something already high in fat to cheese.

The meal isn't big enough for the both of them. Sorry, but this puts the "cheeseburger" on the bad list because the burger part is already contributing quite a bit of fat to the meal. And you can forget about your quiche recipe, because it already had tons of eggs, which are 55 percent calories from fat themselves. Adding lots of Swiss cheese won't help your fat content, not to mention the crust. This also means not topping your pizza with pepperoni or sausage, which would only add more fat. Try vegetables, onions, and mushrooms as your topping.

What we CAN add cheese to is our dear and faithful friends, the complex carbohydrates. If we follow guideline #3, we can add (in a low-fat way) cheese to our baked potato, our bagel, our pinto beans, and our pizza crust—if we don't overdo it—and still eat a low-fat meal.

#3. *Use less cheese.* Keep amounts of cheese more like a "sprinkle." (For this, you'll need to pull out your grater.) Avoid slabs or slices. For example, if you add a tablespoon of Parmesan cheese to 1 1/2 cups of broccoli, it will have about 24 percent of calories from fat (and only 75 calories total). One cup of pasta noodles with 1/8 cup of grated cheddar cheese only has 20 calories from fat, 14 milligrams of cholesterol, and only 225 calories total.

A slice of cheese pizza (1/8 of a 14-inch pizza) has about 230 calories, 32 percent from fat, and 25 milligrams of cholesterol. You can add 1/8 cup of grated cheddar to your baked potato (21 percent calories from fat), an ounce of part-skim mozzarella to your bagel (22 percent calories from fat), or 1/8 cup of grated Monterey Jack (at most) to your refried beans (32 percent calories from fat).

#4. *Try to use lower fat cheeses as much as possible.* It really does make a difference. Adding an ounce of Monterey Jack will add 105 calories, 73 percent of which are from fat, and 26 milligrams of cholesterol. An ounce of part-skim mozzarella (and there are cheeses out now that are even lower in fat than this) adds about 78 calories, 55 percent from fat, and 18 milligrams of cholesterol. By the way, a tablespoon of Parmesan cheese only adds 23 calories, 60 percent from fat, 4 milligrams of cholesterol, and 94 milligrams of sodium.

As long as you "do" pretty much what these guidelines say, you can probably "say cheese" more often than you thought you could.

Just Say Yes to Lean Meats Starting with Beef

In order to have a low-fat diet, do we need to "just say no" to beef? Absolutely not! We should, instead, start saying "yes" to the six leanest cuts beef has to offer.

All six cuts, when trimmed of their visible fat, have less than 42 percent of their calories from fat. This means when served with grains, vegetables, and other low-fat dishes, these cuts CAN be part of a low-fat diet:

(Per 1-ounce, cooked portion, already trimmed of visible fat)

- Top Round, 54 calories, 30.5 percent from fat, 1.8 grams of fat, 24 mg cholesterol (sometimes called London broil)
- Eye Round Steak, 52 calories, 32 percent from fat, 1.8 grams fat, 24 mg cholesterol
- Round Tip, Sirloin Tip, 54 calories, 36 percent from fat, 2.1 grams of fat, 23 mg cholesterol
- Top Sirloin Steak, 59 calories, 40 percent from fat, 2.5 grams fat, 22 mg cholesterol (includes New York steak and strip steak cuts)
- Tenderloin, 58 calories, 42 percent from fat, 2.7 grams of fat, 24 mg cholesterol

Do you trim the visible fat from your meat BEFORE it hits the grill or pan? If so, you're slicing off slightly more calories, fat, and cholesterol than the person who waits to trim off the fat until it hits the plate. Besides bringing only the leanest cuts home with you and trimming off all visible fat before you cook it, there are two other steps you can take to keep meat part of the new low-fat way of eating:

- Cook the meat without fats or fatty sauces. Try grilling, broiling, roasting, or simmering slices in wine or chicken broth. In other words, once you've "cut the visible fat" try to avoid adding any fat back.
- This step might not be too popular with the bigger beef eaters, but it's an important one. Keep your servings to 3

ounces of cooked beef (4 ounces raw weight). That's about the size of a large chicken breast or the palm of your hand. Does this take the fun out of eating meat? I hope not. To be perfectly honest, I think meat has never tasted better. You might think I'm a slightly biased consumer, but now when I think of sirloin, I picture it simmering in red wine with onions and garlic—instead of olive oil or butter.

Here are some tips for cooking lower fat cuts:

- To prevent dryness, try not to overcook.
- Use slow, moist cooking methods, such as braising and stewing.
- Prevent natural juices from escaping. Avoid pricking or searing steaks while cooking.
- Salting meat before cooking tends to delay browning and draws out moisture.
- Marinate meats overnight when possible to increase tenderness. Marinades that include an acid ingredient, such as wine, vinegar, or lemon juice, will help break down some of the protein, making the meat more tender.

Think Lean

Have you ever wondered which red meat cuts have less fat than most? The following cuts have approximately 50 percent less fat (in grams) than the higher fat red meat cuts.

Each of the following cuts has:

- no more than 8 grams of fat per 3 ounce cooked portion (trimmed of visible fat)

    AND

- no more than 80 milligrams of cholesterol

Beef:

Top round (London broil)
    162 calories, 5.3 grams fat, 72 mg cholesterol
Eye of round
    155 calories, 5.5 grams fat, 59 mg cholesterol
Round tip (sirloin tip, tip steak, or tip roast)
    162 calories, 6.4 grams fat, 69 mg cholesterol

Sirloin (top sirloin steak) 177 calories, 7.4 grams fat, 76 mg
  cholesterol
Top loin (New York steak, strip steak) 172 calories, 7.6 grams
  fat, 65 mg cholesterol
Tenderloin (Filet Mignon, Chateaubriand)
  174 calories, 7.9 grams fat, 72 mg cholesterol)

Pork:
Tenderloin 141 calories, 4.1 grams fat, 79 mg cholesterol

Lamb:
Leg, shank portion, 153 calories, 5.7 grams fat, 74 mg
  cholesterol
Leg, sirloin portion, 174 calories, 7.8 grams fat, 78 mg
  cholesterol

Certain meats have, by themselves, less than 30 percent
calories from fat. This would also include most of the fish
department. But first, let's list these low-fat meats, namely
poultry light meat.

These cuts must contain no more than 25 percent calories from fat AND

• no more than 90 milligrams of of cholesterol per 3-ounce
  cooked serving

Skinless chicken breast
  141 calories, 69 mg cholesterol, 19 percent calories from fat
Skinless turkey breast
  132 calories, 62 mg cholesterol, 18 percent calories from fat

Fish Hit the Big Time

One of my favorite less visible, less mobilized food councils
has finally made the big time . . . or maybe I should say
"prime time." The National Fish and Seafood Promotional
Council must have recently gotten their advertising bucks
together because they're hitting television prime time with
some straightforward words about fish.

"Eat fish twice a week" is their main message to faithful
television watchers everywhere, and a powerful message it is.

Let's face it, most people aren't eating that much fish. In fact, most people probably weren't aware that this seemingly large amount of fish was recommended. And the ones who did already know are getting a friendly reminder.

Opting for fish as a source of protein instead of higher fat meat cuts or whole milk dairy products, once in a while, will likely reduce the amount of saturated fat we eat. Of the 40 some odd items sold at a typical fish counter, there usually are at least 10 that have less than 10 percent of their calories from fat.

Read this list of some common fish and see if you hear any of your favorites. These are your lowest fat choices when it comes to finding fish.

Fish 12% or less from fat

Alaska king crab	Perch	Bay scallops
Blue & dungeness crab	Abalone	Clams
Octopus	Grouper	Atlantic pollack
Northern lobster	Cod	Lemon or Flounder sole
Pacific red snapper	Haddock	Yellow fin tuna

Fish 13% to 20% from fat

Whiting	Monk fish	Sea Bass

I fully realize a certain class of fish, shellfish, has become notorious for being horribly "high in cholesterol." Besides squid, topping the high cholesterol fish charts with around 140 milligrams of cholesterol per 3 cooked ounces, shrimp comes in second with about 92 milligrams. Other popular shellfish selections, such as scallops (28 mg), oysters (46 mg), crab (35 to 65 mg), and lobster (57 mg), have reasonably less amounts of cholesterol per 3 cooked ounces.

How does shrimp's 92 milligrams of cholesterol compare with the leanest cut of beef? Three ounces of cooked top round, trimmed of visible fat, has about 72 mg of cholesterol. Surprised? Remember, the latest health guidelines for cholesterol in food recommend eating less than 300 mg a day. There's no reason why 3 ounces of shrimp (not fried, I hope) can't fit into that grand total every now and then.

Salvaging Your Favorite Recipes

Those of us who like to cook have favorite recipes we pull out from time to time. They're the torn ones with all the stains. Those of us who don't cook usually have at least a few dishes we're quite willing to beg people to make for us. And we certainly aren't emotionally prepared to lose these "favorites" to the health cause. However, chances are these "favorite recipes" aren't going to make the cut-offs in terms of fat content.

Since when did anybody "die for" broiled fish, pasta and steamed vegetables, or chicken stew? It's the oven baked lasagna, bacon quiches, and fettucini Alfredos of this world most of us consider our "favorites." And believe it or not, we CAN save most of these from the fat firing line by making some (hopefully not too painful) ingredient substitutions.

There are three ways to cut the fat in a recipe.

Way#1. Reduce the amount of fat called for. If the fat ingredient is a necessary part of the final product, then you may not be able to totally eliminate it. (Oil in pesto sauce is an example.) But you can usually DECREASE the amount added.

Way #2. Remove the fat ingredient entirely. Ask yourself whether the fatty ingredient is there primarily for appearance or out of habit or tradition (such as butter on cooked vegetables or whipped cream on strawberries).

Way #3. Use something else (lower in fat) instead. Is the ingredient there for flavor or texture? Can you get almost the same effect by adding another, lower fat item, such as low-fat yogurt to top your enchilada instead of sour cream or light mayonnaise instead of regular mayo in your tuna salad?

Now try to have an open mind: This might mean using Egg Beaters egg substitute in your quiche (or mixing 6 egg white or so with only 2 egg yolks), adding low-fat milk instead of cream and 1/2 the butter to your fettucini Alfredo, or mixing up a low-fat mushroom gravy for your stroganoff. Here are some suggestions. You can cut this guide out and stick it in your recipe box. Hopefully, in a few years, it too will be torn and stained.

Tip #1.   Instead of butter, shortening or some margarines, USE

- Butter Buds (a powder that looks like melted margarine once you add water) can be used to replace at least half the butter in many ways, except to fry or saute.
- A sprinkle or two of naturally flavored butter sprinkles (such as Molly McButter) over foods you might usually add butter or sour cream to.
- Margarine (where the first ingredient listed is a liquid vegetable oil). But remember, you're still replacing one fat with another, so add less if you can.
- Some or all of the butter, margarine, or oil in recipes can be replaced by another liquid that will add moisture. It all depends on the type of recipe as to how much fat can be replaced and by what (wine, fruit juice, chicken broth, etc.).

Tip #2. Instead of baking chocolate (1 oz), USE

- 3 tablespoons cocoa plus 1 tablespoon oil

Instead of hot chocolate mixes USE

- Hot cocoa mix made from:
  1 cup nonfat dry milk powder
  1/3 cup unsweetened cocoa powder
  3 tablespoons sugar
  (Mix ingredients and store in an airtight container.) To use, put 2 heaping teaspoons of mix into a cup and add hot water. Stir well.

Tip #3.   Instead of cheeses, USE

- Part-skim mozzarella and other reduced fat (lower calorie) cheeses. In most cases you can also use LESS cheese than the recipe calls for.

Tip #4.   Instead of ricotta cheese (whole milk), USE

- Part-skim ricotta cheese or 1% fat cottage cheese, or a mixture of the two.

Tip #5. Instead of cream, USE

- Evaporated skim milk or regular low-fat milk. Add some nonfat dry milk if you need to thicken it. CAUTION! Non-dairy creamers may have "no cholesterol" but most are just as high in percentage of calories from fat as cream.

Tip #6. Instead of cream cheese, USE

- Neufchatel cream cheese or Philadelphia Light, or combine these with plain yogurt, part-skim ricotta, or low-fat cottage cheese.

Tip #7. Instead of creamy dressing or dip, USE

- Almost Fat-Free Creamy Dressing made as follows:

  1 small envelope (1 oz) ranch dressing powder (use "lite" if available)

  1 1/2 cups nonfat milk (or low-fat)

  1/2 cup nonfat plain yogurt, or low-fat

  1 tablespoon "lite" Miracle Whip (or reduced calorie mayo)

  Blend milk, yogurt, mayo and powder together well. Keeps great in refrigerator about five days. Makes 2 cups of dressing.

Tip #8. Instead of eggs, USE

- Three eggs can be replaced by 1 egg beaten with 3 egg whites.
- Egg Beaters (Fleischmann) or egg substitute available in the frozen food section.

Tip #9. Instead of gravy, USE

- Mushroom Gravy Recipe:

  Mix 1 1/2 packets or cubes of low-sodium chicken broth (or beef) with 1 1/2 cups water. Add 3/4 cup raw sliced mushrooms and 1/3 cup diced onions. In a saucepan, simmer until the mushrooms are cooked and onions tender. In a separate pan, melt 1 tablespoon butter or margarine. Mix in 2 tablespoons flour. Add this to the mushroom mixture, stirring for a few minutes until the gravy thickens. Pour in 1/4 cup low-fat milk (or nonfat) and simmer, stirring for a few minutes more.

Tip #10. Instead of mayonnaise, USE
- Plain yogurt
- Reduced calorie types of mayonnaise
- Mock mayo, made as follows:
  1/2 cup reduced calorie mayo with 1/2 cup low-fat plain yogurt
- Low-fat cottage cheese, whipped up in a food processor or blender

Tip #11. Instead of whole milk, USE
- Nonfat or low-fat milk

Tip #12. Instead of oily vinaigrettes or marinades, USE
- For cold salads, try the reduced-calorie Italian dressings or Balsamic vinegar
- For marinades, try beer, wine, tomato puree or low-sodium broths as your marinade base. Add garlic, spices, etc., as usual.

Tip #13. Instead of sour cream, USE
- Nonfat or low-fat plain yogurt (In sauces, add 2 tablespoons flour for each cup of yogurt so the sauce will thicken properly.) For hot dishes, stir yogurt in just before serving, since high temperatures will cause it to curdle.
- Knudsen Nice n' Light sour cream
- Formagg Sour Cream Style or other reduced fat "light" sour creams.
- Substitute part-skim ricotta cheese or low-fat cottage cheese blended with buttermilk.
  CAUTION! Most imitation sour creams have just as much fat as regular sour cream.

Tip #14. Instead of sweeteners
- In some cases, fruit and/or fruit juices or pureed fruits can be used for at least half the sugar called for.

Tip #15. Instead of some or all of the fat for stir-frying, simmering, or sauteing,

- Substitute low-sodium broths, wine, beer, or fruit juice.

Tip #16. Some of the fat in certain recipes

- Substitute rum, whiskey, brandy, or fruit juices and fruit purees (such as mashed bananas or applesauce) or buttermilk.
NOTE: The alcohol in liquor evaporates during cooking.

Tip #17. Instead of bacon or sausage, USE

- Canadian style bacon
- Louis Rich Turkey Breakfast Sausage

Tip #18. Instead of ground beef, USE

- Ground sirloin (less than 13 percent fat)
- Substitute ground turkey breast or ground chicken breast (available in some meat departments).

Making Recipe Changes

Sample Recipe

Eggplant Parmesan

Original:

1 eggplant (about 1 to 1 1/2 pounds)
2 eggs, lightly beaten
1 cup Italian-style bread crumbs
9 tablespoons olive oil
1 clove garlic, minced
1 can (28 oz) crushed tomatoes
2 teaspoons oregano leaves, crushed
1/2 cup grated Parmesan cheese
8 ounces mozzarella cheese, shredded

Modified:

1 eggplant (about 1 to 1 1/2 pounds)

1 egg, 1 egg white, beaten with 2 tablespoons water (reduced by 1 yolk)

1 cup cracker meal or white flour (lower in fat than bread crumbs)

1 1/2 recipe of "15 Minute Spaghetti" as follows:

9 oz tomato paste, 21 oz Italian-style stewed tomatoes, 7.25 oz sliced bottled mushrooms, and seasonings

2 cups cooked pasta (use ziti macaroni or fettucini style). This adds carbohydrates to recipe.

1 1/2 cups grated part-skim mozzarella cheese (about 7 oz) (Lower in fat.)

6 tablespoons grated Parmesan cheese (reduced by 2 tablespoons)

*NOTE: No oil is needed, since eggplant is broiled instead of fried.

Cut off stem and bottom of the eggplant, then slice off the lengthwise ends of the eggplant to eliminate tough skin. Cut the eggplant lengthwise into 1 centimeter-thick slices (usually makes about 10 slices). Coat each slice in egg mixture then cracker crumbs. Place slices on a non-stick cookie sheet and broil each side at medium-high heat for about 3 minutes. Watch carefully so it doesn't burn.

Line a 9 by 9-inch baking pan with 1/2 the eggplant slices. Top with 1/2 the sauce, then 1/2 the mozzarella and 2 tablespoons of Parmesan. Now add the pasta evenly. Top with the rest of the eggplant, then the sauce and cheese. Bake for 15 minutes in a preheated 375-degree oven. Makes 6 servings.

Nutritional Analysis Per Serving (modified recipe)

Calories, 340, Fiber, 5 gm, Cholesterol, 68 mg, Sodium, 590 mg

Percent of calories from: Protein, 24%, Carbohydrate, 53%, Fat, 23%

In other eggplant Parmesan recipes, about 60 percent of calories are usually from fat!

The Art of Healthful Baking

Phase I

Contrary to what my friends think, I was NOT born a nutritionist. According to a certain third grade document entitled "What I Want to be When I Grow Up," I wanted to become a "baker."

Perhaps I was impressed by the hypnotic smell of bread baking, or maybe it was the taste of whipped cream—I don't remember. But the point is something else must have impressed me somewhere between third grade and college. Instead of writing about the "Joys of Baking with Lots of Fat," here I am writing about "The Art of Healthful Baking."

To be a "healthful baker" you have to be committed to minimizing the two favorite baking ingredients: fats (butter, lard, vegetable shortening, oil, take your pick, they're all "fat") and eggs (specifically egg yolks). Remember, eggs have more than 50 percent of their calories from fat, so we're minimizing them not only because they're high in cholesterol but because they are a fatty ingredient. And while we're at it, it's not a bad idea to minimize sugars (white, brown, powdered, or honey) and salt (sodium chloride) when possible.

By making a few ingredient adjustments, we can transform your favorite baking recipe into a more healthful food. You may have to get used to the color, light brown, if half the flour you add is whole wheat. And if you lower fat and sugar, the crumb may not be quite as smooth and moist or the taste as sweet—depending on how much you lower the fat and sugar. In many cases, you can cut the fat and sugar in half without anyone noticing, including you!

Experiment using the guidelines below until you've lowered fat and sugar as far as you can while still maintaining the taste that keeps you making that recipe again and again.

Yeast Breads

These recipes aren't usually the fat and sugar culprits. Only a small amount of sugar (about 2 tablespoons) is added to help the dough rise and brown the crust. Shortening (fat) is not an essential ingredient but is added to give flavor and make the crumb tender. Try to keep it down to 1 tablespoon per loaf.

Quick Breads (nut breads, muffins, cornbread, biscuits)

With quick breads, added fat can be lowered several ways.

• Use nonfat milk instead of whole milk. (Nonfat milk contains all the protein and other nutrients without the fat and extra calories.)

• If eggs are used, keep to a maximum of one per recipe.

• Try not to add too many nuts (only about 1/4 to 1/3 cup per loaf).

• Keep the fat ingredient (shortening, butter, oil, etc.,) to a minimum (about 2 to 3 tablespoons per recipe). With biscuits, you can cut the added fat by a third or a half, but you may then need to use a little more nonfat milk to help mix in the extra flour.

• Sugar can usually be reduced to about 2 to 3 tablespoons per recipe.

Cake Squares (spice and carrot cake, coffee cake, pound and fruit cake)

In cooking circles, these desserts are informally called "butter cakes," and for a very good reason!

You can reduce fat in several ways:

• The first suggestion will probably be the toughest to follow: Strip the frosting off the cake. Frosting is made of only fat and sugar. So the only way to reduce them is to decrease or eliminate the frosting altogether. (You'll be amazed how well carrot or spice cake stands on its own.)

• Depending on the recipe, sometimes you may be able to cut fat in half. (A minimum of about 1/4 to 1/3 cup of added fat usually is essential.)

• If 3 eggs are called for, use 2 instead.

- Sugar may be reduced to a minimum of about 1/3 cup.
- To lighten the cake's texture, you can beat egg whites separately and fold them into the batter toward the end.

Very Important Messages

- Remember, every time you take fat OUT of a recipe you need to add the same amount of fat-free liquid back in to keep it moist and delicious. Fruit juices work well with muffin-type batters and some cake recipes, while liquor (rum, whiskey, sherry, brandy, etc.) works well in others. If you cut oil from 6 tablespoons to 2 tablespoons, you'll need to add at least 4 tablespoons of fruit juice back.
- When substituting whole wheat for white flour, use 7/8 cup instead of 1 cup.

Pies and Pastries

The sugar in the pie filling can, at least, be cut in two. Sometimes only one-fourth of the sugar listed in the recipe is really necessary!

To lower fat:

- Pie crust is made of fat and flour. A quick way to decrease fat is to take the top crust off your pie. Instead, sprinkle toasted oatmeal or graham cracker crumbs on top or cover with a meringue. Also, you could just cover the pie with foil when baking (to prevent loss of moisture). Then serve it with ice milk on top.
- Don't dab any butter inside the pie or on the crust.

Following these guidelines, you can take an ordinary peach pie at 584 calories per serving and 41 percent of those calories from fat and turn it into 311 calories per serving with 34 percent of calories from fat.

Let's take a look at how I changed one of my favorite recipes:

Carrot Cake (without frosting)

Original ingredients
3 cups carrots
2 cups flour
1 cup sugar
1 1/2 cup oil
1/2 cup unsweetened coconut
3 eggs
1/2 cup walnuts
2 teaspoons baking powder
2 teaspoons baking soda
1 teaspoon salt

This recipe contains:
570 calories per serving, 3.5 gm fiber, 80 mg cholesterol, 63 percent of calories from fat.

Modified recipe:
3 cups carrots
1 cup whole wheat flour
1 cup white flour
1/2 cup sugar
1/3 cup oil
1 cup orange juice
8 oz canned pineapple (in juice)
1/2 cup unsweetened coconut (optional)
1 egg and 2 egg whites
1/3 cup walnuts
2 teaspoons baking powder
1 teaspoons baking soda*

*No salt is needed because baking soda and powder already contain sodium

This recipe contains:
215 calories per serving, 2.7 gm fiber, 22 mg cholesterol, 36 percent of calories from fat

Phase II

Something New, Lesson 1.

All that salt the recipes tell you to add? Don't listen to them. It's more than optional; it's totally unnecessary. Only in yeast breads is a moderate amount needed to help control the yeast activity. You're going to get plenty of sodium in your baking powder (247 mg per teaspoon) and baking soda (821 mg per teaspoon). These are not optional unless you like your cakes and muffins flat as a board.

Something New, Lesson 2.

Ration only one egg yolk per recipe. That's usually all you need to keep your batter smooth and blended. Remember every last drop of fat and cholesterol is neatly tucked away in the yolk of the egg. So if the recipe normally calls for 2 eggs, use 1 egg and 1 or 2 egg whites.

Something New, Lesson 3.

Try to get used to a light brown crumb and the nutty taste of whole wheat flour. Just by using 1 cup of whole wheat flour and 1 cup of white instead of 2 cups of white flour, you double the amount of dietary fiber (15 grams instead of 7). And, as a bonus, you get a veritable vitamin bonanza! Indeed, you can double the amount of vitamin B6, folacin, pantothenic acid, copper, phosphorus, potassium, selenium, and zinc and get one and a half times more vitamin E and calcium and two and a half times more magnesium just by using half whole wheat flour in your recipe.

The "Something Old" Lesson

Now for the sake of review, here's a lesson on something old. (It's starting to sound like someone is getting married!) In most baking recipes, you can automatically cut the fat and sugar in half without anyone noticing. Just remember to make up the difference in liquid volume lost by adding a fruit juice. For example, if you cut the amount of added oil in a muffin recipe from 1/2 cup to 1 tablespoon, you'll need to add about 6 tablespoons of orange or pineapple juice.

7

What's the Big "Fat" Deal About Homemade Meals?

The First Meal of the Day—Break-fast

Breakfast, the MOST important meal of the day? Well, that's debatable. (I place my vote for the mid-day lunch.) But for most of us it's obviously the FIRST meal of the day anyway. What we choose to put into our bodies will, in essence, fuel half of our workday. Think about that next time you're feeding yourself before a big meeting!

Certainly, children seem to function better in school with breakfast in their stomachs. Recent clinical research on children suggests they have a definite decrease in problem-solving abilities on mornings when they skip breakfast. But, back to us adults who may not need to master times tables in the morning.

I have some clinical research results to cite for you as well. This may sound a bit extreme, but it makes an interesting point. In a midwestern study, overweight people who received their entire allotment of the day's calories at breakfast actually lost weight, while most of the people who took in all their calories at dinner time gained weight instead.

Many of us tend to do the same breakfast day after day. So I would suggest we make sure whatever it is, it's low in fat. There's a huge difference, for example, between chewing on a croissant or Danish and fixing a bowl of hot oatmeal. And there's something to be said for washing your breakfast down with orange or grapefruit juice instead of creamed and sugared coffee each morning.

Avoiding the buttery croissant or jelly-filled donut and Danish is probably a predictable suggestion. But what about those gourmet muffins or freshly baked bagels that come with at least a one- to two-ounce slab of cream cheese in the middle? Well, I hate to burst your health-muffin bubble, but most commercial muffin recipes (yes, even the bran types) usually have at least 40 percent of their calories from fat, with up to 400 calories each and 30 to 60 milligrams of cholesterol—mainly from eggs added to the batter. A bagel, by the way, with half an ounce of neufchatel cream cheese has about 200 calories, 21 percent from fat, and 11 milligrams of cholesterol.

And now a few words on cereal. Somehow hot cereals have gotten the reputation of being too time-consuming to cook. Not necessarily true. Most are even microwavable or about 5 minutes from start to finish to cook over the stove. This is hardly time intensive. It will take you at least 5 minutes in line at that bakery of yours. Of course, we need to make sure we're not adding too much fat to our cereal. We can add fruits for flavor instead of butter. Dried fruits, such as raisins, or dried apricots or fresh fruits, such as banana coins or peach slices, can be added. Even cooked fruit, such as applesauce or apricots with cinnamon, will make a tasty cereal topping.

We can pour non- or low-fat milk over our cereal instead of "whole milk" where almost half the calories come from fat. Non- or low-fat milk is great for cooking those instant oatmeals in too, instead of water. When we add 1 cup of skim milk to 1 1/2 cups of cooked oatmeal in place of low-fat milk, the percentage of calories from fat jumps down from 24 percent to 11 percent.

On weekends, we're in a different breakfast mode altogether, aren't we? Suddenly we start imagining Belgium waffles decorated with berries and whipped cream, three-egg omelettes, or a stack of pancakes. Pancakes and waffles are workable, but that three-egg omelette is a fat-laden no-no, anyway you top it. The basic ham and cheese omelette without sour cream has about 725 calories—70 percent from fat, and 850 milligrams of cholesterol. See what I mean?

So what do Americans do to these horribly high-fat, cholesterol-rich breakfast entrees? We eat them with more fatty foods, such as bacon, sausage, or hash browns on the side. You might ask, "All right, Elaine, what DO we do?" Split an egg yolk with someone you love. If you eat eggs occasionally, try lightening them up by adding a few egg whites to one whole egg. (This is for two people.) Beat in some nonfat milk and maybe one or two tablespoons of flour or low-fat cottage cheese (to thicken it up) and your eggy entree is MUCH lower in calories and cholesterol and has around 26 percent of its calories from fat. You can even fill your new fluffy omelette with nonfat items (tomatoes, onions, mushrooms, salsa, plain yogurt, etc.).

Breakfast on the Run

Morning after morning, most of us rush, rush, rush around the house to get ourselves out the door on time, just to sit on a freeway somewhere in the typical urban commute. Well, if we're going to be inching along bumper to bumper, we might as well have a nice relaxing breakfast while we're at it.

Having your breakfast on the run does have a couple of shortcomings that we might as well admit to right away. You can't read the newspaper while you eat your breakfast anymore (unless you're in the passenger's seat), and you can't have gooey, messy breakfasts anymore (you know the ones where you really do need to use a fork and knife).

And you'll need to stock your car (now doubling as a breakfast nook on wheels) with a few supplies. Keep your glove compartment well stocked with napkins. Get a beverage holder for your dashboard or center console if you don't already have one. And if you tend to stain your clothing with even the "hard-to-spill" foods, you might want to keep a small towel in the back that you can drape over your clothes while you leisurely eat and drink your breakfast. Of course, we aren't talking about toting the usual "fast" breakfast foods, such as a cheese Danish and coffee or an Egg McMuffin. Here are five low-fat ideas, one for each day of the work week. If you keep things on schedule you can even remind yourself what day it is. "If it's muffins, this must be Tuesday," for example.

#1. Make Your Own Frozen Waffles

You can pop them directly from the freezer into the toaster, wrap them in a paper towel, grab some juice or fresh fruit, and you're out the door. You can use the basic instructions for buttermilk waffle batter, but to keep them low-fat, use about 2 cups of flour (1/2 whole wheat if you want), 1 1/3 teaspoons baking powder, 1 tablespoon sugar, 1 egg yolk, 2 egg whites, 1 3/4 cup buttermilk, and at the most 2 tablespoons oil. If you absolutely need to grease your waffle iron, try using the Weight Watchers or PAM sprays. These waffles come out to about 236 calories each (this recipes makes six waffles), that are 15 percent calories from protein, 60 percent carbohydrate, and 25 percent from fat (using 2 tablespoons of oil). Cholesterol is 45 milligrams and sodium 150 milligrams per large waffle. After cooking, break the waffles into toastable-sized squares, place a serving's worth in a plastic bag, and store in the freezer.

#2. Left-overs Fit for Breakfast

For those craving the atypical breakfast, even cold pizza will do. One slice of cheese or vegetarian pizza, 1/8 of a 14-inch pizza, has about 230 calories, 30 milligrams of cholesterol, and 580 milligrams of sodium. From 30 to 35 percent of calories are from fat, 20 percent from protein, and up to 50 percent from carbohydrate. The less cheese, the better. Because this breakfast is a little high in fat, make sure to drink some fruit juice or eat a piece of fresh fruit with it.

#3. The Way Yogurt Lovers Eat Their Cereal

Figure out a steady place in your car to set your bowl down. Then find a plain nonfat or low-fat flavored type of yogurt. Most flavored yogurts go heavy on the sugar, so watch that, too. If a flavored yogurt has around 150 calories per 8-ounce service (such as Weight Watchers brand), it usually is the lower sugar type. Assuming you've already been using a low-fat, high-fiber cereal, you're ready to add about a cup of your cereal to your cup of yogurt. For smaller eaters, cut down to 3/4 or 1/2 cup of each.

#4. Bagel Delights

Keep your already-split bagels in the freezer. Then in the morning you just need to break them apart and toss them in the toaster. While they're toasting you can get the mystery inside ingredient ready. If you feel like a toasted onion and cheese bagel, you can slice your cheese while your onion bagel is toasting. If it's more of a bagel and cream cheese morning, get your 1/2 ounce of Neufchatel cheese (or Philadelphia Light) ready to spread.

• A toasted onion bagel with an ounce of cheese has 265 calories, 28 milligrams of cholesterol, 500 milligrams of sodium, 21 percent of calories from protein, 49 percent from carbohydrate, 30 percent from fat, and 215 milligrams of calcium. Using a lower fat cheese will help bring the fat down further.

• A bagel with 1/2 ounce of Neufchatel or light cream cheese has about 200 calories, 11 milligrams cholesterol, 310 milligrams sodium, 16 percent of calories from protein, 64 percent from carbohydrate, and 20 percent from fat.

   *If you add 2 tablespoons of Smuckers Low Sugar preserves to the above, it's 250 calories, 13 percent from protein, 70 percent from carbohydrate, and 17 percent from fat.

• An English muffin (or bagel) with 1 tablespoon of peanut butter will be about 245 calories, 0 milligrams of cholesterol, 255 milligrams sodium (if you use the unsalted type), 15 percent of calories from protein, 55 percent from carbohydrate, and 30 percent from fat.

#5. My Favorite Muffins

Think about it: You can take muffins camping, to a picnic, or impress your colleagues and bring a batch to your next early morning meeting. But there is one tiny problem—that three letter word again—FAT.

The muffins you buy in your friendly neighborhood bakery (even the bran types) are usually pretty packed with grease—40 percent of calories from fat or more. This is about the same as a biscuit, and some come close to looking more like a Danish (with 50 percent of calories from fat) than a muffin.

The newer, fancy muffin mixes (Bran & Honey-Nut or Cinnamon Swirl, for example) have vegetable shortening (a saturated fat) listed as the third ingredient. The second and fourth ingredients are sugar in the Cinnamon Swirl case. The Swirl will come out to about 32 percent of calories from fat, but only because the sugar content is so high it brings down the percent of total calories from fat.

What is the answer to the over-fat and sugar-laden muffin? Just three little words. Make your own. It's easier than you think. Make a batch on Sunday night, have a couple for breakfast on Monday, and freeze the rest in individual serving bags. Come Wednesday or Friday morning, you just take one or two out of the freezer and pop them into a microwave or toaster over for a couple of minutes. To make low-fat muffins, follow the "Art of Healthful Baking Guidelines" on pages 150-152.

I also need to qualify that some bakery muffins are better in the fat department than others. So it's possible your favorite bakery muffin is just fine. How can you tell? Well, you can't really tell for sure, but here's a quick clue. Try the muffin grease spot test:

Cut your muffin in half. Take one of the halves and press the just-cut side to a brown paper bag. (You can see the grease spots better if the bag is brown.) Or use a paper towel or napkin if that's what's handy. Then look for grease spots on the bag or napkin.

It doesn't take a trained eye to be able to tell the difference between a grease spot and a water or juice spot. If you're not sure, touch it with your fingers. You can almost always feel the difference.

To get you started on your merry low-fat muffin way, there are two quick and easy recipes for my favorite muffins in the recipe section in the next chapter.

Don't Forget Your Fruit (or Fruit Juice)

A cup of orange, grapefruit, or pineapple juice totals 100 to 140 calories. They're all mostly carbohydrate calories. This helps round off your breakfast on the run. I like making a big enough fruit salad to last a few days. Then in the morning all I have to do is scoop some out into a portable container and off to work I go. Fresh fruit makes a great midmorning snack.

Now for one last quick breakfast tip. Keep some of the microwavable instant oatmeal envelopes (the less sweetened ones) in your desk drawer at work. Then all you need to do is buy some non- or low-fat milk at the cafeteria, pop the cereal and milk into the microwave for two minutes, and you've got yourself a breakfast—or afternoon snack for that matter.

Packing a Low-fat Lunch Box for Your Child

It doesn't matter whether your child is going to school or playing at home. That daily question continues: "What should I fix for lunch?"

It's not a simple question either. You want it to be healthful, you want it to meet their nutrition and growth needs. But most important of all, you want them to like it because chances are they won't eat it otherwise. Which brings me to the subject of VARIETY. It's not only the spice of life, it's the spice of the lunch box too. Back in grade school, I remember bag lunch after bag lunch filled with Nilla wafers, carrot sticks, and those little boxes of raisins. I'm just now (15 some odd years later) getting to the point where I can eat raisins and carrot sticks again. I still can't face Nilla wafers.

The bottom line to a bag lunch is, does your child actually eat it? This makes it imperative your child is included in the "what's for lunch" discussion. This doesn't mean you magically become a short-order cook an hour each day. But try to consider your child's likes and dislikes as best you can. Some kids will gladly share these with you again and again. With other kids, you might have to do some probing. Try asking which type of bread they like best. What are their favorite sandwiches?

Only after my poor horrified mother found two weeks worth of decaying, uneaten sandwiches under my bed did she come to the understanding I hated chewy sticky white bread getting stuck in my teeth and to the roof of my mouth. So here's another question to ask. Do you like your bread toasted or plain?

What are the essential ingredients to a child's healthful bag lunch? It should include some fresh fruit or fruit canned in juice, and some vegetables. Vegetables can be sliced and added to the sandwich or cut up into sticks or circles, washed well, and put into a bag. (Otherwise they dry up by lunchtime.) If the lunch doesn't already include an ounce and a half of cheese on a slice of pizza or in the sandwich, then you might want to add a small carton of non- or low-fat milk or some yogurt. Or give your child the coins to buy that at school.

Dessert? I must admit I definitely remember looking forward to eating the chocolate covering off and unrolling the HO HO every day. The "dessert" or something special concept isn't all that bad. It's the "what" we consider (or what we train our children to consider) dessert or special that gets us into trouble. There are healthier cookies out there and great recipes for muffins and nut breads that can certainly double as dessert. Many are included in the next chapter.

The main feature of your child's bag lunch can obviously be the standard sandwich, but it can also be, your child's preference permitting, something on the order of leftover lasagna, chili with cornbread, or colorful vegetarian pizza slices. Which standard sandwiches should be more standard than others? Believe it or not, the esteemed peanut butter and jelly sandwich can make this healthful sandwich list—with a few minor adjustments. Here are a few of the possibilities:

Peanut Butter and Jelly Sandwich

2 slices whole wheat bread
2 tablespoons peanut butter
2 tablespoons Smuckers Low-Sugar Spread.

Nutritional Analysis:
410 calories, 7 grams fiber, 510 mg sodium, no cholesterol, 15 percent calories from protein, 50 percent from carbohydrate, 35 percent from fat.

CLT (Cheese, Lettuce and Tomato) Sandwich

1 1/2 oz part skim cheese
half a tomato, sliced
2 slices whole wheat bread
several leaves of dark green lettuce
mustard to taste (analyzed with 1/2 teaspoon)

Nutritional Analysis:
300 calories, 4 1/2 grams fiber, 600 mg sodium, 27 mg cholesterol, 25 percent of calories from protein, 48 percent from carbohydrate, 27 percent from fat. (The fat content jumps to 37 percent if regular cheese is used.)

Meatball Surprise Sandwich

10 small meatballs (or 4 medium-sized meatballs) from the "Italian-Style Hamburger or Meatball" recipe found in the next chapter, page 189
1 French or sourdough roll
1 to 2 tablespoons catsup or tomato sauce
1 tablespoon grated Parmesan cheese (That's the surprise).

Nutritional Analysis:
425 calories, 55 mg cholesterol, 780 mg sodium, 26 percent of calories from protein, 52 percent from carbohydrate, 22 percent from fat.

Turkey

2 slices whole grain bread
2 1/2 ounces cooked turkey breast, sliced thin
(You can buy the whole turkey breasts cooked, in the
    packaged meat section of the supermarket)
a few leaves of dark green lettuce,
half a tomato, sliced
mustard to taste or 1 tablespoon cranberry sauce

Nutritional Analysis:

295 calories, 5 grams fiber, 50 milligrams cholesterol, 420 mg
    sodium, 38 percent of calories from protein, 48 percent
    from carbohydrate, 14 percent from fat.

A Few Fruit Ideas

Orange or apple wedges, sliced bananas, pears, canned
apricots (in juice) 100 percent pure orange, apple, or grapefruit juice.

Try mixing and matching the above, such as pineapple
chunks with banana coins and raisins, or apple wedges with
pears and cinnamon.

Some Cuttable Vegetables

Cucumber, zucchini, carrot, and celery strips or sticks,
cauliflower or broccoli flowers, kohlrabi, carrots, cucumber
or squash slices or coins, green or red pepper rings.

Adults Need Lunch, Too

Many of the same principles for your child's lunchbox apply
for you, too—the need for fruits and vegetables, choosing
lower fat snacks and goodies. Perhaps your choice in
sandwich might differ, though. There are a few fancy (low-
fat) sandwich recipes for you in the recipe section in the next
chapter. The lunch tips listed in the Deli Delights section in
Chapter 5 also can be helpful at home.

But "lunch" certainly isn't synonymous with "sandwich." Warmed up chili or casseroles make great lunches from home. This doesn't take any extra time, either. All you need to do is plan for leftovers when you're making dinner. Then package individual portions directly into microwavable storage containers. Keep one for tomorrow's lunch, then freeze the rest. I find people are far more willing to eat "leftovers" at lunch than at dinner two days in a row. Besides, if the recipe is considered delicious, then you and your family will even look forward to lunches.

When I eat out at a restaurant on a weeknight, I usually go so far as to eat half my meal and doggy bag the rest for tomorrow's lunch. You can order a couple of "a la carte" items in addition to your dinner selection, and tell the waiter or waitress to package them to go. And there you have it—your ready-made lunch for tomorrow.

Curious About Condiments?

I can show you how to make a low-fat hamburger patty, but all the trimmings are up to you. And don't underestimate the contribution that condiments can make towards the fat total of the meal. Some of them are definitely NOT benign "extras."

Here's a list of the more popular condiments

	1 tablespoon Sodium (mg)	% Calories from Fat	Calories
Mustard	11	8%	188
Ketchup	16	6%	170
Chili Sauce	16	trace	201
Cocktail Sauce	20	trace	160
Sweet Pickle Relish	21	4%	107
Steak Sauce	18	trace	149
Sweet & Sour Sauce	32	trace	320!
Reduced Calorie Mayonnaise	35-50	90%	115
Tartar Sauce	75	96%	182
Mayonnaise	100	100%	78

Obviously in terms of adding fat, mustard or ketchup is the better choice to spread your bread or bun with than mayonnaise. If mayo is a must, then opt for the reduced-calorie types (giving you half as much fat per tablespoon). And then just "wet the bread", don't smother it with the stuff.

In these tables and recipes we measure condiments in teaspoons and tablespoons, but when it comes to actually spreading, we're measuring in spoonfuls or a knife's worth. So get yourself (and your loved ones) very well acquainted with what a teaspoon or tablespoon really looks like. For most people, one tablespoon doesn't even begin to describe the amount of mayonnaise or tartar sauce they usually add.

CAUTION: Most sandwich shops use large plastic spatulas to spread their mayonnaise. I find the specifications "just barely wet the bread" are much more effective than "spread it light, will ya?" What that person thinks is "light" and what you think is "light" could be tablespoons apart.

Life Beyond the TV Dinner

We think we have to choose between making a laborious dinner from scratch and eating a frozen or fast food dinner. Fortunately, it isn't that simple. This myth lives on because all the recipes we ever come across in magazines and newspapers require at least 10 ingredients. (Many require an extra shopping trip because you certainly don't have half that stuff at home.) Also, many recipes require an hour of preparation time.

Let's fact it. After a long day at work we don't have an hour to give. The solution? New recipes to make at home that require a reasonable amount of preparation time. They say we all basically have 20 recipes we end up making over and over. So I'm asking you to incorporate some new ones (low in fat) into your 20 recipe repertoire AND to revise the rest, using the guidelines listed in the beginning of this chapter. You might find some of your favorites have already been revised in the recipe section that follows, such as low-fat lasagna, macaroni and cheese, and tacos.

Don't be put off by the amount of time some of these recipes require in the oven. This is still FREE TIME for you—time you can use to ride your stationary bike, soak in the tub, read the newspaper, or play with your kids. The bottom line here is that it takes less time in the kitchen, right?

My two favorite quick and easy dinners are "the two P's" pasta and potatoes. I like to buy fresh pasta noodles (you can freeze pasta, too). And while it's boiling, you can get your low-fat sauce and vegetables ready. If I'm really in a hurry, I throw my vegetables in with the pasta and let them both boil. There are a couple of low-fat sauces in the recipe section, but you can also use Ragu Gardenstyle Spaghetti Sauce in a bottle, a reduced-calorie Italian dressing, or just toss a mixture of Parmesan cheese, black pepper, and natural flavored butter sprinkles, such as Molly McButter or Best O'Butter.

Once in a while I'll even spend a Saturday making homemade ravioli (my secret filling recipe is at the end of the next chapter: "Chicken, Basil, Baby Carrot Filling"). Then you freeze a dinner's worth in separate plastic storage bags. All that's required when you come home from work is to take a bag out of the freezer and boil some water. Homemade pasta in minutes!

For a quick potato dinner, you can pop your potatoes into the microwave until they're cooked throughout (5 to 10 minutes, depending on how many potatoes and your microwave). While they're cooking, start getting your filling and topping ready. Fill each potato with vegetables, such as onions, mushrooms, squash, etc., or lean meats, such as leftover London broil or chicken breast. You can even open a can of water packed tuna. Top the potato with Ragu Gardenstyle or other low-fat red sauces, a cheese sauce (see the next chapter for a recipe), Parmesan or part-skim milk cheese.

These are just two examples. There are many more in the recipe section. So without further ado, here are some sample recipes.

8

Cooking Smart: Recipes for Lowering Fat

Breads and Muffins

Lemon Bread

2 cups flour
1 cup whole wheat flour
4 tsp baking powder
3 Tbsp margarine or butter, softened
1 cup sugar
1 egg
3 egg whites
1 cup low-fat milk
finely grated peel of 2 lemons (2 tsp)

Glaze: Filtered juice of two lemons mixed with 2 Tbsp powdered sugar

Preheat oven to 350 degrees. Mix together flours and baking powder. In separate bowl, cream the margarine with the sugar. Stir in egg and egg whites, milk, lemon peel, and any pulp filtered from the lemon juice. Blend with flour mixture and pour into two nonstick sprayed loaf pans (9 X 5"). Bake until toothpick inserted near center comes out clean. (About 30 minutes. Don't overbake!) Brush hot loaves with lemon glaze. Makes 24 slices (12 per loaf).

Nutritional Analysis: Per slice
Calories 113, Fiber 1 gm, Cholesterol 15 mg, Sodium 70 mg
Percent of calories from: Protein 10%, Carbohydrate 75%, Fat 15%

Apricot Nut Bread
1 1/4 cup whole wheat flour
1 cup white flour
1 tsp baking soda
1 tsp baking powder
1 tsp cream of tartar
1/2 tsp salt
2 eggs
1 1/2 cup orange juice
3 Tbsp oil
1/2 tsp vanilla extract
1/2 cup sugar
8 oz dried apricots, chopped
1/3 cup walnuts
Preheat oven to 350 degrees. Lightly beat eggs with orange juice. Add oil, sugar, vanilla. Mix dry ingredients. Add wet and dry mixtures together, not overmixing. Toss in apricot and walnut pieces. Bake for about 45 minutes. Makes 2 loaves, 10 servings per loaf.

Nutritional Analysis: Per Serving
Calories 140, Fiber 3 gm, Cholesterol 26 mg, Sodium 116 mg
Percent of calories from: Protein 8%, Carbohydrate 67%, Fat 25%

Fruit and Bran Muffins

1 egg
1 cup low-fat milk
1 cup wheat bran
1/2 cup whole wheat flour
1/2 cup white flour
1/4 cup honey
1 Tbsp baking powder
1/2 tsp salt (optional, but this recipe was analyzed with it)
1 tsp cinnamon
1 Pippin apple
3/4 cup crushed pineapple (do not drain)
2 Tbsp butter or margarine, melted

Preheat oven to 375 degrees. Put the egg, milk, honey, butter and bran in a mixing bowl and let stand for 5 minutes. Meanwhile, finely chop apple. Add the flours, baking powder, salt, cinnamon, apple, and pineapple. Stir until barely mixed. Spoon into muffin papers, filling each cup until almost full. Bake in the middle of the oven for about 20 minutes. Makes 8 muffins. They can be frozen and defrosted as needed.

Nutritional Analysis: Per Muffin
Calories 170, Fiber 4 gm, Cholesterol 44 mg, Sodium 285 mg
Percent of calories from: Protein 10%, Carbohydrate 67%, Fat 23%

Banana Health Nut Muffins

2 medium very ripe bananas
3 Tbsp butter or margarine, very soft or melted
1/2 cup pineapple juice
1/2 cup sugar
1 egg, 1 egg white
1/2 cup walnut pieces
1 cup whole wheat flour
1 cup white flour
1/4 cup wheat germ
1 tsp baking powder
1/4 tsp ground cloves or 1/2 tsp ground cinnamon

Preheat oven to 400 degrees. Mash bananas thoroughly in mixing bowl. Add the next 4 ingredients and blend, using electric mixer if possible, until smooth. Mix in nuts. In another bowl, mix dry ingredients until well blended. Gradually add dry mixture to liquid mixture, mixing well with electric mixer. Spoon batter into Teflon muffin pan or paper baking cups. Bake until lightly brown, about 20 minutes. Makes 12 muffins.

Nutritional Analysis: Per Muffin

Calories 210, Fiber 2.5 gm, Cholesterol 30 mg, Sodium 80 mg

Percent calories from: Protein 9%, Carbohydrate 62%, Fat 29%

Blueberry Oat Bran Muffins

2 1/4 cups oat bran (a mixture of 1/2 rolled oats
   and 1/2 oat bran may be used)

1/4 cup chopped nuts

1/4 cup raisins

2 tsp baking powder

3/4 cup nonfat milk

1/4 cup honey

1 egg with 2 egg whites, beaten

1 Tbsp vegetable oil

2/3 cup blueberries, raspberries, or chopped apricots
   (frozen berries can be used)

1/2 tsp cinnamon

Preheat oven to 425 degrees. In a large bowl combine first four ingredients. Add remaining ingredients. Mix until dry ingredients are moistened. Fill Teflon muffin pans (or use papers) until almost full. Bake 15 minutes or until golden brown. Makes 12 muffins.

Nutritional Analysis: Per Muffin

Calories 150, Fiber 2.5 gm, Cholesterol 22 mg, Sodium 60 mg

Percent of calories from: Protein 15%, Carbohydrate 59%, Fat 26%

Low-fat Garlic Bread

8 oz part-skim ricotta cheese
2 Tbsp butter or margarine, melted
1/4 cup grated Parmesan cheese
1 Tbsp Best O'Butter (or Molly McButter)
3 cloves garlic, finely minced
1 1/2 lb French or sourdough bread

Preheat oven to 400 degrees. Blend first five ingredients together well. Cut bread loaves into two halves each. Spread the garlic mixture on evenly. Bake for 5 to 7 minutes. (Broil for a short time at the end if you prefer.) Slice into separate pieces. Makes 15 dinner servings.

Nutritional Analysis: Per Serving

Calories 168, Cholesterol 10 mg, Sodium 325 mg

Percent of Calories from: Protein 15%, Carbohydrate 66%, Fat 19%

Easy Cheesy Biscuits

1 cup whole wheat flour
1 cup white flour
4 tsp baking powder
1 cup nonfat milk
1/2 cup chopped onion
3 Tbsp butter or margarine
2.5 oz part-skim cheddar cheese (about 1/2 cup), grated
2 tsp herb of choice (I like to use Italian seasonings)

Preheat oven to 350 degrees. Simmer onions in margarine for about 5 minutes. Meanwhile, mix dry ingredients. Then mix everything together, stirring just until blended. Spoon into Teflon-coated muffin pan. Makes about 12 biscuits. Bake until lightly brown (about 10 to 12 minutes).

Nutritional Analysis: Per Biscuit

Calories 125, Fiber 1.5 gm, Cholesterol 4 mg, Sodium 155 mg

Percent of calories from: Protein 15%, Carbohydrate 55%, Fat 30%

Soups and Salads

Potato Cheese Soup

6 medium-large red potatoes, cooked
3 cups nonfat milk
6 oz sharp cheddar cheese, grated
1 1/2 cups chopped white onion
1 Tbsp fresh parsley, finely chopped
1/4 tsp pepper (or to taste)
1/2 tsp sweet basil leaves, dried
dried paprika (optional)

Mash potatoes and onions together until smooth (as if you're making mashed potatoes) or use a food processor. There might be a few potato chunks, but that's fine. Add to a large soup kettle and mix in the milk and spices (except the paprika). On medium heat, let simmer for about 8 minutes, stirring frequently. Then mix in the grated cheese. Let simmer about 8 minutes longer. Serve in bowls. Lightly sprinkle paprika on top if you like a little pizzaz or color. Makes about 6 servings. Freezes well too.

Nutritional Analysis: Per Serving

Calories 275, Fiber 5 gm, Cholesterol 30 mg, Sodium 247 mg

Percent of calories from: Protein 21%, Carbohydrate 48%, Fat 31%

(When served with bread the percent from fat will decrease a bit.)

Autumn Medley Stew

2 15-oz cans stewed tomatoes
1 yellow onion, cut into strips
2 or 3 medium carrots, sliced into coins
1 green pepper, coarsely chopped
2 potatoes, raw, diced
3 chicken half breasts
2 cups water (with 2 packets low-sodium chicken broth, optional)
4 cups cooked rice
1/2 tsp black pepper

1 tsp rosemary

1 tsp Italian seasoning

4 cloves garlic, crushed

In a large soup kettle, simmer chicken breasts in 2 cups of water (or chicken broth). Add onion to chicken as it simmers. While it's cooking, you can slice other vegetables. When chicken is cooked throughout, remove and set aside. Add tomatoes, potatoes, carrots, peppers, and spices to onion and broth mixture. Continue to simmer. Break chicken into chunks, de-bone, and add to stew. Simmer 30 minutes or until carrots and potatoes are tender. Add rice and simmer 10 more minutes. Makes about 8 servings.

Nutritional Analysis: Per Serving

Calories 214, Fiber 4.5 gm, Cholesterol 22 mg, Sodium 215 mg

Percent of calories from: Protein 24%, Carbohydrate 70%, Fat 6%

Less Fat Potato Salad

4 lbs. white potatoes (or red), microwaved or baked until done, then diced

1 green pepper, finely chopped

1 red pepper, finely chopped

1 cup chopped green onion (use white and part of green)

1 cup thinly sliced celery

1 1/2 cup bread & butter pickles, diced

3 hard boiled eggs, cooled then chopped

Dressing: 8 oz low-fat cottage cheese (use 1% milkfat if available)

3/4 cup reduced calorie mayonnaise

2 Tbsp Dijon mustard

1/2 to 1 tsp dill weed

2 Tbsp parsley flakes (crushed in hand as you add)

1 tsp black pepper

Toss the first 7 ingredients in a large bowl. Using a food processor or blender, whip the cottage cheese until it looks smooth. Then add the mayo, mustard, and spices and whip again until well blended. Stir into potato salad mixture. If you tend to like less "other stuff" in your potato salad, reduce the pepper, celery, and pickles by half. Makes 15 servings at least!

Nutritional Analysis: Per Serving
Calories 190, Fiber 4.5 gm, Cholesterol 55 mg (with eggs), Sodium 290 mg
Percent of calories from: Protein 14%, Carbohydrate 67%, Fat 19%

Garden Rice Salad
1 1/2 cups cooked brown rice (or wild rice blend), cooled
1 1/4 cups chopped tomatoes
3/4 cup lightly cooked peas (microwave frozen peas on high for two minutes)
1/4 cup finely chopped green onions (remove half of green top)
1/4 cup pinenuts (broil for a minute or so to brown first if possible)

Dressing:
2 Tbsp lemon juice
1 tsp walnut oil (or olive oil)
1/4 tsp black pepper
1/8 tsp garlic powder
1/2 tsp oregano flakes
1/2 tsp sweet basil flakes

Toss the first 5 ingredients together in a medium-sized bowl. In a small bowl, mix the dressing ingredients together. Stir the dressing well as you evenly pour over the rice mixture. Toss together and chill in refrigerator until ready to serve. Makes 4 servings.

Nutritional Analysis: Per Serving
Calories 153, Fiber 6 gm, Cholesterol 0 mg, Sodium 12 mg
Percent of calories from: Protein 13%, Carbohydrate 66%, Fat 21%

Macaroni Salad

12 oz uncooked macaroni noodles
1 1/2 cups red pepper, finely chopped
6 green onions
3/4 cup green pepper, chopped
1 1/2 cup celery, slices
1 3/4 cup bread and butter pickles (finely chopped)
1 lemon, squeezed on top of salad and toss (optional)

Dressing
1 1/2 cup low-fat cottage cheese (1% milkfat)
1/3 cup reduced-calorie mayonnaise
1 Tbsp mustard
1 tsp pepper
1 tsp crushed dried basil leaves
1 tsp dill, dried

Cook macaroni as directed on package, drain and cool. While noodles are cooling, chop and prepare the remaining ingredients. Add the cottage cheese to a blender or food processor. Whip until smooth and creamy. Add the mayonnaise, mustard and seasonings to the cottage cheese and mix by hand. When pasta cools, toss with remaining ingredients, add dressing and blend. Serves 12.

Nutritional Analysis: Per Serving
Calories 170, Fiber 2.5 gm, Cholesterol 3 mg, Sodium 335 mg
Percent of calories from: Protein 18%, Carbohydrate 71%, Fat 11%

Quick Tuna Salad

1 6 1/2-oz can water-packed tuna, drained
1 apple, diced
3 Tbsp reduced calorie mayonnaise
2 cups shredded salad greens

Toss tuna, apple, and mayonnaise together, Serve over salad greens (or on bread for a sandwich). Makes 2 servings.

Nutritional Analysis: Per Serving, with salad greens
Calories 230, Fiber 3 gm, Cholesterol 52 mg, Sodium 409 mg

Percent of calories from: Protein 44%, Carbohydrate 36%,
   Fat 20%

Creamy Fruit Salad

2 cups assorted fresh fruit (for example, 1 cup strawberries,
   1 sliced peach, 1 sliced banana)
1/2 cup lemon or vanilla low-fat yogurt
Dash cinnamon or nutmeg
Toss yogurt with fruit. Top with cinnamon. Makes 2 servings.

Nutritional Analysis: Per Serving
Calories 142, Fiber 4 gm, Cholesterol 3 mg, Sodium 39 mg
Percent of calories from: Protein 10%, Carbohydrate 82%,
   Fat 8%

Sunshine Salad

4 cups fresh spinach
2 nectarines, sliced
1 cup fresh strawberries, halved
6 Tbsp reduced calorie vinaigrette
1 Tbsp sunflower seeds, roasted
Toss first 4 ingredients together. Sprinkle sunflower seeds on
   top. Makes 4 servings.

Nutritional Analysis: Per Serving
Calories 81, Fiber 4.4 gm, Cholesterol 0 mg, Sodium 220 mg
Percent of calories from: Protein 13%, Carbohydrate 62%,
   Fat 25%

Smoked Fish Pasta Salad

3 oz smoked salmon or trout, sliced thin and cut into pieces
2 cups cooked pasta (twisties if available), drained
1 cup asparagus tips, cooked (canned are fine if available)
1 cup raw, sliced summer squash
1/4 cup green onions, chopped
1/2 avocado, sliced (optional)
1 tsp dill
Pepper to taste

1/4 cup your favorite reduced calorie creamy bottled dressing
Mix all the ingredients together gently. Makes 2 entree salad
servings or 4 side salads.

Nutritional Analysis: Per Entree Salad
Calories 292, Fiber 4 gm, Cholesterol 30 mg, Sodium 840 mg
Percent of calories from: Protein 25%, Carbohydrate 59%,
Fat 16%

Tabbouleh Salad
1/3 cup chopped walnuts or almonds
1 cup dry bulgur
2/3 cup chopped green onions
1 cup diced tomato (or quartered cherry tomatoes)
1/3 cup lemon juice
2 cups shredded romaine lettuce leaves
1/4 cup chicken broth
pepper to taste
Pour enough boiling water over bulgur to just cover. Let sit 30
minutes (until water is absorbed). Add remaining
ingredients, except lettuce. Toss thoroughly. Cover and chill
at least 2 hours. Toss in lettuce and serve. Makes 6 servings.

Nutritional Analysis: Per Serving
Calories 162, Fiber 4 gm, Cholesterol 0 mg, Sodium 40 mg
Percent of calories from: Protein 12%, Carbohydrate 63%,
Fat 25%

Cucumber & Tomato Salad in Garlic Yogurt Dressing
1 lb cucumbers (about 2 medium), peeled and sliced
1/2 lb tomatoes, chopped
4 scallions, minced
1/2 cup fresh mint, chopped fine
1/2 cup fresh parsley, chopped fine
3 Tbsp lemon juice
2 cloves garlic, crushed
1 cup plain low-fat yogurt
Black pepper to taste

Mix the lemon juice, yogurt, garlic, pepper, mint, and parsley together. Pour over cucumber and tomato mixture and stir. Serve within an hour for best taste. Makes 6 servings.

Nutritional Analysis: Per Serving
Calories 45, Fiber 1 gm, Cholesterol 2 mg, Sodium 35 mg
Percent of calories from: Protein 24%, Carbohydrate 63%,
    Fat 13%

Chicken Salad Tropicale

5 cups cooked rice
4 leftover BBQ chicken breasts, boneless, skinless,
    and shredded into bite-sized pieces
1 (8-oz) can unsweetened crushed pineapple, drained but
    reserve juice
2 cups jicama, finely chopped, or use sliced water chestnuts
2/3 cup green onions, finely chopped
2 1/2 cups celery, sliced
1/2 cup roasted peanuts (or other nuts)
spinach or romaine lettuce

Tropical Dressing
    1 cup plain low-fat yogurt
    1 cup reduced-calorie mayonnaise
    2 to 3 Tbsp pineapple juice
    1/4 cup honey
    2 tsp finely grated fresh ginger
In large bowl, combine rice, chicken, pineapple, jicama, onions, and celery. In another bowl, blend all dressing ingredients until smooth. Pour dressing over rice mixture and toss. Serve on a bed of spinach or romaine lettuce leaves and sprinkle with roasted peanuts. Serves at least 12. This can be made a day in advance.

Nutritional Analysis: Per Serving
Calories 275, Fiber 2 gm, Cholesterol 30 mg, Sodium 160 mg
Percent of calories from: Protein 20%, Carbohydrate 53%,
    Fat 27%

Carrot Sauce
(Great with pasta, chicken, fish, or vegetables)
1 Tbsp butter
1/2 cup low-fat milk
1 1/2 finely grated carrots
4 Tbsp low-fat milk
2 tsp cornstarch
3 Tbsp Romano or Parmesan cheese
1/2 tsp oregano flakes
pepper to taste
Puree grated carrots in blender or food processor with 1/2 cup milk. Melt butter on medium high heat in Teflon fry pan. Add carrot mixture and let bubble for a minute. In a small dish, mix 2 tsp cornstarch with 2 Tbsp milk. Then add 2 Tbsp more milk. Add to carrot mixture, stir frequently, and let bubble a few minutes more. Reduce heat to simmer. Sprinkle cheese and spices on top, stir, and let simmer several minutes. Makes 3 servings of sauce.

Nutritional Analysis: Just the sauce per serving
*Also analyzed with 1 cup pasta noodles per serving

Calories 112, *285, Fiber 1.6 gm, *2 gm, Cholesterol 22 mg, Sodium 165 mg
Percent of calories from: Protein 16%, *15%, Carbohydrate 32%, *62%, Fat 53%, *23%

Cheese Sauce
1 cup part-skim ricotta cheese
1/2 cup skim milk
1/2 cup Parmesan cheese, grated
Mix ricotta cheese, skim milk and Parmesan cheese in microwave-safe dish. Microwave on high for a few minutes until hot and bubbly. Pour over at least 1 cup of pasta, potatoes, seafood, etc. Serves 4.

Nutritional Analysis: Per serving of sauce
Calories 140, Fiber 0 gm, Cholesterol 28 mg, Sodium 280 mg
Percent of calories from: Protein 34%, Carbohydrate 15%, Fat 51%

*When each serving is served with 1 cup of pasta there are: 310 calories, 0.5 gm fiber, 29 mg cholesterol, 285 mg sodium, and 24% calories from fat, 23% from protein, and 53% from carbohydrate.

Honey Mustard BBQ Sauce

2 Tbsp honey
1/3 cup Dijon-style mustard
1 Tbsp finely chopped parsley or parsley flakes
1 Tbsp white wine Worcestershire sauce
1/8 tsp black pepper

Combine all 5 ingredients, mixing well. Brush over steak, chicken or turkey while on the grill. This recipe gives you enough sauce to generously coat 8 chicken breasts.

Nutritional Analysis: Per serving of sauce
Calories 25, Cholesterol 0 mg, Sodium 150 mg
Percent of calories from: Protein 8%, Carbohydrate 76%, Fat 16%

Side Dishes

Seasoned Rice

1 cup uncooked brown rice
1 1/2 cup water
1 packet low-sodium chicken broth (or 1 cube)
1 cup chopped onion
1 1/2 cups vegetable pieces (grated carrots, broccoli, or a combination of others)
2 tsp parsley flakes
1/2 lemon, sliced (used as garnish when serving, great squeezed on top of the rice)

Mix low-sodium chicken broth with water in a medium-sized saucepan. Add the rice, onions, parsley, and mix. Spoon the vegetable pieces on top and cover saucepan. Let boil. Then reduce heat to a simmer. Let simmer until rice is cooked and most of the water is gone (about 25 minutes). Stir vegetables into the rest of the rice mixture and serve. Serves 4.

Nutritional Analysis: Per Serving
Calories 195, Fiber 6 gm, Cholesterol 0 mg, Sodium, 25 mg
Percent of calories from: Protein 10%, Carbohydrate 84%,
  Fat 6%

Oil-Free Hash Browns
2 cups red potatoes, chopped in 1/3" cubes
1 1/2 cups water
1 packet (or cube) low-sodium chicken broth
1/2 cup chopped onion
1 or 2 cloves garlic
1 Tbsp parsley flakes
*Optional: 1/3 cup grated sharp cheddar cheese
Heat water and broth powder, onion, garlic, parsley, and
  potatoes in medium saucepan until boiling. Drop to
  medium heat and let simmer until water evaporates (do
  not cover) and potatoes are tender (about 15 minutes).
  Add cheese if desired. Makes 2 servings.

Nutritional Analysis: Per Serving (with cheese)
Calories 255, Fiber 6 gm, Cholesterol 20 mg, Sodium 220 mg
Percent of calories from: Protein 16%, Carbohydrate 62%,
  Fat 22%

Country Bread Stuffing
12 ounces turkey breakfast sausage (or other ground meat)
2 cups onions, chopped
2 cups mushrooms, sliced
2 cups celery, chopped
1 stick butter or margarine (1/2 cup)
2 cups grated carrots
4 cups low-sodium chicken broth
21 ounces Pepperidge Farms Herb Seasoned Stuffing
  (or similar bread cubes with almost no fat added)
2 Tbsp parsley flakes
Heat sausage for about 4 minutes on medium heat in large
  Teflon frying pan, breaking meat up into pieces. Add
  onions, celery, mushrooms, and butter. After sausage

browns and vegetables become tender, add grated carrots and parsley. Heat for another couple of minutes, stirring frequently.

While you are waiting for the sausage-vegetable mixture to cook, boil 4 cups of chicken broth in a large saucepan. Remove pan from heat and pour in 21 ounces of stuffing cubes, stirring quickly to evenly moisten the stuffing with broth. When vegetable-sausage mixture is cooked throughout, add to bread cubes and stir well.

To finish cooking or to reheat later, place saucepan on low heat for about 20 minutes, stirring often. Makes about 12 servings.

Nutritional Analysis: Per Serving

Calories 295, Fiber 1.5 gm, Cholesterol 35 mg, Sodium up to 1000 mg (depending on bread cubes)

Percent of calories from: Protein 18%, Carbohydrate 48%, Fat 34%

Carrots with Apricots

1 cup dried apricots

3 cups carrots, cut into 1/2" rounds

3 Tbsp water

1 tsp butter or margarine

pinch of sugar

chopped fresh parsley or dill for garnish

Soak apricots in hot water for 1 1/2 hours to soften or microwave in water on high for a minute or two. Pat dry and cut in julienne strips. In a skillet or fry pan with a tightly fitting lid, combine carrots, water, margarine, and sugar. Cover and cook over medium heat for 12 to 15 minutes or until carrots are tender. Stir occasionally to prevent sticking. Stir in apricots and heat through. Serve garnished with parsley or dill. Serves 4.

Nutritional Analysis: Per Serving

Calories 70, Fiber 1 gm, Cholesterol 0, Sodium 46 mg

Percent of calories from: Protein 7%, Carbohydrate 85%, Fat 8%

Elaine's French Fries
2 large russet potatoes (or 3 medium)
1 tsp vegetable oil
salt as desired (analyzed without salt)
Seasoning suggestions: garlic, finely chopped or Italian
   herbs, or if you like it hot, try some chili powder, cayenne
   red pepper, or paprika.
Preheat oven to 400 degrees. Cut potatoes into shoestring-
   sized strips. Spread the oil evenly on Teflon baking sheet
   with plastic spatula. Lay potatoes in a single layer on
   sheet. Bake for 10 to 15 minutes or until lightly brown.
   Flip potatoes to other side with spatula, sprinkle salt on
   top if desired, and bake about 10 minutes more. Makes 2
   large servings.

Nutritional Analysis: Per Serving
Calories 160, Fiber 4 gm, Cholesterol 0 mg, Sodium 2 mg
Percent of calories from: Protein 9%, Carbohydrate 78%,
   Fat 13%

Sandwiches

Chicken Sandwich with Salsa
1 chicken breast, cooked, without skin
1 French roll
green leaf lettuce
About 1/8 cup salsa

Nutritional Analysis: Per sandwich
Calories 450, Cholesterol 70 mg, Sodium, up to 700 mg,
   depending on salsa
Percent calories from: Fat 12%

Special Turkey Sandwich
3 ounces cooked turkey breast (use smoked, if desired)
1/8 cup cranberry sauce
green leaf lettuce
1 French roll

Nutritional Analysis: Per sandwich
Calories 450, Cholesterol 60 mg, Sodium 580 mg
Percent calories from: Protein 30%, Carbohydrate 57%, Fat
   13%

Lowered Cholesterol Egg Salad Sandwich

6 large eggs
2 Tbsp reduced-calorie mayonnaise
1/4 cup chopped green onions
1/4 cup finely chopped celery
pepper to taste
Dijon mustard to taste (optional)
1 tomato, sliced
dark green lettuce leaves
8 slices whole wheat bread

Set eggs in medium saucepan, cover with water. Heat to a
boil. Let boil for 5 minutes. Let eggs cool and remove
shells. Remove 3 of the yolks and throw them away. Take a
fork and gently shred the remaining 3 whole eggs and 3
egg whites. Add the reduced-calorie mayo, onion, celery,
and mix. Then add pepper and mustard to taste. Spread on
slices of bread and garnish with tomato and lettuce. Makes
4 sandwiches.

Nutritional Analysis: Per Sandwich
Calories 265, Fiber 5 gm, Cholesterol about 150 mg, Sodium
   480 mg
Percent of calories from: Protein 19%, Carbohydrate 58%,
   Fat 23%

Lite Chicken Salad Sandwich

4 boneless, skinless chicken breasts, cut into bite-sized
   chunks
2 cups chicken broth
1/2 cup diced jicama (or water chestnuts)
1 green onion, finely chopped
1/4 cup and 1 Tbsp plain low-fat yogurt
1 1/2 tsp Dijon mustard
1 tsp parsley flakes

1/2 tsp dill
pepper to taste
1/4 cup grated sharp cheddar cheese
2 whole tomatoes, sliced
1/2 whole cucumber, sliced
12 slices sourdough bread (or whole wheat)
Saute chicken chunks in 2 cups chicken broth until thoroughly cooked. Drain and let cool. Mix yogurt, mustard, onion, parsley, and dill together well. Add chicken chunks and cheese. Pepper to taste. Serve on bread with slices of tomato and cucumber. Makes 6 sandwiches.

Nutritional Analysis: Per Serving
Calories 250, Fiber 1 gm, Cholesterol 6 mg, Sodium 630 mg
Percent of calories from: Protein 15%, Carbohydrate 70%, Fat 15%

Breakfast Entrees

Buttermilk-Oatmeal Pancakes
1 1/4 cup buttermilk
1 Tbsp oil
1 egg beaten with 2 egg whites
1 Tbsp honey
1 cup rolled oats
1/2 cup whole wheat flour
1/2 tsp baking soda
1/2 tsp cinnamon
Combine the buttermilk and rolled oats in a bowl and let stand about 5 minutes. In another bowl, stir the dry ingredients together. Add eggs, oil, and honey to the bowl with buttermilk and oats. Add dry ingredients to wet. Stir to moisten. Pour 1/4 cup batter for each pancake into medium hot Teflon pan. Turn pancakes when top is bubbly and edges are slightly dry. (Be patient. These pancakes tend to take a bit longer to cook because of the oats.) Makes 3 large servings.

Nutritional Analysis: Per Serving
Calories 310, Fiber 4 gm, Cholesterol 90 mg, Sodium 300 mg
Percent of calories from: Protein 19%, Carbohydrate 55%,
   Fat 26%
Topping Ideas: Try to skip the butter and add instead: pureed
   fruits, non- or low-sugar preserves, lite syrups, or plain
   yogurt with chopped apples and almonds or bananas and
   pecans.

Low-Fat Pigs in Blankets

4-oz cooked turkey breakfast sausage links   (about 5 1/2 oz
   uncooked)
1/4 cup Aunt Jemima Buckwheat Pancake and Waffle Mix
   (or similar "incomplete" whole-grain mix)
1/4 cup Aunt Jemima Buttermilk Pancake and Waffle mix
   (or similar "incomplete" mix)
1/2 cup nonfat milk
1 egg white

Separate the raw turkey sausage into 6 links and cook over
   medium heat in a large frying pan. While meat is cooking,
   mix the pancake mixes together, add egg white and milk,
   and beat well. (Do not follow the directions on the box.)
   When sausage is cooked throughout and edges are
   browned, set aside. Make 3 pancakes, using 1/2 the batter.
   Repeat with remaining batter. Serve 3 pancakes with 3
   links to make a serving. This recipe makes 2 servings.
   Serve with fresh fruit or juice to bring down the
   percentage of calories from fat.

Nutritional Analysis: Per Serving
Calories 265, Fiber and cholesterol information not available
   on product labels, Sodium 1090 mg
Percent of calories from: Protein 29%, Carbohydrate 41%,
   Fat 30%

The 5-Minute Low-fat Omelette

1 egg
5 Tbsp nonfat milk
3 Tbsp flour

1 Tbsp green onions, chopped

2/3 cup sliced vegetables. (I like using 1/3 cup artichoke hearts and 1/3 cup winter squash.)

1 Tbsp grated sharp cheddar or Parmesan cheese

1/4 cup plain low-fat yogurt

pepper, parsley, or other herbs or spices to taste

Beat egg with milk until smooth. Add flour and seasonings and beat until smooth. Mix in onions and vegetables and spices or herbs. Pour into a heated Teflon fry pan over medium heat. When underside is done, flip over and cook other side. Then flip one half over and top with yogurt and grated cheese. Serve with fruit garnish, such as 1/2 cup apple slices, orange wedges, or strawberries. (Strawberries were used in analysis.) Makes 1 omelette.

Nutritional Analysis: Per Serving

Calories 330, Fiber 9 gm, Cholesterol 250 mg, Sodium 210 mg

Percent of calories from: Protein 22%, Carbohydrate 51%, Fat 27%

(Note: To lower cholesterol further, replace half the egg yolk with another egg white.)

Lunch and Dinner Entrees

Italian Style Hamburgers or Meatballs

12 to 14 ounces of ground sirloin (less than 13% fat)

4 green onions, chopped

1 egg white

1/4 tsp black pepper

3 cloves garlic, minced (optional)

1/3 cup fresh parsley, finely chopped

5 Tbsp cracker meal

For Hamburgers:

Mix ingredients well with a large spoon. Pat into 4 burgers. Grill or fry (not adding any extra fat) until cooked throughout. Serve on a bun or with slices of bread. Add dark green lettuce leaves and tomato for freshness. Moisten bread with a bit of mustard or catsup, if you like.

Nutritional Analysis: Per hamburger with bun
Calories 355, Cholesterol 60 mg, Sodium 340 mg
Percent of calories from: Protein 29%, Carbohydrate 43%,
   Fat 28%

For Meatballs:

Mix ingredients together well with large spoon. Roll by hand
into about 50 meatballs. Over medium heat, cook in large
fry pan until brown on all sides and cooked throughout.
Serve as an hors d'oeuvre or toss into a tomato sauce and
serve with pasta. Makes 50 meatballs (about 10 servings).

Nutritional Analysis: Per 5 Meatballs
Calories 90, Fiber 1 gm, cholesterol 25 mg, sodium 50 mg
Percent of calories from: Protein 41%, Carbohydrate 26%,
   Fat 33%

Fish Sticks

13 oz sea bass, raw (or other thick and firm white fish)
1/2 cup cracker meal or crumbs
1/4 tsp pepper
1/2 tsp Italian seasonings
1 tsp parsley flakes
2 egg whites mixed with 3 Tbsp low-fat milk
2 tsp oil

Preheat oven to 375 degrees. Cut fish into 1/2-inch thick
   sticks (about 2 to 3 inches in length and about an inch in
   width). In a medium-sized bowl, mix cracker meal with
   spices. Beat egg white with milk in another medium-sized
   bowl and set aside. Coat a Teflon baking pan with the oil.
   With fork, coat each fish piece in the egg-white mixture,
   then in the crumb mixture. Place them on baking sheet.
   Bake until golden brown—about 15 minutes. (You may
   need to flip them over to brown the other side.) Serve with
   spicy mustard or catsup. (Stay away from the fatty tartar
   sauces and mayonnaise.) Makes 3 servings.

Nutritional Analysis: Per Serving
Calories 245, Fiber 0.6 gm, Cholesterol 63 mg, Sodium 110 mg

Percent of calories from: Protein 48%, Carbohydrate 28%, Fat 24%

Broiled Fish with Tomato

3 orange roughy fillets (12 ounces, raw)
    or other boneless white fish such as sole or snapper
1 tomato, sliced

Broiling sauce:

    2 Tbsp Oriental Chef-Delicate Sesame salad dressing or
        similar-type bottled salad dressing
    1 tsp reduced-sodium soy sauce
    1 tsp honey

Lay fish fillets on foil-covered baking sheet. Gently spoon half of broiling sauce evenly over fish. Broil for several minutes, watching carefully. Flip fillets to other side. Place tomato slices around fish fillets and dress both with the remaining sauce. Continue broiling until fish is cooked throughout. Makes 3 servings.

Nutritional Analysis: Per Serving
Calories 135, Sodium 280 mg
Percent of calories from: Protein 62%, Carbohydrate 16%, Fat 22%

Seafood with Lemon Sauce

2 tsp margarine
2 Tbsp lemon juice
1 clove garlic
1 tsp basil flakes, crushed in hand while added
4 Tbsp champagne or white wine
2 tsp cornstarch
1 Tbsp low-fat milk
16 oz raw scallops
pepper to taste
4 cups cooked pasta

Melt margarine with garlic over medium-high heat. Brown for about a minute. Add scallops, lemon juice, champagne, basil, and pepper. Cover and let cook for a few minutes.

Meanwhile, mix milk and cornstarch. When scallops are almost tender throughout, add milk mixture, stir, then lower heat to a simmer. Let cook, uncovered, for a couple minutes more. Serve over pasta. Makes 4 servings.

Nutritional Analysis: Per Serving
Calories 300, Cholesterol 43 mg, Sodium 320 mg
Percent of calories from: Protein 33%, Carbohydrate 57%, Fat 10%

Beef Tacos
8 corn tortillas
7 oz uncooked lean ground beef
     (Use ground sirloin with less than 13% fat, if available.)
1/2 cup onions, chopped
1 cup canned kidney beans, drained
1/4 to 1/2 tsp chili con carne seasoning
pepper to taste, 1/4 to 1/2 tsp
1 cup grated carrot
2 tomatoes, diced
1 cup grated part-skim cheese (use less to lower fat)
2 cups loose leaf lettuce, shredded
Add beef, onions, and seasonings to Teflon fry pan over medium heat until cooked throughout. Add beans and let simmer a couple minutes longer. Soften tortillas by placing each on in a Teflon fry pan on medium heat. Flip to other side and continue heating. Then remove and repeat with other tortillas. Fill tortillas with beef, carrot, tomatoes, cheese, and lettuce. Makes 4 servings (2 tacos each).

Nutritional Analysis: Per Serving
Calories 390, Fiber 11 gm, Cholesterol 40 mg, Sodium 225 mg
Percent of calories from: Protein 25%, Carbohydrate 45%, Fat 30%

Generic Stir Fry
2 tsp sesame oil
2 to 3 Tbsp low-sodium chicken broth or white wine

2 chicken breasts, skinned and boned, cut into cubes
  (or use 7 oz shellfish, turkey, or lean beef cuts)
1 clove garlic, minced
1 or 2 slices fresh ginger, chopped (or 1/8 tsp powdered)
1/2 cup low-sodium chicken broth
3 cups vegetables (your choice)
1 1/2 tsp reduced-sodium soy sauce   .
1 to 2 tsp cornstarch, dissolved in a little water
3 cups cooked brown rice
Heat wok or large Teflon frying pan until very hot. Add oil,
turning pan to coat. Add chicken pieces, 2-3 Tbsp chicken
broth, garlic, and ginger, stirring constantly until chicken
is white. Add more broth if more moisture is needed.
Remove chicken and set aside.
Add the rest of the chicken broth and any "long cooking"
vegetables, such as carrots, broccoli, or cauliflower. Bring
to a boil. Cook about 4 minutes, stirring constantly. Add
any medium-cooking vegetables, such as green peppers or
squash, and cooked chicken. Stir and cook about 2
minutes. Add any quick-cooking vegetables (bok choy,
spinach leaves, bean sprouts) and soy sauce. Stir
vegetables for a minute or two. Add more chicken broth if
more moisture is needed. Thicken by pushing the
vegetables to one side and stirring in the cornstarch
mixture. Heat and stir until thickened. Stir in the
vegetables to coat with sauce. Serve on bed of cooked rice.
Makes 3 servings.

Nutritional Analysis: Per Serving
(Analyzed with 1 1/2 cup broccoli and 1 1/2 cups carrots)
Calories 395, Fiber 13 gm, Cholesterol 47 mg, Sodium 290 mg
Percent of calories from: Protein 26%, Carbohydrate 58%,
  Fat 16%

Lemon Chicken Parmesan

1 1/2 oz dried tomato slices (Add warm water and set aside
  for 20 minutes to reconstitute slightly.)
4 skinless, boneless chicken breasts
1 lemon

1/2 tsp black pepper
1 tsp dried rosemary flakes or 2 tsp dried basil leaves
(Crush in hand while adding.)

Cheese Sauce:
1 cup part-skim ricotta cheese
1/2 cup nonfat milk
2/3 cup Parmesan cheese
Serve over 6 cups cooked pasta (about 9 oz fresh pasta)
Place dried tomato slices in 9" square baking dish to make a
bed for the chicken breasts. Add chicken breasts evenly,
laying completely flat. Squeeze juice of 1 lemon over all of
the chicken. Sprinkle pepper and basil or rosemary on top.
Cover dish with foil and bake in preheated 350-degree
oven until tender (about 45 minutes). Mix cheese sauce in
microwave-safe dish. Microwave on high for 2 minutes
until hot and bubbly. Pour over chicken when done. Bake
uncovered for 5 minutes. Broil for the last minute or so to
lightly brown the top, if desired. Serve each portion over 1
1/2 cups cooked pasta. Makes 4 servings.

Nutritional Analysis: Per Serving
Calories 590, Fiber 3 gm, Cholesterol 100 mg, Sodium 455
    mg
Percent of calories from: Protein 34%, Carbohydrate 45%,
    Fat 21%

Dijon Chicken
About 1 lb raw boneless chicken breasts, skinless
1 Tbsp butter or margarine
3/4 cup white wine
2 leeks, white part only, thinly sliced
3 Tbsp Dijon-style mustard
2 Tbsp evaporated low-fat milk mixed with 1 Tbsp flour
3 cups cooked brown rice (or white, if you prefer)
Cut chicken breasts into 1/2" strips. Saute in 1 Tbsp butter
    and 1/2 cup wine until cooked throughout (about 4 to 5
    minutes). Remove chicken pieces with a slotted spoon.
    Saute leeks in pan drippings for about 3 minutes. Add the

rest of the wine, mustard, milk, and flour mixture and simmer until the sauce thickens slightly (about 5 minutes), stirring frequently. Add chicken chunks. Serve over rice. Makes 3 servings.

Nutritional Analysis: Per Serving
Calories 530, Fiber 5 gm, Cholesterol 105 mg, Sodium 343 mg
Percent of calories from: Protein 35%, Carbohydrate 45%, Fat 20%

Quick Quesadillas

2 flour tortillas
1/2 cup grated part-skim cheese of choice
1 Tbsp tomato sauce, salsa, or bottled spaghetti sauce
1/4 cup chopped green onions
1/2 cup chopped fresh tomatoes
1/4 cup low-fat plain yogurt

In a Teflon pan, heat both sides of one tortilla until it is soft and hot. Spread 2 Tbsp of sauce down the middle of the tortilla. Sprinkle half the grated cheese evenly over the tortilla, followed with onions and tomatoes. When tortilla browns, and cheese starts to bubble, fold one side toward the middle and then the other side. Top with 1/8 cup yogurt. Then repeat with rest of ingredients.

Nutritional Analysis: Per Quesadilla
Calories 215, Fiber 1.5 gm, Cholesterol 45 mg, Sodium 480 mg
Percent of calories from: Protein 24%, Carbohydrate 43%, Fat 33%

At Home Fajitas

4 fajita flour tortillas
12 oz raw chicken breast, round steak, skirt steak or even swordfish

Marinade:
1 cup chicken broth
1 Tbsp reduced-sodium soy sauce (if available)
1 tsp Worcestershire sauce

1 clove garlic, finely chopped

1/2 tsp pepper

1 tsp lemon juice

Salsa Guacamole:

1/2 avocado, mashed

3 Tbsp plain low-fat yogurt (or nonfat)

2 cups loose leaf lettuce, shredded

1 cup chopped tomatoes

Cut meat into 1/3-inch thick strips. Mix marinade and add meat to it. Marinate for about 4 hours in the refrigerator. (If you're out of time, skip the long marinate time.) Make guacamole mixture and set aside in a serving bowl. Remove meat strips and set in Teflon fry pan with half the marinade. (Throw the other half away.) Simmer until the meat is well done and the marinade has almost boiled off. Quickly remove meat into a serving bowl. To soften tortillas, place in non-stick fry pan on medium-high heat and flip to other side when lightly brown and soft. Makes 4 fajitas.

Nutritional Analysis: Per Chicken Fajita (round steak values in parentheses)

Calories 260 (275), Fiber 2 gm, Cholesterol 53 mg (56 mg) Sodium 470 mg (will be much less if reduced-sodium soy sauce is used)

Percent of calories from: Protein 37% (35%), Carbohydrate 35% (33%), Fat 28% (32%)

Tuna Enchiladas

4 corn tortillas

1 6 1/2-oz can solid white tuna, water packed, drained

2 Tbsp green onion, chopped

1/2 cup grated part-skim cheese

1/3 cup Ragu Gardenstyle spaghetti sauce

1/8 tsp chili powder

1 (more) cup Ragu Gardenstyle spaghetti sauce to pour on top

1/2 cup plain low-fat yogurt

6 olives, cut in half

Preheat oven to 375 degrees. Mix tuna with green onions, cheese, 1/3 cup sauce, chili powder. Heat each tortilla in a Teflon pan to soften. Spread remaining cup of spaghetti sauce in baking pan. Roll 1/4 of tuna mixture in one tortilla and repeat with remaining 3 tortillas. Place in pan. Bake for 10 to 15 minutes. Cool a couple of minutes before serving. Top each enchilada with 2 Tbsp yogurt and 3 olive halves. Serves 2.

Nutritional Analysis: Per Serving
Calories 473, Fiber 6 gm, Cholesterol 85 mg, Sodium 705 mg
Percent of calories from: Protein 36%, Carbohydrate 38%, Fat 26%

Chicken with Asparagus
4 chicken breasts, skinned and boned
1/2 cup cracker meal (cracker crumbs or flour)
1/4 tsp black pepper
1 tsp parsley flakes
1/2 tsp thyme
1/2 oz Butter Buds (one small packet) or use skim milk
1 1/2 cups asparagus, cooked
2 1/2 cups pasta, cooked

Gravy:
1 1/2 cups low-sodium chicken broth
3/4 cup raw sliced mushrooms
1/3 cup diced onions
1 Tbsp margarine, melted
2 Tbsp flour
1/4 cup skim or low-fat milk
1/4 cup grated Parmesan cheese

Preheat oven to 400 degrees. Mix the cracker meal and seasonings together in a medium sized bowl. Mix up the Butter Buds, following directions on package, in a separate bowl. Dip chicken breasts in Butter Buds, one at a time, then dip in crumb mixture and place on Teflon baking sheet. Bake for about 30 minutes, turning chicken after 15 minutes. While chicken is baking, boil pasta and asparagus and make gravy. Simmer mushrooms and onions in broth over medium-high heat until tender. Add margarine mixed with flour and cook until thickened. Add milk and simmer a few minutes longer until creamy. When chicken is ready, arrange 4 nests of pasta on a serving dish and lay a chicken breast on each next. Garnish the edges with cooked asparagus spears. Pour gravy evenly over chicken and pasta. Sprinkle top with Parmesan cheese. Serves 4.

Nutritional Analysis: Per Serving
Calories 395, Fiber 3 gm, Cholesterol 75 mg, Sodium 270 mg
Percent of calories from: Protein 37%, Carbohydrate 45%, Fat 18%

Chicken Pesto Lasagna
4 boneless, skinless chicken breasts, cut into bite-sized pieces
1 packet low-sodium chicken broth mixed with 3/4 cup water
2 tsp Italian seasoning
2 cups grated zucchini
2/3 cup (5 oz) Pesto For Pasta (or other pesto. If it has excess oil, please drain the oil off.)
1 1/2 cup part-skim ricotta cheese
1/2 cup Parmesan cheese
2/3 cup chopped green onions
12 oz (dry weight) lasagna noodles
8 oz part-skim mozzarella cheese, grated
1 1/2 cups Ragu Gardenstyle Spaghetti Sauce
Preheat oven to 375 degrees. In frying pan, simmer chicken pieces in broth and Italian seasonings over medium heat until cooked. While chicken is cooking, mix the ricotta and Parmesan cheese with green onions in a bowl. Using a slotted spoon, remove chicken pieces from pan. Lightly shred chicken in food processor with pesto and zucchini. Cook noodles until just tender. To make lasagna, first spread 1 cup Ragu on bottom of 9 by 13-inch pan. Add 3 strips lasagna. Spread on half the chicken mixture and add 3 strips lasagna on top. Then spread the cheese mixture and top with 3 strips lasagna. Then spread the rest of the chicken mixture and top with 3 strips lasagna. Spread

1 1/2 cups Ragu on top and sprinkle with the grated mozzarella. Bake for 25 minutes. Makes 12 servings.

Nutritional Analysis: Per Serving
Calories 335, Fiber, not available, Cholesterol 45 mg, Sodium
    500 mg
Percent of calories from: Protein 28%, Carbohydrate 44%,
    Fat 28%

Super Quick Spaghetti Sauce
15 oz extra lean ground beef (less than 13% fat)
1 1/2 cups chopped yellow onion
2 cups grated yellow crookneck squash or zucchini
3 cloves garlic
1 tsp dried oregano flakes
1 tsp lemon pepper (no salt blend) or just 1/2 tsp pepper
1 jar Ragu Chunk Gardenstyle Spaghetti Sauce (32 oz)
Cooked pasta (about 6 to 9 cups)
Cook beef with garlic, onions, and spices. Then stir in the
    grated squash for about 5 minutes. Add a bottle of
    spaghetti sauce and let simmer for 5 minutes more. Serve
    over cooked pasta. Makes 6 servings.

Nutritional Analysis: Per Serving
Calories 415, Fiber, not available, Cholesterol 45 mg, Sodium
    575 mg
Percent of calories from: Protein 22%, Carbohydrate 58%,
    Fat 20%

**Chicken, Basil and Baby Carrot Filling
(for pasta, dinner crepes, etc.)**
4 chicken breasts (skinned, boned, cut into strips and
    simmered in 1 cup low-sodium chicken broth)
2 green onions (white and part of green stem), chopped
1/4 cup fresh parsley, finely chopped
1 cup lightly packed fresh basil leaves
1 1/2 cups chopped baby carrots, cooked
1/3 cup grated Parmesan cheese
1/4 tsp black pepper

Remove cooked chicken from broth mixture with slotted spoon. Mix all ingredients together and then process until finely ground. Refrigerate until needed.

Nutritional Analysis: Per Complete Recipe
Calories 975, Cholesterol 300 mg, Sodium 1095 mg
Percent of calories from: Fat 21%

Holiday Leftover Casserole
2 cups mashed potatoes (made with milk only)
1 cup cooked peas (or any other leftover vegetable)
1 1/2 cup cooked rice
1 cup leftover cooked turkey, chopped into bite-sized pieces
1 recipe mushroom gravy, or use 1 1/2 cups leftover gravy
In a saucepan, simmer 1 1/2 cups low-sodium chicken broth with 3/4 cup sliced mushrooms and 1/3 cup diced onion until mushrooms are cooked and onions are tender. In a separate pan, melt 1 Tbsp butter or margarine. Mix in 2 Tbsp flour. Add this to the mushroom mixture, stirring occasionally for a few minutes more.

Preheat over to 350 degrees. Spoon mashed potatoes into a casserole dish that holds 1 1/2 to 2 quarts. Add peas, rice, turkey, and 1 cup gravy. Then stir. Pour the remaining gravy on top. Bake in oven until heated throughout, about 15 minutes. Serves 3 as main entree.

Nutritional Analysis: Per Serving
Calories 400, Fiber 11.5 gm, Cholesterol 55 mg,
    Sodium 700 mg
Percent of calories from: Protein 23%, Carbohydrate 59%,
    Fat 18%

Snacks and Desserts

Pear 'N Raisin Crisp
1/2 cup Quaker Oat Bran cereal, uncooked
1 Tbsp packed brown sugar
1/2 tsp cinnamon
1 Tbsp margarine, melted

6 cups thinly sliced pears (about 6)
1/2 cup raisins (or other dried fruit, chopped)
1/4 cup water
1 Tbsp lemon juice
1/4 cup packed brown sugar
2 Tbsp flour
1/2 tsp cinnamon
Heat oven to 375 degrees. Combine oat bran, brown sugar,
cinnamon, and margarine; mix well. Set aside. Combine
pears, raisins, water, and lemon juice in large bowl. Add
the remaining ingredients, stirring until pears are evenly
coated. Arrange in 8-inch square baking dish; sprinkle oat
bran topping evenly over pears. Bake 25 to 30 minutes or
until pears are tender. Makes 8 servings.

Nutritional Analysis: Per Serving
Calories 180, Fiber 4 gm, Cholesterol 0 mg, Sodium 20 mg
Percent of calories from: Protein 4%, Carbohydrate 86%, Fat
  10%

Rhubarb Crisp
1/2 cup walnut pieces
7/8 cup flour
1/3 cup brown sugar, lightly packed
1 Tbsp sugar
1/4 tsp cinnamon
2 Tbsp softened butter or margarine
1/4 cup reconstituted Butter Buds, chilled
5 to 6 cups diced fresh rhubarb (or use frozen)
2/3 cup sugar
3 Tbsp flour
Toast walnuts in 375 degree oven for about 5 minutes (until
lightly brown and smelling nutty). Let cool then chop in
food processor or by hand into 1/4-inch chunks. Mix 7/8
cup flour with 1/3 cup brown sugar and 1 Tbsp sugar and
cinnamon. Work in butter and Butter Buds until mixture
holds together. Add walnuts.

For filling, wash rhubarb, cutting off leaves and brown tips. Cut into 1/3 to 1/2-inch slices. Add to strawberries along with sugar and flour. Empty the bowl, including loose flour or sugar, evenly into a 9-inch pie plate or similar dish. Sprinkle with topping. Bake in preheated 375-degree oven for about 45 minutes. (Juices should bubble thick around the edges, and the top should be golden brown.) If the top browns before the filling has finished baking, cover the top with foil and continue baking. Makes 6 servings.

Nutritional Analysis: Per Serving

Calories 250, Fiber 3.5 gm, Cholesterol 8 mg, Sodium 35 mg

Percent of calories from: Protein 7%, Carbohydrate 67%, Fat 26%

Frozen Fruit Bars

2 cups summer fruit

1 Tbsp sugar

1 tsp lemon juice

Puree fruit in blender, adding a tablespoon or two of water if needed. Add sugar (if desired) and lemon juice and blend. Pour into bar molds or small cups and insert sticks. Freeze until solid. For most fruits it'll be less than 50 calories each (mostly carbohydrate). Makes 4 bars.

Lemon Strawberry Yogurt Whip

2 1/2 cups strawberries, cut in half

1 6-oz container each Weight Watchers A La Francais lemon and strawberry nonfat yogurt (or similar)

6 oz La Creme whipped topping, slightly thawed

Lightly puree strawberries in food processor or blender. Pour into large mixing bowl. Add both yogurt and the whipped topping. Blend with mixer. Gently spoon into separate serving dishes. Refrigerate one hour before serving and serve within 24 hours for best consistency. Serves 8.

Nutritional Analysis: Per Serving

Calories 125, Fiber 1 gm, Cholesterol 30 mg, Sodium 30 mg

Percent of calories from: Protein 6%, Carbohydrate 62%, Fat 32%

Hot Applesauce Cake
4 Tbsp margarine, softened
2/3 cup sugar
3 egg whites, 1 yolk, lightly beaten
1 cup white flour
1 1/2 cup whole wheat flour
3/4 cup orange juice
2 cups applesauce, unsweetened
2 tsp baking soda
2 tsp cinnamon*
1 tsp ground cloves*
1 tsp ground allspice*
1/4 tsp nutmeg*
1/4 tsp mace*
  *(Or use 4 tsp "pumpkin pie spice" for the spices above)
1 cup raisins
1/2 cup walnuts (or other nuts)
Preheat oven to 350 degrees. In large mixing bowl, cream margarine, slowly adding sugar; beat until smooth. Add egg mixture, mix well. Mix dry ingredients together (flours, soda, spices), add to creamed mixture along with applesauce, orange juice, raisins, and walnuts. Beat until well blended. Pour into non-stick bundt (or similar) pan. Bake 40 to 50 minutes (or until toothpick inserted in center comes out clean). Cool 10 minutes, then turn out onto plate or rack to cool completely. If desired, sprinkle cake with powdered sugar. Makes 12 servings.

Nutritional Analysis: Per Serving
Calories 270, Fiber 4 gm, Cholesterol 22 mg, Sodium 200 mg
Percent of Calories from: Protein 8%, Carbohydrate 67%, Fat 25%

Cream Sherry Walnut Cake (Homemade and With Mix)
With Mix:
1 yellow cake mix (incomplete)
1 egg and 1 egg white
1 cup cream sherry

1/2 cup walnut pieces
1/3 cup and 2 Tbsp water
1 Tbsp vegetable oil
1/8 cup powdered sugar sifted on top of cake for decoration
(optional)

Do not follow mixing directions on cake mix. Preheat oven to
350 degrees. Add cake mix to a bowl and beat in eggs,
sherry, walnuts, water, and oil until smooth. Pour into a
non-stick bundt or similar-sized pan (or use non-stick
cooking spray). Bake for about 35 minutes. Do not
overbake! Makes 12 slices.

Nutritional Analysis: Per Slice
Calories 250, Sodium 290 mg
Percent of calories from: Protein 6%, Carbohydrate 63%, Fat
31%

Homemade:
1 3/4 cups flour
1 cup sugar
2 1/2 tsp baking powder
1 tsp salt
1/3 cup butter or margarine, softened
1/2 cup low-fat milk
1 egg
2/3 cup cream sherry
1 tsp vanilla extract
1/2 cup walnuts

In a large mixing bowl, mix first 4 ingredients. Blend in
butter and milk for about 1 to 2 minutes at medium speed
with mixer. Add and mix in egg, sherry, and vanilla for 2
minutes more. Scrape bowl constantly. Pour the batter
into a Teflon or spray coated bundt or similar-sized cake
pan and bake 25 to 35 minutes, until toothpick inserted in
center comes out clean. Makes 12 slices.

Nutritional Analysis: Per Slice
Calories 235, Fiber 1 gm, Cholesterol 35 mg, Sodium 300 mg
Percent of calories from: Protein 7%, Carbohydrate 58%, Fat
35%

Chocolate Whiskey Cake (With Mix)

1 box Duncan Hines Swiss Chocolate Cake mix (or use another chocolate cake mix where they ask you to add the eggs and oil yourself)

3 egg whites, 1 egg yolk, lightly beaten

1/3 cup and 1/4 cup whiskey

3/4 cup water

Preheat oven to 350 degrees. Pour box mix into large mixing bowl. Add whiskey, egg mixture, and water. Beat well. Add to a nonstick bundt pan (or similar) or use non-stick cooking spray. Bake for about 35 to 40 minutes (until toothpick inserted in center comes out clean). Lightly sift and sprinkle powdered sugar on top if you like. Makes 12 servings.

Nutritional Analysis: Per Serving

(Exact values depend on mix used.)

Percent of calories from: Protein 9%, Carbohydrate 69%, Fat 22%

Oatmeal Raisin Cookies

1 1/4 cup rolled oats

1 cup oat bran

1/4 cup chopped nuts

3/4 cup raisins

2 tsp baking powder

1/2 tsp cinnamon

3/4 cup nonfat milk

1/3 cup honey

1 egg beaten with 2 egg whites

2 Tbsp vegetable oil

Preheat oven to 375 degrees. In a large bowl combine first six ingredients. Add remaining ingredients. Mix until dry ingredients are moistened. Portion half of the batter and spoon 15 cookies on a Teflon pan. Bake until lightly brown, about 8 minutes. (If you want them chewy, bake only 5 minutes.) Repeat with rest of batter. Makes 30 cookies.

Nutritional Analysis: Per Cookie

Calories 65, Fiber 1 gm, Cholesterol 9 mg, Sodium 26 mg

Percent of calories from: Protein 10%, Carbohydrate 65%,
  Fat 25%

Mint Chocolate Chip Cookies

1/4 cup butter or margarine, softened
1/2 cup reconstituted Butter Buds (a low-calorie butter
  substitute), chilled
1/2 cup brown sugar
1/2 cup sugar
1 egg and 1 tsp vanilla, beaten
3/4 cup whole wheat flour
3/4 cup white flour
1/2 tsp baking soda
9 oz mint chips (or other flavor)

Preheat oven to 350 degrees. Cream butter with sugars and
  Butter Buds mixture. Add egg and vanilla; beat until fluffy.
  Combine flours with baking soda, mixing into creamed
  mixture. Stir in chips. Drop onto a Teflon baking sheet.
  (Each cookie should be a little less than a tablespoon.) Bake
  for about 6 to 8 minutes. Watch carefully, taking them out
  of the oven BEFORE they're cooked through to keep them
  chewy. Cool on paper towels. Makes about 30 large cookies.

Nutritional Analysis: Per cookie
Calories 100, Fiber 0.6 gm, Cholesterol 13 mg, Sodium 55 mg
Percent of calories from: Protein 4%, Carbohydrate 60%, Fat
  36%

Rum Berry Topping

2 Tbsp Smuckers Low-Sugar Boysenberry Spread
  (or use one of their other flavors)
1 Tbsp rum
Serve over
  1 cup vanilla ice milk,
  low-fat frozen yogurt, or
  angel food cake

In a saucepan over medium heat, simmer the preserves with the rum for about 5 minutes, stirring frequently. Pour over dessert of choice. Makes 1 serving.

Nutritional Analysis: Per Serving, including ice milk
Calories 265
Percent of calories from: Protein 8%, Carbohydrate 73%, Fat 19%

Oaty Apricot Tart
Crust:
    1 1/2 cup flour
    1/2 cup melted butter or margarine
    6-7 Tbsp cold water
    1 Tbsp Molly McButter (or other natural butter-flavored sprinkles)—optional
Mix butter into flour with fork. Add water, tablespoon by tablespoon until ingredients start sticking together. Pat into Teflon-coated pie or quiche dish.

Filling:
    5-6 cups apricots, quartered
    2/3 cup sugar
    1/2 tsp ground cinnamon
    1/4 cup flour
Mix ingredients together and pour evenly into crust shell.

Topping: 1 1/2 cups rolled oats (or low-fat Muesli cereal)
    1/2 cup reconstituted Butter Buds, chilled
    2 Tbsp melted butter or margarine
Mix topping ingredients and spread evenly over filling.
Bake tart in preheated 425-degree oven for 15 minutes. Reduce to 350 and bake about 30 minutes longer, until crust browns and the juice bubbles thick around the sides. Makes 12 servings.

Nutritional Analysis: Per Serving
Calories 270, Fiber 3 gm, Cholesterol 27 mg, Sodium 170 mg
Percent of calories from: Protein 7%, Carbohydrate 60%, Fat 33%

Reduced Fat Blueberry Cheesecake (or other fruit)

Crust:

1 cup flour
1/4 cup margarine, melted
1/4 cup nonfat milk (or low-fat)

Filling

1 8-oz package Philadelphia Light Cream Cheese (in tub)
1 cup nonfat milk
1/3 cup sugar
1 egg

Topping

3 cups fresh or frozen blueberries (or other fruit in season:
   strawberries, kiwis, etc.)
2 Tbsp cornstarch

Preheat oven to 350 degrees. Combine crust ingredients and press into Teflon 9-inch pie tin (or use spray coating). Using a mixer or food processor, blend filling ingredients until smooth. Pour over crust. Bake for about 20 minutes. Meanwhile, in a saucepan, cook blueberries with cornstarch (adding about 1/4 cup water if necessary), stirring until thickened.

After cheesecake has baked for 20 minutes, pour blueberry mixture evenly over the top and bake for about 20 minutes more (until cream cheese filling has set and crust has lightly browned). Cool. Serves 12.

Nutritional Analysis: Per Serving

Calories 173, Fiber 2 gm, Cholesterol 32 mg, Sodium 170 mg
Percent of calories from: Protein 10%, Carbohydrate 50%,
   Fat 40%

(Just for comparison's sake: A certain chef's refrigerator cheesecake with blueberries has more than 300 calories per same size slice, with 70% of calories from fat and 133 mg cholesterol!)

Very Berry Smoothie
1 cup fresh or frozen berries (If frozen, thaw slightly)
1/2 cup nonfat milk
3/4 cup low-fat frozen yogurt* (Breyers, Rhapsody Farms,
   Yoplait, etc.)
*Use strawberry or other berry flavors.
Put all 3 ingredients in a food processor or blender. Blend
until smooth. Serves 2.

Nutritional Analysis: Per Serving
Calories 135, Cholesterol 6 mg, Sodium 72 mg
Percent of calories from: Protein 14%, Carbohydrate 70%,
   Fat 16%

CHAPTER

9

The Healthy
Happy Hour

You walk in and look around. As you're greeted with a cup of eggnog, you try to remember if this is your third or fourth holiday party this week. You grab a handful of those green and red covered chocolate pieces on your way to talk with a friend. While talking you nibble on a couple handfuls of potato chips with dip and some crackers and cheese.

Later, when champagne is passed around, you try pieces of the English toffee and fudge sitting on the coffee table, on top of the handfuls of almonds and several toothpicks of speared Vienna sausage that you had somewhere between the chocolate and the champagne. You unsuspectingly walk out of the party carrying a grand total of around 2200 calories, most of which are from fat.

I'm not suggesting we all roam around each party clasping our calculators and calorie counter booklets and chewing on a celery stick. But we can save ourselves from "the party guilts" by partying with a little extra food wisdom.

The Party Goers Guide to Healthful Eating

#1. Make better choices

When confronted with the typical party nibblings (nuts, dips, chips, hor d'oeuvres, appetizers, etc.), know which ones are lower in fat and calories and choose these when you can. As far as hor d'oeuvres and appetizers go, stay away (or limit yourself to a taste) from the cheesy, pastry, eggy or meaty types. What's left? For other party snacks, you can scrutinize the following table.

	Calories	% Calories from Fat
Crackers:		
Ritz, 1	18	48
Wheat Thins, 2	18	36
Saltines, 1	12	25
Bread: (anything in this category is a better choice)		
Sourdough, 1/2 slice	35	7
Bagel halves, 1	82	6
Pita bread halves, 1	95	5
Pastries:		
Fruit turnover, 1	340	53
Cream puff with custard, 1	300	54
Danish, 1	275	50
Dips:		
Sour cream, 1/4 cup	123	86
Yogurt, low-fat, 1/4 cup	35	22
Light sour cream, 1/4 cup	90	60
Guacamole, 1/4 cup		
Refried beans, 1/4 cup	75	26

	Calories	% Calories from Fat
Chips: (1 oz is about 2 handfuls, depending on the hand)		
Potato, 1 oz	163	62
Tortilla, 1 oz	139	47
Pretzels, 1 oz	111	11
Cheese twists, 1 oz	153	56
Nuts:		
Peanuts, 1/4 cup	210	73
Almonds, 1/4 cup	246	77
Spreads:		
Pate, 1/4 cup	41	73
Cheese spread, 1 Tbsp	50	77
Cream cheese, 1 Tbsp	50	90
Sweets:		
Sugar cookies, 1	60	45
Chocolate chip cookie, 1	95	47
Fudge, 1 oz cube	195	78
English toffee, 1 oz	195	78
M & M Peanuts, 1 oz	145	45
Meats/Deli Platter:		
Vienna sausage, 1 small	45	82
Chicken nugget, 1	52	54
Bologna, 1 oz	90	82
Salami, 1 oz	70	72
Ham, 1 oz, trimmed of fat	45	33
Turkey breast, fresh, 1 oz slice	45	19
Cheese, 1 oz slice	115	74
Brie (or other soft French cheeses), 1 oz	95	75

	Calories	% Calories from Fat
Fruit Platter (all items in this category are better choices):		
Apple, 1/4 whole	20	5
Pineapple chunks (in juice), 1/4 cup	38	1
Melon balls, 1/4 cup	14	6

Vegetable Platter (all items in this category are better choices):

	Calories	% Calories from Fat
Broccoli, 1/4 cup	11	10
Cauliflower, 1/4 cup	4	3
Mushrooms, 1/4 cup	4	14
Carrots, 1/4 cup	10	6
Tomato slices, 1/4 whole	6	6
Green or red pepper, 1/4 cup	12	8
Cucumber, 3 slices	2	5
Celery, 1/4 cup	4	5
Green beans (lightly cooked), 1/4 cup	9	5
Squash strips, 1/4 cup	6	4

#2.—Keep portions to a minimum

Remember to eat slowly and enjoy it. The problem with snacks and spreads is they slowly, without notice, add up over the evening. If you saw what you ate during the party's duration piled all together on a plate, you would probably be shocked. Instead, you can fill a small plate with just a taste of the foods you want to try.

#3.—Offer to bring food low in fat

Rolls and nut breads can be a great alternative to the typical high-fat party fare. You can bake many festive (and healthful) breads by following the "Art of Healthful Baking" section in Chapter 6.

A lower fat dip can be made by substituting plain, low-fat yogurt for sour cream or using 1/2 light sour cream and 1/2 nonfat yogurt. A spinach dip can be made by mixing frozen spinach, minced onion, diced jicama, and spices with yogurt and serving it in a hollowed sourdough bread round (using the cut-out pieces of bread as dippers). Another quick dip can be made by mixing dried soup mix (onion types work well) with plain, low-fat yogurt. However, only use half the amount of soup mix you would normally add to sour cream. The salty flavor is more pronounced when yogurt is used.

The amount of fat in fancy spreads such as crab or salmon can be reduced by cutting the amount of cream cheese called for in half, by using Philadelphia Light in the tub, or by adding low-fat yogurt, part-skim ricotta cheese, or buttermilk until you get the desired consistency.

You can also offer to bring fruits and vegetable platters to the party so you know there will be something you can nibble on. Lemon or vanilla low-fat yogurt can be used as a dip for fruit.

A special section on cheese and crackers will be found later in this chapter. So keep reading.

#4.—Don't spend all your calories at the bar

Usually we're not thinking too much about "extra" calories or the effect of too much alcohol when we order a double martini or a pitcher of Margaritas. And you certainly aren't thinking about how alcohol calories can easily be converted and stored as fat in the body. Why do you think there's such a thing as a beer "belly"?

Think about what you usually drink during the course of an evening party—or Sunday barbecue, for that matter—and add the damage up, using the table below.

	Calories	
Eggnog, 1 cup	342	(49% from fat)
Wine, 1 cup	259	
Champagne, 1 cup	180	

	Calories
Cordials and liqueur, 1 oz	97
Martini, 1 1/2 oz	140
Daiquiri, 3 1/2 oz	125
Other cocktails, 3 1/2 oz	140-180
Beer, 12 oz	145-160
Light beer, 12 oz	100-120
Grapefruit juice, 6 oz	70-80
Orange juice, 6 oz	75-85
Apple cider, 1 cup	110
Fruit punch, 1 cup	132
Sweetened seltzers, 6 oz	70-85
Tonic water, 6 oz	60-70
Assorted soft drinks, 6 oz	70-95

The following items are unsweetened

Club soda	0
Sparkling water	0
Seltzer	0

But for those of us who DO think about these extra (potential fat) calories, or those who have ever been, or will be, elected "DD" (Designated Driver) by friends, here are some tips to help you join the party without necessarily downing all the alcohol and extra calories.

If You Prefer Not to Drink ANY Alcohol:

• Order or make an orange or cranberry juice spritzer, with half orange or cranberry juice and half club soda. A 12-ounce orange spritzer has 75 calories (from carbohydrate) and about 75 mg of vitamin C as a bonus!

• Order club soda or sparkling water (for absolutely no calories) and ask for a twist of lemon or lime to add flavor and festivity to your drink.

• Order decaf or regular coffee (with a dab of whipped cream if you want it to look fancy).

- If you're giving the party, try the Sparkling Punch, Apple Sangria, or Peachy Punch at the end of this chapter. Or make up some of your own!

And then there are some of us who just want to drink fewer calories or less alcohol. Call it a security blanket, but we're the people out dancing or at a party who tend to always have a glass in our hand. If you're one of these perpetual sippers, the following tips are especially for you:

Order a wine spritzer instead of wine or a wine cooler. A wine spritzer is wine with club soda (zero calories in the soda). A wine cooler is wine with regular 7-Up or a similar soda added. A 12-ounce wine cooler will cost you about 170 calories. A wine spritzer will only run about 125 calories. But 12 ounces of wine "straight" will give you twice the alcohol and cost you around 250 calories!

- If you like mixed drinks, try ordering the first one regular and the rest without alcohol. You can usually order a strawberry daiquiri without the alcohol—remember the ones your parents used to order for you before you turned 21? Or you can trade off: one mixed drink, one club soda, one mixed drink, one club soda.

- What about all the veteran beer drinkers? I'm sure there are a bunch out there who poo-poo "light" beers. But what exactly ARE the benefits of saying "Bud Light please" instead of "I'll have a Budweiser"? Well, the benefits are mostly caloric, since the alcohol content is only slightly lower. Take a look at the table above. What does this mean in terms of a possible evening's worth of beer? If you order three Miller Lites (one of the lite beers with the lowest number of calories) instead of 3 regular beers, for example, you will save yourself about 160 total calories but only 37 calories from alcohol.

Be aware, though, that some beers are called "light" because of their light color, not their calorie content. If you order a Lowenbrau and the bartender says "Light or dark?" he or she means the color. So I suggest if you're interested in drinking a beer lower in calories, get to know which brand you like and order it by name.

Lightening Up Your Holiday Feasts

Why lighten up the meal you've been looking forward to all year long—that holiday feast that serves as a painful reminder of why relief products such as Alka Seltzer were invented? Why bother? Because you can prevent the pain or regrets the night of and the morning after and because it's easy to do. So why not?

Generously filling a dinner plate with typical holiday fixings and a slice of pie adds up to around 2200 calories, half of which come to you courtesy of the nutrient FAT. That's the bad news. The good news is that by making a few minor adjustments in the kitchen and at the table, you can cut the calories in half, while still maintaining the holiday custom of covering your entire plate with food and ending the evening with a festive dessert. So here goes.

- Choose white turkey meat, if possible.
- Before you thicken the meat juices to make a gravy, skim as much of the visible fat as you can (fat floats, so look for it on the top).
- Reduce fat in your stuffing by adding real bread cubes (croutons, etc., have fat added to them), and keeping added butter, margarine, and bacon or sausage grease to a minimum. (If you need some moisture, add low-sodium chicken broth.) Keep stuffing outside the bird. This way the turkey fat drips into the pan instead of your stuffing. If you're extremely motivated, you can replace 1/4 of the bread cubes called for with steamed, cut-up vegetables or grated carrots.
- Serve bread-type rolls instead of the crescent style rolls (high in fat) and skip the butter at the table. You can serve fancy fruit preserves instead.
- Those innocent fruit and vegetable side dishes can quickly contribute fat calories via added butters and ingredients such as cream cheese, sour cream, cheese sauces, cream, fatty gravy, etc. Instead, serve sweet potatoes, for example, baked with apple slices and apple or orange juice. Steam or microwave a medley of vegetables and toss with lemon juice, herbs, and a sprinkle of Parmesan cheese. Serve fruit warmed with fruit juices, spices or liqueurs. Fresh fruit

pieces tossed with champagne or nonfat yogurt (vanilla or lemon flavors) also work nicely.

• Make mashed potatoes by simply mashing potatoes. Use skim milk to help soften them. You don't NEED to whip in butter or margarine.

• See the recipe section in this book for a delicious recipe (the low-fat rendition, of course) for Pumpkin Custard Pie.

Cheese and Crackers

The usual cheese and cracker rendezvous—a popular party cracker such as the "Ritz" or "Trevor Triscuit" meets up with the soft French-looking dish called "Brie." Separately they're dangerous enough—but together? Well, don't expect "some enchanted evening." Expect a fattening one.

Most of us know that crackers tend to be loaded with fat and salt. But that doesn't mean we never find ourselves buying crackers. A lot of the spreads we cover our crackers with are also high in fat and sodium, and who knows what else.

One ounce of your basic cheddar cheese (about the size of a processed cheese slice) at 115 calories, 74% from fat, lined up with 4 fatty crackers, such as Ritz (72 calories, 48% from fat) gives you a total of 190 calories, 64% from fat. What did you expect to get when you put two fatty things together? You get even more fat. I don't even want to think about the highly processed types that have so many "other" things added that they have to take on names such as "cheese food." By the way, these squirtable cheeses have 85 to 95 calories per ounce, about 350 mg of sodium, and more than 65% of calories from fat.

If you choose a low-fat cracker, at least you have a running start. Consult Chapter 3 for a list of low-fat crackers (with less than 30% of calories from fat). Now on to the cheese part of the equation.

	Calories	% Calories from Fat
Cream cheese, 1 Tbsp	50	90
Sour cream, 1/4 cup	123	86
Light Philadelphia cream cheese (in tub), 1 Tbsp	30	75

	Calories	% Calories from Fat
Cheese spread, 1 Tbsp	50	65
Light sour cream, 1/4 cup	90	60
Refried beans, 1/4 cup	75	26
Low-fat yogurt, 1/4 cup	35	22
Low-fat cottage cheese, 1/4 cup	50	20
Nonfat cottage cheese, 1/4 cup	35	<5

It's obvious the last six are your skinny dip possibilities. For example, a lower fat dip can be made by substituting plain low-fat yogurt for sour cream or at least using 1/2 sour cream and 1/2 yogurt. One quick dip idea is to mix dried soup mix (onion types work well) with plain low-fat yogurt. Use only half the amount of soup mix that you would normally add to sour cream. The salty flavor is more pronounced when yogurt is used instead of sour cream.

Fancy spreads such as crab or salmon can be lowered in fat by cutting the amount of cream cheese called for in half (or even lower by using Philadelphia Light in the tub—a third less fat) and by adding low- or nonfat cottage cheese, part-skim ricotta cheese, or buttermilk until you get the desired consistency.

Cheese is one of our favorite foods. Whether it sits on a cracker, tops our tortilla, or is layered in our lasagna, let's face it, we love it! Unfortunately, cheese IS "fat city." You can cut your fat per ounce almost in half simply by buying the part-skim (reduced fat) types. Who can refuse an offer like that? To be considered lower in fat, cheese must have 5 grams or less of fat per ounce.

You'll also find a list of lower fat cheeses in Chapter 3. So let's try the revised cheese and cracker rendezvous. Four saltine crackers paired up with 1 ounce of Laughing Cow Reduced Calorie cheese equals 95 calories, 40% from fat. You could use even less cheese per cracker and lower the percentage of fat even more.

Having a healthy happy hour can be simple if you follow the general party-pointer rules outlined in this chapter. These rules will save you from the party guilt of unwanted extra fat, sodium, and calories by allowing you to view the party with a little extra food wisdom. Here are some recipes to help send you on your way!

Entertaining with Health (Low-fat Recipes galore!)

Appetizers

Potato Rounds

3 red potatoes, just cooked in the oven
1/3 cup grated sharp cheddar cheese
1/2 cup part-skim ricotta cheese
1/4 cup chopped green onions

Cut the potatoes lengthwise into four rounds each. Mix the remaining ingredients. Spread about 1 tablespoon on each round. Broil for a minute or two (until cheese bubbles). Makes 12 rounds. These can be served as an appetizer on a bed of lettuce or parsley.

Nutritional Analysis: Per Round
Calories 60, Fiber 1 gm, Cholesterol 7 mg, Sodium 33 mg
Percent of calories from: Protein 18%, Carbohydrate 56%, Fat 26%

Chicken Meatballs

14 to 16 ounces of ground chicken breast, uncooked
1 egg white
1/2 cup crackermeal
1/4 cup green onions, finely chopped
3 Tbsp BBQ sauce
2 cloves garlic, minced
1 Tbsp freshly chopped parsley

Mix all ingredients well in a medium-sized bowl. Shape into 1-inch meatballs. Heat in Teflon skillet until brown all around (on medium stove setting). Makes about 30 meatballs, or 5 servings of 6 meatballs each. Serve with spaghetti, as appetizers, with bread as a sandwich, etc.

Nutritional Analysis: Per Serving
Calories 160, Fiber 1/2 gm, Cholesterol 50 mg, Sodium 130 mg
Percent of calories from: Protein 55%, Carbohydrate 28%, Fat 17%

Baked Chinese Egg Rolls

Egg roll wrappers (available packaged usually near the produce section)
1 cup cooked chicken breast, prawns, or tofu, diced
1/4 cup low-sodium chicken broth
4 finely minced scallions
1 1/2 cup slightly cooked cabbage or spinach (boil or steam briefly)
1/2 cup grated carrots
1/2 cup bean sprouts
1/3 cup water chestnuts, chopped
1 clove garlic, minced
1 tsp chopped fresh ginger or 1/4 tsp ground ginger
1 Tbsp "lite" soy sauce (or 1 1/2 tsp regular soy sauce)
1 1/2 tsp sesame oil

Preheat oven to 450 degrees. Simmer 1 cup meat or meat substitute in chicken broth and 1/2 tsp sesame oil until cooked throughout . (If using cooked meat, simmer about 3 minutes.) Add more broth if needed. Add everything but the rest of the sesame oil, simmer 5 more minutes. Let mixture cool about 10 minutes. Place 1/4 cup filling in a rectangular shape on the center of each egg-roll wrapper and fold up envelope style (first each of the ends, then the bottom and top flap). Seal the last flap with a paste made of 1 Tbsp flour and 2 Tbsp cold water.

Place on a Teflon baking sheet, greased with 1 tsp sesame oil. (You can spread it evenly with a plastic spatula.) Flip egg rolls over once to coat each side with a bit of oil. Bake for 5 minutes more, or until brown, then turn rolls over and bake 5 more minutes, again until brown. Makes 8 egg rolls. Serve with Chinese mustard or sweet and sour sauce.

Nutritional Analysis: Per Egg Roll (not including sauce)
*This recipe was analyzed using prawns as the meat item.

Calories 70, Fiber 2 gm, Cholesterol 40 mg, Sodium 370 mg
Percent of calories from: Protein 34%, Carbohydrate 48%,
   Fat 18%

Broccoli Quiche Squares

1 lb broccoli (about 2 sections), steamed or microwaved until
   barely cooked, then chopped into small pieces
4 Tbsp white flour
2 eggs
2 oz part-skim mozzarella, grated (or other part-skim cheese)
1/4 cup chopped parsley
1/2 tsp dried oregano,
1/2 tsp dried basil
1 cup low-fat cottage cheese
1 cup part-skim ricotta cheese
1 Tbsp lemon juice
1/4 tsp pepper
1/3 cup Italian-style bread crumbs (other types can be used)
Whip flour with beaten eggs. Add broccoli and the remaining
   ingredients (except bread crumbs), mixing gently. Coat a 9-
   inch square pan with cooking spray (or use a non-stick
   pan). Pour in the mixture. Sprinkle bread crumbs on top.
   Bake 35 to 40 minutes. Cool for a few minutes. Cut into
   squares. Makes about 25 squares.

Nutritional Analysis: Per Square
Calories 45, Fiber 1 gm, Cholesterol 25 mg, Sodium 120 mg
Percent of calories from: Protein 35%, Carbohydrate 29%,
   Fat 36%

Pesto Cheese Rounds

4 rolls (about 8 oz altogether)
2 Tbsp Pesto for Pasta (frozen pesto)
   or use other pesto but drain off some of the oil
4 oz part-skim mozzarella cheese, grated
Preheat oven to 400 degrees. Cut rolls in half, then remove a
   little of the inside bread (to make a cavity). Melt pesto if

frozen. Spread pesto evenly on the 8 halves. Sprinkle each half with grated cheese. Bake for about 4 minutes. Turn oven to broil, placing rolls about 3 inches from the broiler unit, and broil about one minute, watching carefully. Makes 8 appetizer servings.

Nutritional Analysis: Per Serving
Calories 120, Cholesterol 9 mg, Sodium, not available
Percent of calories from: Protein 21%, Carbohydrate 57%, Fat 22%

Dried Tomato and Cheese Appetizers

16 cracker rounds or squares (Use low-fat crackers, such as saltines, melba rounds, etc.)
2 1/2 ounces (about 1/2 cup) chevre (fresh goat cheese)
16 slices of dried tomatoes (if packed in oil, drain WELL)
Garnish of fresh basil leaves, shredded or chopped
Spread 1 Tbsp of cheese over 2 crackers. Top with 2 slices of dried tomato. Garnish with fresh basil pieces. Makes 8 appetizers of 2 crackers each.

Nutritional Analysis: Per 2 crackers
Calories 60, Fiber 1 gm, Cholesterol 8 mg, Sodium 90 mg
Percent of calories from: Protein 19%, Carbohydrate 46%, Fat 35%

Mini Pizzas

2 11-oz cans Pillsbury Soft Breadsticks
25 Tbsp Ragu Gardenstyle Spaghetti Sauce
1 cup part-skim mozzarella cheese, grated
1 cup Kraft Light & Natural cheddar cheese, grated
1/2 cup grated Parmesan cheese
1/2 cup finely chopped sun dried tomatoes
1/2 cup finely chopped colorful vegetables (such as green pepper, carrots, etc.)
Preheat oven to 375 degrees. In bowl, mix cheeses together. Open can of breadstick dough. Roll out strips in one piece, on lightly floured surface, to form one large rectangle. If you use a round cookie cutter 2 1/2 inches wide, you should cut about 13 pizza rounds per can. Place on Teflon

cookie sheet. Spoon on 1 Tbsp Ragu per round. Evenly sprinkle with cheese mixture and garnish each round with your finely chopped vegetables of choice. Bake until crust is lightly browned and cheese bubbled (about 10 to 15 minutes—but watch carefully). Makes 26 mini pizzas.

Nutritional Analysis: Per Mini Pizza
Calories 90, Cholesterol 8 mg, Sodium 270 mg
Percent of calories from: Protein 22%, Carbohydrate 47%, Fat 31%

Chicken Apple Champagne Sausages

2 small to medium red or green apples, cored and grated
1 onion, finely chopped
1 cup crackermeal or bread crumbs
1/2 cup dry champagne or sparkling dry white wine
1 lb ground chicken or turkey breast
1/8 tsp pepper
1/2 tsp powdered curry (optional)

Cook the apple and onion in a non-stick skillet over low heat, covered, until they are soft (about 4 minutes). Combine cracker meal and champagne in bowl. Add the ground chicken, pepper, curry if desired, and apple-onion mixture and mix well with spoon. Shape sausage meat into 20 to 24 patties about a half-inch thick. Heat a non-stick skillet over medium heat and cook the patties until the undersides are brown. Then turn patties over and brown other side (about 5 minutes total). Makes 8 servings. Serve with brunch, as appetizers, etc.

Nutritional Analysis: Per Serving
Calories 150, Fiber 1.5 gm, Cholesterol 35 mg, Sodium 35 mg
Percent of calories from: Protein 43%, Carbohydrate 46%, Fat 11%

Dips and Spreads

Salmon Spread

7 1/2 ounces of freshly cooked salmon or smoked salmon (or use canned salmon, pick out pieces of skin and bone)

1/2 cup Light Philadelphia (in tub) cream cheese
1/4 cup part-skim ricotta cheese
1/3 cup (heaped) jicama or water chestnuts, finely chopped
1/4 cup white onion, finely chopped
1 Tbsp parsley flakes
1/2 tsp black pepper
1 loaf French bread, cut into 16 slices

Mix all ingredients, except bread, VERY BRIEFLY in food processor or blender. Stir the mixture around and briefly blend again if necessary. Keep well chilled. (You can make this a day before you need it.) Spread 1 Tbsp of spread on each 1/2 slice of bread. (Makes about 2 cups of spread.)

Nutritional Analysis: Per Serving (1/2 slice of bread)
Calories 68, Sodium 140 mg, Cholesterol not available
Percent of calories from: Protein 20%, Carbohydrate 60%, Fat 20%

Crab Spread

6 oz fresh crab, shredded
1/2 cup Philadelphia Light cream cheese, at room temperature
1/4 cup low-fat yogurt, plain
1/3 cup chopped water chestnuts or jicama
1 Tbsp onion flakes
1 Tbsp parsley flakes
1/2 tsp pepper
1/8 tsp salt
1 loaf French bread or low-fat crackers

Mix crab, cream cheese, yogurt, and seasonings together. Add water chestnuts. Makes about 2 cups of spread. Spread about 1 Tbsp of crab mixture on each half slice of French bread.

Nutritional Analysis: 1/2 slice of bread
Calories 65, Fiber 0.1 gm, Cholesterol 6 mg, Sodium 165 mg
Percent of calories from: Protein 18%, Carbohydrate 62%, Fat 20%

Almost Fat-Free Creamy Dip

1 small envelope Hidden Valley Ranch "lite" dressing powder
1 1/2 cup nonfat milk
1/2 cup nonfat plain yogurt
1 tsp reduced-calorie mayonnaise
Mix the ingredients in a blender or food processor.
Makes about 2 cups of dip or dressing.

Nutritional Analysis: Per 2 Tbsp
Calories 20, Cholesterol 1 mg, Sodium 210 mg
Percent of calories from: Protein 21%, Carbohydrate 72%,
   Fat 7%

Spinach Dip

1 cup nonfat yogurt, plain
1/2 cup light sour cream (such as Knudsen Nice N' Light)
1 Tbsp reduced-calorie mayonnaise
1/3 to 1/2 cup finely chopped white onion (depending on your
   taste)
1 tsp garlic powder
1 tsp black pepper
1 tsp basil flakes, dried
1 1/2 cup finely chopped jicama or water chestnuts
1 10-oz box frozen chopped spinach, thawed (Drain well by
   squeezing the excess water out with your hands.)
1 round loaf of sourdough bread (24 oz)
Blend the first 7 ingredients together well in a medium-sized
bowl. Add the jicama and well-drained spinach. Carve out
the center of the bread round, as if to make a pie shell.
Cut the bread you removed from the center of the loaf into
squares for dipping. Spoon the spinach dip into the bread
shell and serve. Dip can be made 10 hours in advance.
Works great for a party of 15.

Nutritional Analysis: Per Serving (15 servings total)
Calories 160, Fiber 2 gm, Cholesterol 3 mg, Sodium 300 mg
Percent of calories from: Protein 15%, Carbohydrate 70%,
   Fat 15%

Party Drinks

Banana Eggnog

2 ripe bananas
2 eggs
1 tsp sugar
2 cups chilled skim milk
2 tsp vanilla extract
ground nutmeg

Peel and mash bananas. Add egg and sugar and blend until smooth. Add milk and vanilla and continue to mix until just combined. To serve, pour into chilled glasses and sprinkle top with nutmeg. Makes 4 servings.

Nutritional Analysis: Per Serving
Calories 126, Fiber 1 gm, Cholesterol 54 mg, Sodium 95 mg
Percent of calories from: Protein 25%, Carbohydrate 63%, Fat 12%

Apple Sangria

1 orange and 1 lemon, cut into slices
juice of one lemon
1 cup orange juice
1/4 tsp cinnamon
1 6-oz can frozen apple juice concentrate, thawed
25-oz bottle sparkling apple cider, well-chilled
2 cups (or more) sparkling water or club soda

Place orange and lemon slices in a large pitcher. Sprinkle with cinnamon. Blend in rest of ingredients, adding the sparkling water at the end to taste. Serves 8.

Nutritional Analysis: Per Serving
Calories 90, Fiber 0.6 mg, Sodium 10 mg
Percent of calories from: Protein 2%, Carbohydrate 96%, Fat 2%

Sparkling Punch

2 cups orange juice
3 Tbsp lemon juice (juice of 1 lemon)

6 oz unsweetened pineapple juice
1 cup unsweetened apple juice
12 oz sparkling mineral water or club soda
In a large pitcher, combine the fruit juices and sparkling water. Pour over ice. Makes about 4 10-oz servings.

Nutritional Analysis: Per 10-oz serving
Calories 110, Fiber 1 gm, Sodium 10 mg
Percent of calories from: Protein 4%, Carbohydrate 93%, Fat 3%

Peachy Punch

2 lb frozen sliced peaches, partially thawed
12 oz apricot nectar, chilled
1/4 cup lime juice
1/4 tsp almond extract
32 oz club soda or sparkling mineral water
Place peaches in processor or blender. While running, add nectar to form a puree. Add lime juice and extract. Add this to a punch bowl, straining first if you want. Gradually mix in club soda to taste. Makes about 10 servings.

Nutritional Analysis: Per Serving
Calories 60, Fiber 2 1/2 gm, Sodium 6 mg
Percent of calories from: Protein 5%, Carbohydrate 94%, Fat 1%

10

Cutting Fat Forever

Well, you've made it this far, so I know you know that you need to know to cut the fat in your diet—for now. Why not forever? Because forever is a long time. And in order for you to voluntarily eat the low-fat way for the rest of your life, a few things need to happen.

You need to not only believe that a low-fat diet will improve your overall health and reduce your risk of heart disease and cancer, but you have to really want this for yourself. Unfortunately for many people, something drastic (like a death in the family or an extremely high serum cholesterol test result) has to scare them into realizing it can happen to them. Time and time again I've seen a thankfully nonfatal heart attack transform a patient into someone filled with conviction and discipline.

Secondly, it has to be easy. I've said it before, and I'll say it one more time: Few people are willing (or able for that matter) to give up their busy, on-the-go lifestyle. So for the new low-fat way of eating to last beyond a month of mere good intentions, it has to fit into your present way of life. And as luck would have it, you have just been shown how the low-fat eating guidelines can be easily incorporated into every eating experience, from fast food to quick meals at home, simply by making smarter choices. You don't necessarily need to change where or how you eat, just change what you eat.

Of course, in order for anything to last forever (including low-fat eating), you have to love it. You have to actually enjoy eating food lower in fat. No one is going to voluntarily sentence themselves to a life of bland, boring food. But now you know that low-fat eating can include most of America's favorite foods, such as pizza, lasagna, and tacos.

Once you've had some practice, ordinary fatty food may even seem very unappealing to you. To me, there is nothing appetizing about finding oil floating around in the bottom of a pasta salad or watching mayonnaise turn yellow on a summer picnic, or being able to see all the white fat globules, clear as day, in fatty sausage or a slice of salami. I don't even like the feeling of immobilizing "fullness" that unavoidably arrives after a cream laden French or Italian dinner. Maybe someday soon you'll feel the same.

Once You're Living a Life Low in Fat

Once you are really and truly living a life low in fat (less than 30 percent of calories from fat), there are better fats you can choose that might help lower your serum cholesterol level even further. Generally the "better fats" are the less saturated fats. Perhaps you've heard the terms "polyun-saturated fats" or "monounsaturated fats."

Fats are composed of fatty acids that can either be a monounsaturated fatty acid (with one unsaturated chemical bond), polyunsaturated fatty acid (with more than one unsaturated chemical bond), or a saturated fatty acid (with all chemical bonds saturated). So the "less saturated" fats are your mono- and polyunsaturated fats.

But don't get sucked into the good fat–bad fat sales pitch either. Remember: all fat in excess of 30 percent calories from fat is probably bad for your overall health.

The Great Vegetable Oil Wars

Americans are fickle when it comes to vegetable oils. Five years ago the magical oil was safflower because it was "high in polyunsaturates." A year ago, it was olive oil because monounsaturated fats were the fatty acid of choice. Today, canola oil has hit the spotlight because it's the oil "lowest in saturated fat" while tropical oils are on the outs because they're high in saturated fat.

While "fat" on our bodies or in our food has clearly become the big no-no of the nineties, somehow vegetable oil has managed to surface unscathed in the eyes of the public and media. We all seem to be forgetting that oil is 100 percent fat! And that goes for all the "light" and "no cholesterol" oils, too. Why is it so easy for us to get sold on the oil of the week? Because people desperately want to believe fats are okay as long as they're using the "right"fat.

Sorry, but if reducing your risk for obesity and some cancers happens to be a concern, then the low-fat diet, which means a diet low in vegetable oils too, is the ONLY way to go. Recent animal studies have shown that a diet high in polyunsaturated fats may be linked to certain cancers. And other new studies are showing that fat calories are more likely to turn into body fat than carbohydrate calories.

But within a low-fat diet (with less than 30 percent of total calories from fat), some fats are better than others. It's the polyunsaturated and monounsaturated fats that are preferred to saturated fats. This is mainly because saturated fats are potent raisers of blood cholesterol levels, even more so than cholesterol-containing foods.

Now for the tricky part. Most vegetable oils are naturally unsaturated (either high in polyunsaturates or monounsaturates) except for the tropical oils (coconut, cocoa butter, palm, and palm kernel oil), which are extremely high in saturated fats. Tropical oils are commonly used in processed foods, such as cookies, cakes, pastries, and nondairy creamers, because they're less expensive and have a longer shelf life. Some food companies also say people prefer the way these oils taste.

Other vegetable oils (corn, soy, and sunflower) can also become uncharacteristically saturated by undergoing a solidifying process called "hydrogenation." This occur when margarines or shortenings are made. More of their beneficial unsaturated fats then become saturated.

Are some oils absorbed into food less readily than others during frying? (This would mean less fat actually gets into your bloodstream.) Despite commercials advertising otherwise, a *Consumer Reports* study several years back showed all oils are absorbed more or less the same.

This vegetable oil stuff is such a hot topic that I just received information on yet another brand new oil. This one says it's the best because it has the "highest monounsaturated fat content." It's called Trisun oil and is only being marketed to food processors so far. So don't be surprised to see this unusual oil listed as an ingredient on your box of cereal or crackers in the near future.

True, it wins the contest for the most monounsaturated fat, but it doesn't win the lowest in saturated fat award. That title still belongs to the other unusual sounding oil, canola.

Is it true some oils shouldn't be used at higher temperatures, such as for deep frying or stir frying? Yes, certain oils have a lower smoke point (the temperature at which the oil starts to foam or smoke). Smoking or foaming is an indication that oxidation and chemical breakdown has begun. The highest temperatures recommended for deep frying are 380 to 390 degrees. Among the sunflower and safflower oils tested by *Consumer Reports*, none had a smoke point below 450 degrees. Olive oils, however, range from 315 to 400 degrees smoke point, depending on the brand. These probably should be avoided for high temperature cooking. The peanut oils tested did not smoke below 425 degrees, except for Planters brand, which smoked around 400. According to the Canola Council of Canada, canola oil's smoke point rests safely above 445 degrees.

Here's a list of the various vegetable oils on the market today, with their proportions of polyunsaturated, monounsaturated, and saturated fats.

Vegetable Oils: Ranging from Lowest to Highest in Saturated Fat

Type of Oil	Percent Saturated	Percent Polyunsaturated	Percent Monounsaturated
Canola (rapeseed)	6	28	62
Almond	8	17	70
Safflower	9	74	12
Walnut oil	9	63	23
Sunflower	10	66	20
Corn	13	59	24
Olive	14	8	74
Sesame	14	42	40
Soy	15	37	43
Peanut	17	32	46
Wheat germ	19	62	15
Cottonseed	26	52	18
Palm	49	9	37
Cocoa butter oil	59	3	33
Palm kernel oil	81	2	11
Coconut oil	87	2	6

*The percentages may not total 100 when added together because of the conversion factors from grams of fat to percent of total fat.
Source: Food Processor II computer software, ESHA Research.

Putting the Squeeze on Margarine

Life without butter is a life condemned to butterless popcorn, bread from the oven or a hot baked potato with something else on it. To me, anything BUT butter IS "something else." But then butter and I go way back.

Have you ever been madly disappointed because someone asked you if you would like some "butter," only to realize they really meant "margarine"? Well, I'm sorry, but margarine is not butter. Margarine is margarine. Which brings us to the question, "Is margarine really that much better for you?"

I'm afraid this is one of those "yes, but . . ." answers. Some of you might be blurting out, "Of course the answer is yes. What could possibly be just cause for a 'but'!"

This may come as a surprise to some committed margarine users, but margarine has just as much fat (and just as many calories) per teaspoon as butter. Both are made up of approximately 80 percent fat and 20 percent water. Both, of course, have all of their calories from fat. Margarine's claim to fame has to do with the fact it offers less saturated fat and no cholesterol.

So the one "but" to the "Is margarine better for you" question is that some people tend to use "more" margarine because it has less flavor than butter. And if lowering the total amount of fat in your diet is really the most important diet recommendation, then there are times when butter might be better!

What about the saturated fat and cholesterol you get from butter and not margarine? If you're eating a diet low in fat and saturated fat (using table fats sparingly and cooking with almost no added fat), then it's possible the amount of saturated fat and cholesterol you would get from this incidental table butter may not add up to anything worth worrying about.

If the worst thing that could happen is you use one teaspoon of butter a day, we're talking about adding 10 milligrams of cholesterol. (The daily recommendation is to eat less than 300 milligrams.) The one teaspoon of butter adds about 2 1/2 grams of saturated fat to your day's total.

If you're laughing yourself silly over the concept of only one teaspoon a day, then perhaps you're a candidate for the make-it-with-margarine club. Up to 27 percent of margarine's total fat is from saturated fat, compared with butter with around 64 percent.

First there were butter substitutes and the product line "margarine" was born. Well, now there are even substitutes for margarine— the "spreads" or "diet margarines." These products basically can't legally be called margarine because they contain less than the federally required 80 percent fat (by weight). Spreads, for example, are usually between 45 and 75 percent fat by weight. How does this 5 to 35 percent fat magically disappear? Food manufacturers not so magically just add more water.

Then there's the "whipped" butter or margarine (where air is incorporated into the product during the whipping process). These products also have less fat per teaspoon. So take your pick. You can replace some of the fat with air or with water. But it only counts (in terms of health) if you use the same amount or less than you would normally.

In case you're in the market for a good tasting margarine, *Consumer Reports* recently conducted a taste test on the subject. The top three were, in this order:

#1. I Can't Believe It's Not Butter (stick)

(Per tablespoon: 90 calories, 95 mg sodium and 20% saturated fat)

#2. Parkay (stick)

(Per tablespoon: 100 calories, 155 mg sodium, 18% saturated fat)

#3. Blue Bonnet

(Per tablespoon: 100 calories, 95 mg sodium, 18% saturated fat)

I keep hearing there are people who actually prefer the taste of margarine, but I have yet to meet any. Perhaps these top tasting margarines will make the difference.

You have to make up your own mind. Obviously we all should by using much less fat overall, on the table and in our cooking. If we would add the same amount of either, then a less saturated margarine would be the spread of choice.

"Hydrogenation"— a Sign of Saturation

The "hydrogenation" process, commonly used to produce shortening and more solid margarines (from a liquid vegetable oil), actually "saturates" some of an oil's poly- or monounsaturated fats.

This hydrogenation process has also infiltrated the packaged food industry. You'll find it in your crackers, cookies, frozen dairy desserts, etc. You'll find the words "hydrogenated" or "partially hydrogenated" vegetable oil listed on the ingredient label if it's there.

When an oil is "hydrogenated" or "partially hydrogenated" it undergoes a processing procedure where hydrogen ions are pumped into a vegetable oil, changing some of its "unsaturated fatty acids" (either mono- or polyunsaturated) to newly "saturated fatty acids." Theoretically, the softer, more liquid margarines are less saturated because they need less hydrogenation.

Summing It All Up

Before we wrap up this course on low-fat eating, how about humoring the teacher in me and taking a little quiz?

(Ah, come on! It's true or false.)

1. When you eat a Big Mac, you are really swallowing the equivalent of 7 teaspoons of oil!

2. Turkey ham, advertised as "95% Fat-Free", really is a high-fat product (51% of its calories are from fat). The ad phrase "95% Fat-Free" really refers to it being 5% fat BY WEIGHT, but 51% of its calories are still from fat!

3. Thirty percent of ALL CANCERS in this country are thought to be preventable through changes in our DIET.

4. The typical evening party goer, without any extra effort, can walk out of a party having eaten a minimum of 2200 calories, most of which are from fat.

5. The chef salad that people often order when they're watching what they eat is really one of the fattiest,

highest calorie choices they could make. (Approximately 800 calories each, 72% of which are from fat.)

6. By making simple changes to a chocolate cake mix, you can bake an irresistible chocolate whiskey cake that has only 200 calories a slice and 22% of calories from fat, compared with the usual cake mix recipe with 300 calories a slice and 48% of calories from fat.

7. You can cut the fat almost in half in some of the fast food sandwiches, such as the Fillet-O-Fish at McDonald's, just by taking off the mayonnaise, fatty secret sauces, or tartar sauce.

8. Taco Bell's Taco "Light" has twice the calories and more fat than the regular taco.

9. Two comprehensive, research-based, government health reports were released to the public during the last two years and both focused on the importance of lowering the fat in the American diet.

10. Cheese and beef aren't necessarily "bad" foods. They CAN be part of a low-fat dish when smaller amounts of the lower fat options (part-skim cheese and the leanest beef cuts) are eaten along with complex carbohydrates with a limited amount of added fat.

Did you think all of the statements were TRUE?

Congratulations. If you got most of them right, then you should feel good about what you've learned over the last nine chapters. Which brings me to the final requirement for fighting fat forever—self-confidence. You need to feel as if you fully understand the basic steps to eating a low-fat diet.

Never let down your guard because it really is a "fight" against FAT. Fat wears many different disguises. It comes by way of the kitchen table (from table fats such as butter, margarine, sour cream, gravy, salad dressing) or stove (deep fat frying, fats added in the pan). We are most often fooled by the "hidden fats," those in foods that protect their presence well, such as crackers (even "baked" wheat thins), frozen waffles, bakery muffins, ice creams, and many others.

I'm having a difficult time ending this book because the road to low-fat eating never really ends. There will always be newly discovered (delicious) low-fat recipes to share, new products to tell you and warn you about, new fast food items and new trendy type restaurants to give you tips on. But for now you definitely know the basics.

And if, per chance, your health and your vigor for low-fat eating change positively because of this book, then please share your enthusiasm and experiences with someone you love. It could make a big difference in their lives, and in yours.

I N D E X

If you found this book helpful and would like more information on this and other related subjects, you may be interested in one or more of the following titles from our Wellness and Nutrition Library:

Fast Food Facts, 3rd Edition: Nutrition and Exchange Values for Fast Food Restaurants (200 pages)

Fast Food Facts, pocket edition (184 pages)

Making the Most of Medicare: A Personal Guide Through the Medicare Maze (170 pages)

Fight Fat & Win: How to Eat a Low-Fat Diet Without Changing Your Lifestyle (200 pages)

The Guiltless Gourmet Cooks Ethnic: Low-Fat Ethnic Recipes, Menus & Nutrition Facts (250 pages)

When a Family Gets Diabetes: Art Therapy to Help Kids and Families Understand Diabetes (50 pages)

Expresslane Diet: Weight Loss with Convenience and Fast Foods (176 pages)

Retirement: New Beginnings, New Challenges, New Successes (140 pages)

Whole Parent/Whole Child: Raising a Chronically Ill Child (175 pages)

Diabetes: A Guide to Living Well: A Program of Individualized Self-Care (396 pages)

Adult Braces in a Gourmet World: A Consumer's Guide to Straight Teeth (148 pages)

I Can Cope: Staying Healthy with Cancer (202 pages)

Managing the School Age Child with a Chronic Health Condition (350 pages)

Pass the Pepper Please: Healthy Meal Planning with Low Sodium (66 pages)

The Guiltless Gourmet: Recipes, Menus for the Health Conscious Cook (170 pages)

The Joy of Snacks: Good Nutrition for People Who Like to Snack (270 pages)

Convenience Food Facts: Help for the Healthy Meal Planner (188 pages)

Learning to Live Well with Diabetes: Your Complete Guide to Diabetes Management (392 pages)

The Physician Within: Taking Charge of Your Well-Being (170 pages)

Exchanges for All Occasions: Meeting the Challenge of Diabetes and Weight Control (250 pages)

Managing Type II Diabetes: Your Invitation to a Healthier Lifestyle (170 pages)

Diabetes 101: A Pure and Simple Guide for People Who Use Insulin (110 pages)

The Wellness and Nutrition Library is published by Diabetes Center, Inc., in Minneapolis, MN, publishers of quality educational materials dealing with health, wellness, nutrition, diabetes, and other chronic illnesses. All of our books and materials are available nationwide and in Canada through leading bookstores. If you can't find our books at your favorite bookstore, contact us for a free catalog.

DCI Publishing, Inc.
P.O. Box 47945
Minneapolis, MN 55447-9727